A BOOK OF

CW01432174

–

THE TWO REALITIES

THE PHYSICAL REALITY
(Part One)

THE SOUL REALITY
(Part Two)

BY DEE WELDON BIRD
and
ACHO AND RAMINI my guides
(and this UNIVERSE ITSELF)

Strategic Book Publishing
www.sbpra.net

For information about special discounts for bulk purchases, please contact Strategic Book Publishing, Special Sales, at bookorder@sbpra.net.

ISBN: 978-1-63410-254-4

INTRODUCTION

THE BACK STORY

Hi, let me introduce myself.

I am Dee. I arrived on Earth's space on 17th August 1967. This makes my physical body nearly fifty-seven years old as of now, 6th August 2024.

I started here like everyone has through the centuries. My soul took its first breath and connected with my chosen physical body.

The first year gave my parents a chance to adjust to parenting again. My mum, in her mid-forties, thought she was going through her change, and my dad in his mid-sixties, retiring more his focus.

A premature body of two pounds, three ounces eased them in while I stayed in hospital.

I surprised them with my arrival while on holiday.

After a year, Mum's schizophrenia got worse. They hospitalised her to see what tablets would stabilise her enough to live a family life.

This left my dad no choice but to put me into care as he had to work.

For a year, I stayed weekdays at the foster home and on the weekends with my parents.

When I reached two, my dad wanted me back home full time as I was getting confused with who my parents were, between the foster carers and them.

My dad brought so much love and fun to my little world. My heart missed a beat when my dad passed. That whole year bestowed me with the connection of love that we shared.

This left just myself and my mum living together.

Her tablets had helped but not quite enough.

I won't go into it now as it has been written about in my previous books.

Thirteen months after my dad's passing, and five days before Christmas, I found my mum dead.

Becoming an orphan overnight was tough. It burst the magic of Christmas.

The next six months I went on to face mental abuse, sexual and physical abuse, and I was whipped and starved.

At four years old, I switched from living a childhood to surviving to live.

Finding my mum dead unsettled my life in the physical so much that I turned to my soul naturally, like flowers turn to the sun — it's all energy.

From that moment, staring at death in my mum's eyes opened up my two realities between the soul and the physical.

Think of it like a split screen.

The universe cloaked me as I grew up. My guides guided me through the confusing physical atmosphere of situation and circumstance.

An atmosphere that I didn't relate to because none of it made sense to my soul.

If only I had physically remembered everything then as I do now about soul reality, it would have made it easier, but easier doesn't mean you understand it. There are no short cuts; experience makes it your own.

It took my physical self fifty-three years to catch up with my soul.

Around the age of eleven I got fostered. Living in a family environment after living in an institution bubble was like mixing with a reality I had not been totally exposed to.

Suddenly, I had to adjust to life from the view of a family while gaining access to more of the external everyday life.

I asked a lot of questions in my head that I hadn't had a chance to ask at three years plus when growing up.

After a year being fostered, I started to observe the teachings being taught in the physical and the C of E church lifestyle while staying at the vicarage.

I had previous experience being around nuns and Catholicism while at the children's home.

Teenage years invited me into my own self-discovery.

I remember walking down the road at twelve years old just looking at the world around me as I walked. This heaven they talk about at church, I realised, is not a place you have to wait for when you pass.

Heaven is in plain sight around us.

For the first time I had some space to myself to view more than my everyday life.

I saw how what is taught didn't match what I could see in my soul. The bigger picture past the physical, this energy got my attention.

That day of viewing the bigger picture is what started my journey to find out more about life, curiously in a subconscious way.

Back then I didn't realise how big the path was. Now I understand it's totally infinite, a path with no end in sight.

There is always more.

This brings me to the present now.

All my questions and answers and experience over fifty-seven years has helped me piece it together. Now, I understand it enough to share it.

The physical is confusing and will never make sense to the soul because it is nothing like the soul.

Two realities that don't match.

The universe works in pairs, matching you with your chosen experiences, so the fact the physically taught script doesn't match the soul is a massive red flag.

Sharing my experiences about both realities highlights the bigger picture because of this distortion.

Sitting here amongst years of notes stored in my soul I wondered, how do I share it all in writing?

And ... keep it simple, as I can waffle on.

Looking at my notes within me I found my answer.

I will write it as my notes.

Liken it to a diary, but without dates for each entry just stick to the content.

Yes, there are dates in my original notes that are on paper, but you don't need to hold onto dated history as it is about living in the now, not past or future.

Enough of me waffling, enjoy exploring the two very different realities.

PS: I am not teaching you anything. I am sharing my facts from my experiences. These notes don't have to resonate with you because the universe is infinite.

My view isn't the only view. It's one of infinite many.

Whatever you take from my notes, I trust it will guide you back to you.

Oh, and you may read repeated words because you may have missed it previously or the meaning behind it, so it gives you a chance to spot it further in the book. It may then feel familiar.

It is, and not your imagination.

Like me, you know everything about this universe this is why you are here now.

WHAT MY SOUL BROUGHT WITH ME

My character and personality.

If I was a tin of food, this is what it would say on my label.

Independent, not a shy soul, but can be physically shy, say it how it is, faces what is ahead, a giggler, childlike, curious, inquisitive for truth, level view, holds her own, explorer and quirky.

Not forgetting morals, manners and authenticity, a soul traveller and soul reader.

PREFACE

These notes cover the physical and soul and how they fit into the bigger picture of this universe.

These notes are written from my real-life experience.

There are many languages used on earth.

There is one language of this universe.

The language of this universe consists of four elements.

Element one CONNECTION to the self.

Element two PULSE sharing from the self.

Element three WAVE – action work jobs.

Element four VIBRATION completion – this element overseas the other three elements.

The physical consists of the human form.

The soul consists of energy your signature frequency, your vibe.

AUTHOR'S NOTES

We are taught so much on how we should live, but what came naturally to me in my soul wasn't talked about in the physical, how a soul lives by gut instinct and knowing organically.

What humans handed down was a legacy of dos and don'ts with many labels that contradict.

By observing and experiencing I followed my path of self-discovery.

This uncovered to me the magic of totality in this universe.

It's not a secret. It's your reflection around you.

Once you see the magic for yourself you embrace freedom.

PS: This book is written from my soul reflecting on my experience here. Each page is written in the now and raw, a bit like bullet points, not as a story but has my real life in it, covering many different angles.

I will write I, they, we, them, and us, etc., but the moral and meaning is from my experience and observation. My life views are just that, mine, but I trust my journey so far will encourage you to view your own self-discovery in this universe.

It may read a bit differently, but I trust that how I write it is how it's meant to be. I trust you will receive it with an open view, even if it is quirky, but above all I trust you will enjoy seeing life through my soul, a welcome break if nothing else.

Much happiness, Dee xx

www.deeweldonbird.com

ACKNOWLEDGMENTS

Thank you, universe, for bringing infinite possibilities into experience because of the magic and connection of space around us.

Through my experiences I gathered knowledge and wisdom.

TABLE OF CONTENTS

PART ONE

THE PHYSICAL REALITY

CHAPTER ONE – CONNECTION to the physical self

(Element number one)

Introducing ourselves

HOW DID WE GET HERE?

The physical and soul relationship has been one-sided, where the physical has encouraged us to forget about our soul, even though it is the powerhouse that brings everything to life here.

The soul is only mentioned in passing.

The soul is infinitely alive. Nothing kills it off.

I realised I had soul gut instinct when I found my mum. Something inside of me knew she was dead, although I had not been taught about it back in the early seventies in the physical.

This knowing subtly got my attention and became embedded in me to pick up later.

How the physical body comes to life.

No matter our body age, at some point we are taught about the birds and the bees, or bluntly put, procreation and sex education.

When humans want to have a baby, they have intercourse to get pregnant.

If they are energetically on the same page, then the body will grow nicely inside the mother's womb. But if they are not on the same page energetically then they won't have enough invested energy to create the body. If there is not enough energy, the woman will experience miscarriage, because there isn't enough energy for the body to grow.

If there is enough energy, then the body grows inside the womb, because nothing works here without a soul connection.

The woman's soul breathes through the placenta and through the umbilical cord into the body that is growing.

Liken it to blowing air inside a balloon.

The woman's soul makes sure the body is in working order during the pregnancy ready for the soul when it connects. This is why the movements of the body while it is growing is felt inside the womb.

The soul waiting to connect with the body will visit it during the pregnancy. If the soul likes the look of the body and feels it can use it for its intended experiences, then the soul will wait for the birth.

Sometimes a soul doesn't like the look of a body and will decide sooner rather than waiting for the birth.

If the waiting soul decides to wait for the next one, the soul of the woman knows this and disconnects from the growing body. This is why stillbirth occurs.

Sometimes a soul has not made the decision until birth itself, even after birth, if it decides not to connect with the first breath. This is why stillbirth happens after birth.

If you have experienced birth or witnessed one, you will know this for yourself. It surprised me how no one asks why the body growing inside the woman hiccups and moves inside the womb, but as soon as it is born it does not work.

The new body lays in silence, until the soul takes the first breath, and the body comes alive and starts to cry and move again.

If a body arrives crying during the birth, then the transfer between the souls have already occurred.

This is how we get here.

Some souls are eager to arrive here, some souls are not.

I was told growing up that the eyes are the window to the soul. My eyesight isn't great. I am more or less blind in one eye, and due to being premature, I have a lazy eye.

I thought, well, there are blind people, so how does this work?

Once I started to have babies myself, I soon noticed this after my first daughter was born. I remember looking at her and it felt like I was holding my breath, waiting for the soul to connect with the first breath.

I didn't understand what it meant until I was in my late forties.

But I had a sigh of relief when the soul did connect, and that first cry was heard.

It wasn't a one-off either. It happened with all my four girls.

The same happens the other end.

When my mum took her last breath, her body no longer worked. It doesn't matter your age. As soon as you take your last breath, the physical body no longer works.

Looking back, I realise that the breath is the window to the soul and not the eyes after all. This is why we breathe constantly regardless of our other faculties.

Nothing works without soul.

This was my second red flag. We are taught to put all our energy into the physical body, yet the soul is the master of it.

We are walking souls not walking humans.

If the physical body worked independently on its own then you could argue this, but fact is it does not. You could say what you want about life support, but it is machines keeping the breath going instead of the body's muscles. Where there is breath there is connection with the soul.

A soul instinctively knows how to take the first breath and how to take the last breath.

This is why we see evidence of this with sudden death syndrome or passing in the sleep.

Souls that remember and know how to take their last breath will not need help.

Back to the physical body birth.

When humans hold their babies and bring them home, they think they are bringing home a human.

They are actually bringing home a pure, 100 percent total soul connected to a physical body via the breath.

This pure soul is connected to the universe totally. Why, it is often noticed how children have imaginary friends. They are only imaginary to humans who are not using their connection to the totality of this universe.

To souls it comes naturally.

A soul connecting with a body does not leave the universe in which to come here.

It expands in reflection. Again, I will go into this further in my notes.

On the physical side, the parents prepare for the baby during the pregnancy, so they have what they need in which to physically look after it once home.

Before the pregnancy the soul prepares even before choosing a body. A soul will meet up with a soul reviewer and create their map as a guide for their chosen experiences. It's a bit like when you book a holiday you may plan every detail before you go or wait until you get there to decide. This is the same for souls, when souls choose what they would like to experience. For when they are here and have chosen their chord from the language of this universe, they pack this information in their soul and bring it with them together with their character and personality.

Your soul map tells you and the souls you come in contact with, as they can see from a soul's perspective where you are at on your unique soul path.

The soul feels the physical heartbeat of the human body, but it knows its own signature frequency beat/rhythm that flows from its soul.

The soul will know how the body works past the physical breath.

It knows it comes in two modes: sleep for energy charging and eating and drinking for cell regeneration.

It does not have to entertain the brain because the soul knows the brain is purely for the body to communicate with itself.

This is why the brain rests at the top of the spine, connected at the top of the spinal cord.

I found out recently that the brain has no nerve receptors that detect pain. This means it doesn't feel pain. I observed this while I saw a clip on brain surgery. The lady was playing a musical instrument during the procedure while she was awake.

This is why the body can experience accidents and not feel pain until the brain has registered the incident, either by seeing visually the blood or break, etc., or seeing the reaction of others. Once registered, the pain sensors bad signal information.

Some souls physical body has the ability to not feel any pain. Makes me wonder if everything defaulted by memory and are we playing constantly what to expect from memory.

The soul being infinite can be whatever it wants to be, and experience what it believes in the moment.

Maybe this is where the placebo effect comes into play.

I have seen documentaries where surgeons tested this out without telling the patient but told them later.

The surgeon cut the patient open and then sewed them back up again without doing any medical procedure.

The patients' stitches healed and so did the injury, and they were fine after as if they had had the surgery.

The power of our souls and what we connect with alters the physical experience.

It is an infinite possibility reality after all, so it would make sense why it's not a one experience fits all.

All of these anomalies are in plain sight.

The focus is mainly on the body parts and not the soul energy connecting it together. The physical image distracts from the circuit of it.

An amputee will tell you that they can remove a limb, but they cannot remove the energy. They still feel the limb energetically. Often, they are given tablets to manage the sensation of the phantom limb.

You can cut the body and incinerate it or bury it, but you cannot destroy the energy.

We are walking souls of energy.

This is why we are infinite.

My first awareness of my soul body was at age four years old. It was while I was going through sexual and physical situations. My little body had gone through and faced enough; it needed a break. The universe always provides what you need. I zoned out, or you could say, I spaced out from my physical body. I zoned in, or you could say, I tuned in to my soul. This gave me some space from the situation. It was then when I looked up, I was watching the scene like a film. It felt natural to me being a soul. I smiled in the safety cocoon of my soul noticing I felt nothing to do with the body. In a way, the body was nothing to me; it was just a body and not me. Energetically, I zoomed in closer to the situation and was laughing in my freedom, saying to myself in my consciousness you can't touch me. You can touch my body, but you can't touch me. Armed with this knowledge it empowered me with a strength where fear did not overshadow me anymore. I now realised I had the freedom over the physical script. I put this experience in my soul notebook within my soul when I would piece everything together.

As souls we have the ability to connect with many bodies at different intervals, even in the same lifespan. For example, I have come across souls in my soul readings that are connected to a body that is age two and another body age eighty-three. The soul chooses this if they want to get a lot done in one period. Saves them waiting for one life experience to complete before connecting again with another body. When we let go of the body, our soul stores what we have experienced from our own invested energy. Your soul will match up and store what stems from you.

The universe doesn't copy or repeat. It has no need because it is infinite.

Humans can physically be busy actually doing nothing but are filling time. Not everything you do day-to-day is stored; it is known but it is not stored. If it doesn't have your energy on it, then it's not stored, and you can't own it as your own. It's just a memory.

Humans fight for justice and souls do not, because of space. Everything is seen and known in the universe. You cannot hide a thing.

Getting back to after the birth and once you go home with your parents or carers to their address.

Your soul connects with the physical body in gut instinct knowing. You don't come with an instruction manual because you know how to master the physical body as soon as you take your first breath. You bring your knowing with you.

You know if you're hungry you eat, if your thirsty you drink, if you're tired you rest.

It's pretty much the same as the animal kingdom. They have many babies in their litter. You don't see the mum chasing after her babies to feed them. Yes, she provides food, but she waits for them to come to her when they are hungry. If they are tired, she leaves them to sleep.

This isn't like this with humans in the physical. The physical doesn't stick with the natural knowing but instead they are given a script to follow since their first breath.

The script changes here and there, but the one I know is if they don't wake up after four hours, wake them up and feed them. The physical forgets the body is in sleep mode and when it is in sleep mode it won't want to eat. This is why they wake up grumpy and may have colic and wind because energetically they are in sleep mode not eat mode.

It doesn't stop there.

This script goes on and on, covering all the dos and don'ts on how to become a physical human.

Pre-2018, it would take souls roughly twelve years to learn how to become physical. I have called it the fear station/taught script and, like the film *The Truman Show*, the emperor's clothes story.

With lots of frustration and tears, the soul through repetitive memory learns how to switch from soul instinct to follow the brain script, like everyone has been doing around them for centuries.

The two realities coexisted – the soul lives in the now, the soul learnt and adapted to also live in the past and future. The soul reality is real. It matches the universe, the physical human script, the non-matching one, gives you the illusion of separation and division. If you follow the energy, you can't separate energy from itself.

The physically taught way of life is the total opposite to how you are as a soul – there is no resemblance at all. From January 2024, I have used the film *The Truman Show* with Jim Carrey as an example to call it out because it is a taught reality that doesn't match your energy.

For fifty-seven years I have humoured the Truman taught reality, visiting it daily. I must admit, mixing with it this long, it does rub off on you. I am in the process of weaning myself from the memory of it. I will share about that in part two, the soul reality.

THE PHYSICAL REALITY – QUESTIONS?

Let's start here with the physical, as it's what we have been taught to believe is the be all and end all of life.

Then I will go onto the soul.

My awareness of life here started with my memory from two years old. Young for many I know, but I was meant to remember largely due to my soul path. It's nothing to do with ability, etc.

The first two years of my life I don't remember, but I know what happened in those two years when I was told my history from my niece as a teenager.

So, we don't always remember all the pieces of our physical history.

We don't always have access to it if no one is around who was there at the time.

(Luckily, our soul knows everything).

What I forgot in facts for the first two years, I remembered in feelings, the important bits, of love and connection with my dad. What impacts us isn't what we think should matter, but what aids our own personal growth on our own path.

So, for me, what impacted me was how I was loved and seen by my dad, a connection I loved. This impacted my soul and stayed with me, even if I forgot the physical side of the story.

What I needed to remember for my future I did.

My first impressions started with observing my parents and family members. This stirred up questions such as, why does my dad keep buying me toys that are too big for me?

I remember photos being taken of me in the garden wearing and loving my new red shoes while holding a watering can, next to our poodle dog.

Eating from my dad's plate rather than my own, waiting for the Sunday roast to be served up and asking for a slice of meat.

A day out at the seaside and asking for some chips.

Snippets of memories, these memories remind me that I was there and lived it. These memories may sound random, but pieced together went on to create my moral compass.

(Red being my favourite colour and the meaning soul wise is my energy in colour, I am a feeder, and I love animals, and I love toys and gadgets still at fifty-seven years old), situations that impact us bring out our character and meaning which lays the foundation in our life.

Even if I am not playing with toys, I am creating them.

We bring our character and personality with us.

What impacted me the most was my dad, being consistent and focused on what mattered to him. He had a sense of loyalty and commitment with himself.

More questions about life continued.

My first important question to my mum, after my dad's passing, "You will never die, will you?"

Her reply, "No."

This innocent reply was my first taste of a lie through the eyes of a child at three years old. As an adult I understand it was out of love, but to the child in me it was devastating as I believed her, especially after losing my dad.

Thirteen months after my dad passed, she passed too, which resulted in me being an orphan. This lie became a moral gift to me. I just didn't know it until years later. The impact of this question and answer laid an important foundation for me on my physical journey that I connect with authentically even if the truth hurts.

The question and answer were a thorn in my side for many years, but once I started viewing the bigger picture, I then saw the gift in everything and soon realised once I understood the bigger picture of my life that actually the everyday scenes and events are only part of the story. What is important is the meaning and the message behind it.

NOW THE QUESTIONS I HAD ARE PAST MY PERSONAL FAMILY LIFE BUT LIFE AROUND ME, THE WORLD.

After I found my mum dead, I had to hold my own and grow up quick. It felt like my bubble of being a child stopped overnight. I had to be a responsible parent to myself.

I noticed my soul, thanks to facing my mum's soul when I found her.

Yes, for a moment our souls got my attention before the physical drama took over. If you're wondering how, it's because I knew she was dead, not because of her body and that it wasn't moving. It was because her essence her soul wasn't shining through it. What faced me was her space of where her soul once was. This space reflected my own soul back to me. This opened the doorway of this universe even wider. Her soul's energy was still present when I connected, which is why I still felt her in the room with me. I just wanted her to shine through her body and move it again. I knew instantly this wasn't going to happen, then the physical part of the situation took over and became my focus. The reality kicked in of being alone with a body that no longer worked. I cried and cried not because of my mum's passing, but because I was left with a body and I didn't know

22

what to do with it, because it didn't work. Suddenly, my life became duality. I had the physical reality going on around me, but I had opened the door to this universe even wider. I became instantly aware of both and unable to only focus on the physical as a single reality. I understood from this moment on at three odd years old that the physical reality isn't all there is. It wasn't a theory of probability, but in my reality a fact, her passing revealed to me the reflection of this universe and I connected with it. This doorway of this universe had widened as my physical side grew. Her passing left me with the gift of this universe. It impacted me more than her passing and I could not ignore it. This became my main question – where am I and why am I here? – and not in another part of this universe where my mum and dad are. Why do I have to stay here and be left behind?

My life split open like a Y-junction or fork in the road.

I adjusted to juggling and surviving the physical dramas of my life, while focusing on the curiosity of the questions that arose in me about the physical reality and soul reality of this universe, that is called heaven (church being highlighted from a young age due to my situation and circumstance of being in the care system).

Many questions that arose were to do with how things match or pair up, meaning what is said do they match up with the actions. I soon realised that adults had many intentions, but it didn't mean they meant it or committed to it.

The first twenty-five years were a mind field. Yes, I said *mind* and not *mine* deliberately. The mind literally is confusing to say the least when you have to guess what is meant – contradictions and miscommunication are optional daily.

I continued to have a lot of questions, but I pushed these to one side for a bit, so I could observe my way through my life experiences.

With each situation I found myself in, I got used to change and took each moment as it came. I wasn't able to settle for too long. My energy went on trying to fit in and adapting to new people.

I observed every detail, facial expressions, the tone of voice, the way things were said. I suppose you could say I started observing the world around me like animals do, in a sixth sense manner, as the five senses were not reliable.

Without realising it, from a young age I tuned in to life to be able to work it out. I realised that taking life at face value didn't mean a thing. Even in writing, it didn't always hold much value. Words came and went, together with many labels and judgments. Fitting your soul into a physical reality is impossible because they don't match.

The physical way of life, the surface doesn't tend to like anything too deep or too intense in feeling. Yet, ironically, the physical fills time with overthinking and under-thinking in a convincing repetitive way.

When many are doing the same thing it's rarely questioned, even if it doesn't make much sense. The fact many are doing the same thing. This alone makes it okay.

You may wonder, where I am going with this?

I am heading in the direction of the SELF.

The first element of frequency the language of this universe.

The SELF.

Who are we?

What are our morals and foundation, etc.?

Observing humans while growing up highlighted how many do not know who they are or what they like, never mind love. Taboo subjects came up, like death, sex and many more. Even being honest at times is discouraged to avoid in case of upsetting someone.

The soul knows you cannot upset or offend another soul when its truth, because it is known and understood as a real connection. The physical not recognising this will easily be offended and class it as an opinion or judgement and not a truth. Truth isn't personal but opinions are.

Humans growing up are so distracted with learning that they forget to notice themselves.

IMPACTING FIRST IMPRESSIONS

As a child growing up, I saw how adults treated themselves and how they interact with others, how what is followed from others or from themselves, even if deep down they don't believe it to be true.

First impressions of when you first became conscious of yourself. Soul side it would be prebirth, but the physical side it is often not at the birth but years later. I myself remember back to two years old in stored memory. My soul, however, remembers many past life experiences. Some may only remember bits and pieces of their childhood.

The worry parents go through providing everything and only some of it is remembered by their children anyway.

WHY IS IT THAT EVEN FUN MEMORIES ARE NOT REMEMBERED?

Why this selective remembering?

What is remembered is down to your soul maps. This is why some humans can go through extreme situations and brush themselves off unscathed and not be affected. Some humans can get a slight knock back and it is the end of their world.

It depends if it aids our soul path or not. If it has nothing to do with our soul map, then it passes us by with no reason to remember it.

I will give you my true-life experience to help explain this concept.

My true-life example.

After I found my mum dead and started growing up in the care system, I had blocked out my memory. You could say I put it into storage, like we do with food and freeze it.

I had buried it and chosen to focus on the everyday life.

At school one day we had homework. We were told to do a family tree. Well, being an orphan, I didn't know much about my history. I knew the sad horrible bits but not all the other facts.

I didn't know much about my parents only their ages.

So, I could not fill in the questions and left a lot blank. At break time, my best friend asked me what my mum died of and what was it like being an orphan. I replied, I didn't know any different, what was it like having parents? As to the other question, I said I don't know. I think it's because she was fat.

I didn't have a wide range of information about her, so I said it how I understood it.

This must have triggered a nerve, as this conversation stayed logged in my memory.

(The link with FOOD that is).

My mum starved me, due to her illness, schizophrenia, and living in different realities, but there in this memory was the connection to do with food.

Then I remember at four years old complaining that I was fat when I was in the bath, pulling at my skin with my fingers. I wasn't fat I was the opposite. I didn't understand what the word fat meant at this age, but the words together with life-changing experiences impacted me like a thorn in my side.

For the most part it was buried with everything else – the FOOD/FAT words – but every now and then life experiences would trigger them to my surface reality.

For me it was the meaning behind it, not the visual look of food or fat or body shapes. So, I knew it wasn't about this side of things.

It was the concept of feeling safe and accepted and fitting in with life around me, having the space to be just me comfortably.

This is why food became a signpost, an important marker, a piece to my many pieces that would aid my awareness of energy and our connection to everything.

PAST PAIN VS. FOUNDATION AND SURVIVAL

Having a regular meal at school and at the children's home set me up a healthy connection with food. It was wonderful having the freedom to just enjoy food without having to think about it.

It was wonderful that food wasn't a weapon. It was lovely I had the chance to enjoy the flavours.

I didn't know it back then but looking back I see it clearly now.

I was such a skinny child, so I had been told, hollow legs you could say. I spent my lunch break going back for seconds and thirds. The food was delicious. I even got a doll for eating so much once.

Yet, I was so skinny.

I felt safe which enabled me to build a small part of my foundation. Okay, it was a small layer but still an important one, a base that was strong enough to hold survival and pain. Yes, emotion comes next in element number two sharing from the self. I will go into that next after this element of the self.

I had seven odd years of space to enjoy my food and even have seconds at school.

We had a hearty breakfast at the children's home: cereal, a boiled egg, and one slice of bread and butter, washed down with a cup of tea.

Lunch, a proper meal at school, and back at the homes, a meal of potatoes and protein and veg.

The potatoes at every meal in some shape or another stands out.

The only thing I didn't like was gooseberries. We had lots of blackberry puddings in the winter after picking them in the summer. Staff would freeze them once we had picked them.

I have fond memories with food in those years.

My relationship changed once I reached teenage years.

Suddenly, the space in which to just enjoy food closed in on me with words.

WORD CUD

I have recently called added extra words word cud.

Unnecessary added dialogue.

I chose the word cud because words just get chewed over and over and over, not going anywhere.

Living with a foster family where there were children older than me changed my lifestyle from a simple one to a more complicated word environment.

I loved just being in the moment and having fun, as I enjoyed it over being sad. Laughing got me into a lot of trouble, but it didn't stop me.

Suddenly, food wasn't just enjoyable food anymore. The fat word came back into play.

You will get fat eating that, or that's not good for you or that's bad for you. It wasn't the food. It was the words I matched up with past events.

Pain – survival – hurt –bad – sad – fat ... I didn't want to relive my sad past that these words highlighted to remind me. So, I avoided eating foods with bad words associated with them, then being self-conscious and trying to be a shape I wasn't.

Wow, life was so simple as a kid where eating was concerned.

Memory kicked in, which then creates a pathway. Whether you love it, or like it, or hate it, you're on it, the slippery slope.

At sixteen I came full circle, when my social worker thought it would be a good idea for me to do a family tree and to face my past and history.

This was like lifting a tomb off the dead for me.

I didn't want to wake the monster pain of the past. I lived it, survived it, and got over it.

Why wake it up?

I was shown my parents' death certificates and why they died, but I wasn't told about my mum's schizophrenia. This came later.

This brought up all my buried pain like a volcano.

I felt emotionally out of control in my life. I didn't feel settled and the only thing I could control is food.

My once healthy relationship and foundation with food changed.

I didn't want to be fat because I didn't want to die. Even though I knew the facts being that my mum had deep vein thrombosis and died in her sleep, this did not override what I felt. To me, the reason she died was because she had been fat.

At sixteen years old around this time of facing my past, my social worker got me in touch with my remaining relatives.

We connected and I got on well with my niece who was eighteen years older than me.

She shared my history and how my mum just ate chocolate all day while I was being starved.

This is where my meaning got confirmed, not the cause but some of the meaning with the word fat.

Then I focused on my own life, adapting to teenage reality and other relationships.

The pressure of looking a certain way—in my head, I would be loved if I looked a certain way and rejected if I didn't. I had already experienced a belly full of rejection and I wasn't about to eat my way into experiencing more. But my small internal healthy base clashed with my external world.

My healthy base loved food and a lot of it.

My external reality now was about making sure I looked a certain way so I would not be rejected.

I had already experienced being starved so this was easy for me.

I worked out a way of how I could blend both.

I ate what I loved and binged but then made myself sick to avoid rejection or even worse death.

My life became a daily battle within my own reality.

WHAT HAD SHIFTED?

What had shifted is not how the food was dished up or what I ate but my connection to myself shifted.

I started my life totally being myself. By the time I reached teenage years and adulthood, I had to split myself into sections to learn to get on in life.

Before I was in my zone and connected to myself, while I ate and mixed with others, not much distorted me. Yes, I continued to master myself in the sense of self responsibility, so I could hold my own.

This shift was different.

What had happened was instead of sharing life with others from a viewing distance, suddenly other people's opinions, attitudes and remarks got my attention.

I hadn't had to fit in when I lived in the children's home. We just accepted each other regardless of how we looked or our history, etc.

Suddenly, my life was filling up with confusion, manipulation and miscommunication.

Like I mentioned earlier, it wasn't about shape or size or fat. What it's about is having the freedom and space to be ourselves.

Our natural organic selves and being comfortable with this.

COMFORTABLE WITH OUR SKIN AND BONES

The past used to be about striving for perfection in the physical. I remember my school reports each year it was the same. "You must try harder," "She doesn't pay attention," or "She giggles or chats too much." Some of these mentioned in my report would actually go on to aid my career. If I hadn't been a chatterbox, as I was frequently told, then I would not have been able to do my job as it involves a lot of talking.

So, the physical may have seen some traits in me back then as not beneficial for my life ahead once I left school. But my soul knew all along what it was doing, even if it got me into trouble the physical side.

The shift happened in 2018. This is something I have already written about in my previous books, so I won't go back into that now.

Up until 2018 the focus was on trying harder and being perfect and successful.

The physical forgets that each soul is already perfect regardless of the body it connects to for its experience. The body to the soul is like getting dressed at birth when it connects with the first breath. It's an expression of choice, of character and personality. We don't strive to change our physical bodies to look like our clothes.

This is how the soul views it.

In the here and now, I am on a journey of self-discovery, following the energy behind everything, to understand how infinite totality works, in the vastness of space in this universe.

This book is mainly about introducing you to the two different realities between the physical and the soul. You may think you're just physical and that's it, but as you can see and most probably have seen for yourselves if you have witnessed a birth, the physical body does not work without a soul. When someone passes, the physical body does not work once the last breath has been taken. The physical body does not work independently on its own.

Yes, you're a walking, breathing soul connected to your chosen body. It should have been a one soul reality while being connected with it, but the physical teachings expanded creating two dual realities.

The focus on the physical has overshadowed and distracted you from your magnificent soul self.

Getting back to being comfortable, how often are you uncomfortable in your day-to-day?

UNCOMFORTABLE

I feel uncomfortable in meetings, I feel uncomfortable out of a routine, I feel uncomfortable in these shoes, that person makes me feel uncomfortable, the atmosphere is uncomfortable.

I am sure at some point you have felt being uncomfortable.

Often this gets mixed up with being shy, or not confident.

When such times happen, we want to get the situation over with as quickly as possible, to remove ourselves from uncomfortable, and back to feeling comfortable.

When I started to put pen to paper to write all my books, I felt comfortable with the content, but the process of writing felt out of my comfort zone of ability. I had been told since a child I was uneducable and was in the dunce class, as it was called back then, throughout all my school years. I struggled with a lot of the subjects. English was one of my worst. Ironically, home economics, which is cooking, was one of my best.

So, writing a book seemed totally out of reach with my lack in English and grammar abilities.

Luckily, I soon found out my inabilities didn't stop me from publishing a book, as they have a wonderful team who edit and sort everything out. What a relief this was! I did feel sorry for them with my lack of punctuation – literally zero present – but it's improved over the years.

I didn't get told off or told to try harder, and I didn't get turned away, because they saw the content.

I have published all my books with my publisher, Strategic Book Publishing. If you have a book in you, I highly recommend them.

I have stayed with them because I have felt comfortable. Yes, they are a business, but it feels more friendly than just business. I have enjoyed talking to them and feel listened to. It is wonderful to connect with humans not just the computer.

I appreciated them so much for giving me the chance to express my writing flare.

I feel we connect with those around us when both sides benefit from the connection. The universe works in pairs and matches energy up.

ONE WAY ISN'T TEAMWORK

I have often heard it's one-sided, but if we really look at the totality of a situation, we will see whoever is involved in any situation will be gaining something from it, making it impossible to be one-sided.

Totality covers everything, not just an action or a thought or even a feeling, but a chance for us to be guided back to ourselves.

Life is teamwork. Teamwork is going on constantly. Like my experience with publishing books, it was teamwork that got the books completed.

In every career other souls are needed for it to exist. The totality of this universe includes every soul. There is no separation or exclusion in this universe. This includes earth because it's part of this universe.

Each soul stands out in this universe because of space around each soul.

In the physical we try hard to stand out from the crowd or try hard to hide amongst it. Both options coexist. We select what we want to experience.

Although there is only one of you in this infinite universe, can you handle your infiniteness?

Life as we have known it so far has been like a tug of war – want it, don't want it; love it but hate it; feel it but don't. Often it isn't a hundred percent; it's fifty-fifty or some percentage.

Your soul lives a hundred percent, the physical lives in percentages and portions, etc.

This leads me to selection and choice.

SELECTION AND CHOICE

It is not one-way fits all. If it was, you would not have the placebo effect. All human bodies would be affected the same way with what is eaten or experienced and we know it's not the case.

You have obvious effects of sweetness, bitter, loud, quiet – the basic variety ranges within choices.

If the human body is made up of skin, bone, organs etc., then what makes each body unique and causes the different outcomes is the placebo effect. It's not a case of one size fits all, which is why words such as could have this outcome. The could word covers many a possibility.

The only thing that would make it variable is the energy connection, the first element of frequency, the connection to self.

And what is connected to the human body first at the birth? You got it, your soul.

So going back to the beginning to come forward, it's the soul's energy that makes all the difference.

Our souls create the variety of choice, which makes sense considering the soul is an infinite energy of this universe.

If the physical selection of choice were a 100 percent sure thing, then this would mean the soul matches up with the physical body totally.

We know it does not have this total connection because the mind is changing its mind constantly due to the storage of memory.

Not being dialled in to the physical, a 100 percent the connection causes a wobble in creation, a distortion of a bit of this and a bit of that.

If you were around in the seventies and eighties, you would be familiar with having to tune in manually your radio and television sets.

As long as you knew the radio station or television channel and whether the station was AM or FM on the radio.

By selecting these you could tune in to find your chosen station. But while tuning in, the static and interference of distortion would be heard. Sometimes you would hear a bit of one station and a bit of another as you turned the dial, but it wasn't clear.

The station is clear to hear once tuned in 100 percent.

If you chose to listen to a station not fully tuned in because it was too hard to find, you would succumb to listening to it amongst the static noise around it.

Now setting up a radio or television is automatic, unless you choose otherwise, if manual is an option.

Peeling back the front cover on everything it leads me back to a power source. Nothing works without it.

FOLLOW THE ENERGY NOT THE GOODS

The physical focuses on pictures and words. This has been going on for centuries, even going back in history when hieroglyphs have been found.

Words come and go and change with every century, so what makes sense to us today most probably would not be the same as way back when.

Even the spoken word isn't always reliable, hence the phrase Chinese whispers (meaning a piece of information is passed from one person to the next and is changed sightly each time it is told).

Seeing isn't always believing either. I have seen black families have white children biologically.

So, are we all races within us? Again, this would make sense if the physical were created from soul energy, which holds all infinite possibilities. In our soul we can be whatever we want to be. This choice can override the physical possibilities. When this happens it's called a miracle, a once in a lifetime happening, etc.

But is it?

If the physical doesn't exist without a soul, and the brain is for the cells to communicate with itself, then the brain doesn't hold knowledge, it holds memory. Therefore, soul is where the knowledge is. Infinite knowledge.

THERE IS NOTHING NEW IN THIS UNIVERSE

This may surprise you to read this and it may even blow your mind.

But if we are to get to the facts of reality, we must go way back and follow the energy.

If you're an ant, you see reality from that perspective.

If you're a larger animal, you see reality from that perspective.

If you're a human, you see reality from that perspective.

If you're a bird, you see reality from that perspective.

If you're a plane, you see reality from that perspective of vast space.

Everything below looks small in comparison.

Even when travelling by plane it doesn't look that busy with traffic. I noticed this when I looked out of the plane window this summer.

I saw lots of clouds, and not many passing planes. The odd one I did see it was hard to spot and looked very small unless I saw a plane parallel with us.

I did wonder why more planes were not seen on our journey considering how many are taking off and landing.

I am not a pilot and so I do not have the answer. I can only guess it's because of flight paths in different alignments plus speed and, of course, the vastness of space. Maybe to a trained pilot, they could see what I could not.

As you can see by my random questions that I have on my journey of life, it covers every detail in all areas.

Life is a huge subject matter. It's not an easy subject to write about, partly because I can only share my view but not cover all views at once.

Yes, we are connected to totality all now at once, but sharing it is like watching a plane travel across the sky and chat about the content on the ground, every house and every detailed experience going on down below. It is not possible in writing but is possible to know in connection, so I guess the next best option is an overview from that bird's eye view.

So, this book won't cover every day-to-day detail, because every soul here on earth is having infinite experience.

I have chosen to go beyond the day-to-day, but I have had to cover part of the day-to-day to bring you up to speed.

The reason why I feel there is nothing new in this universe is because, on an energetic level, there isn't. This infinite universe already holds every possibility energetically. Think of it like an energy universe shopping mall. It has everything stocked. Your soul selects and chooses to experience something, and your connection of your choice is matched up and paired to the same choice in this universe shopping mall. This connection brings this chosen event to your reality, not governed by time or days but space.

If your space within you and around you are off, it causes distortion so it's hard to see or feel or interact in any way with your selection. In a nutshell, if the energy of your soul within the space surrounding you isn't tuned in 100 percent to your choice, this then causes offshoots of experience, like a frayed piece of material, creating delays in receiving what you initially chose.

STILLNESS OF COMMITMENT

Stay still and you will feel the vibe or buzz of your own energy, some call it chi. It's your own soul running through every cell of you.

You give off energy.

You receive information.

Through your flow and by being still you connect with your knowing.

The words still and stillness may confuse things here, so I will swap stillness with commitment.

Commitment comes under the fourth element of frequency completion.

I will cover all the elements in due course.

When you are self-dialled/tuned into your own self station, then everything from the shopping mall universe aligns with you quickly without the physical getting in the way.

Your soul is a frequency. It's your vibe and your personal station and hub.

When you connected with your chosen body, you connected your frequency to it through the breath. You breathe constantly so this means your soul station is playing constantly. There is no off switch. The universe never sleeps.

As you breathe, your soul transmits and plays through your physical body.

Your soul is your station, and the human body is like the radio set.

If your connection with your own body choice is off, then everything is off.

Yes, your life always comes back to yourself.

This is why element number one is the self.

Your life is in your own frequency transmission.

How you connect with it is how your life plays out.

When a soul is dialled into itself 100 percent, then the pathway is clear.

No obstructions.

The soul in a committed self-connection holding its own frequency in its own space, like a pilot holding the controls of a plane, will follow its soul path and stay on course.

We move within our space holding our frequency, once we connect in our space through the channel of our frequency, we then make a selection of what we want to experience next. This sends a signal out to the universe shopping mall, which picks up your choice. This is then brought back to you to receive in manifestation/materialisation.

If you confuse your order or keep changing your mind, this universe brings you all of it until you are 100 percent sure.

It has nothing to do with wrong, right, good or bad or even ability. It has everything to do with your frequency and alignment.

We are like walking computers; we have the front cover where all the action is. But what holds that action is not the screen. Take off the front cover you have a circuit board. This is where it all happens.

This is what I am sharing, the circuit energy board of life. The front cover of every day stuff is part of it, but not all of it.

THE FRONT COVER

We are taught in the physical about presentation back in the day. It was putting on your Sunday best or smart dress for work, etc. In the last few years, I have heard the words aesthetically pleasing.

The focus is on the image, the look not so much about the content.

Cycles have come and gone. Back in the day, newspapers were read daily. They were an integral part of the day. Books and magazines, cartoons, films. Entertainment, not forgetting words, creating lyrics for music, manifesting wonderful songs. This combined with movement created different forms of dance.

I loved watching films growing up. I still do. They are a wonderful way of escaping from the physical into a world of imagination and visualisation.

We believe everything we see or hear so it must be true, but is it?

The only way you're going to find the truth and the meaning is by gathering all the layers of information. It is not a test sheet or a multiple-choice answer.

It's real life, not what could be or might be but gathered information of facts, and what is now.

I noticed while growing up that humans want the truth but don't want it either.

The dual life of reality is definitely like a duel. Okay, I am pushing it with words, but the meaning is there.

Front covers give us a presentation of how life should look on paper, but we know from experience anything on paper is not how it necessarily turns out.

You get unforeseen circumstances.

As you can see while I peel away the layers of life, you will understand why one size does not fit all.

This is why many things used as tools here, whether medical, education or interests, often come with the word could.

This could happen, this might happen, the reason being is because anything external to you does not have access to your personal frequency station of yourself, only you do.

Because of space around every single frequency no one has access only themselves.

Liken it to the actual radio station when tuning it in manually.

PROGRAMS AND INSTRUCTIONS

Humans are taught everything, how to walk, how to eat, how to think, how to even breathe.

Over the centuries trends come and go in all areas, cooking, home lifestyle, celebration themes, clothing, toys and interests.

Many have repeated over the years.

Religion was once an important part of family life. Now it's gadgets.

Growing up as a psychic in the seventies and eighties, the spiritual movement back then wasn't so accepted as it is now, in many areas.

You have many different things you can learn and join now that aren't even about talking to the dead.

The world is ready now to understand more about reality past the trends of the moment.

You can learn something from a book or from a tutor, but it doesn't mean you necessarily understand it or know it. Memorising something a pattern or a sequence of words isn't the same as energy knowing it.

When your physical triggers your soul, knowing it will automatically trigger a lot of questions. This is why children ask a lot of questions. Asking questions as you get to adulthood is often seen as a weakness as if you should know it already.

Yet asking questions in truth is an amazing strength. It shows your soul is working with your physical body in connection.

If you have no curiosity and no questions then your quite happy going about your day and not delving too deep into anything to not upset routine, an autopilot of continuation. Holding the fort, you may say. This last sentence is said loosely as it covers one aspect not all angles. Being consistent is stability. I guess what I missed out in the last sentence was variety. Once you're used to a way of life or a lifestyle you are used to it and can do it with your eyes shut.

You're experienced in what you know so far.

This is a different angle again. There are so many ways of looking at things, which is why I can only touch on many aspects; otherwise, this book would never get completed, as there is always more.

I will touch on what my soul feels is relevant to help with understanding the global changes of the shift we are all going through, both personally, physically and globally.

Huge change isn't just happening here on earth's space, it is also happening in locations closely around earth too.

IT'S ALL AROUND YOU

The taught human reality has rubbed off on us all; it's ingrained. It's going to take until at least 2056 for this to rub off.

Words are everywhere. You can't just do anything without words or instructions getting in the way.

Whatever we pick up or do, words are staring at us. This sparks our memory and this joins in too.

The landscape around us does not have instruction manuals; animals and wildlife don't either. They have physical bodies just like us, physical meaning material organic matter. Okay, they don't speak like us with words, but they have something that is superior: the gut instinct, their soul suitcases, or with plant life. It's pure energy.

They get on with life and adapt with their knowing.

They don't label a thing or categorise.

They just get on with living.

Humans don't.

Humans have been encouraged to follow the written word. This sentence reminds me of the bible. I heard this sentence in relation to this when I was told to follow the written word of the bible when growing up.

Nothing is right or wrong or good or bad. If it works for your life go with it.

But for me when I connected with anything in the physical, it stirred up many more questions than answers.

Each angle of life that I went down gave me piles of questions about life itself, which had nothing to do with the actual subject heading. These became like pieces of a big jigsaw puzzle that I started to piece together from fourteen years old, collecting more pieces as each year passed.

Travelling on this road of self-discovery, I have come to the realisation that it never ends, because infinity doesn't.

So instead of branching out through all infinite experiences, looking at life around me from the physical reality aspect and the soul universe realty, I realised now that I feel like I am in a big library of all experiences, totality manifesting its total infinite knowing.

This would explain why every soul and everything is known in this universe. If you listen to NDE (near death experiencers), they often say the same I was told.

I now wanted to find out about how to get to the new, and this is where this next journey is taking me.

Past the library of infinite possibilities out into space to the core of point zero. Point zero to me is where every soul is connected in this universe, like the pupil of an eye.

This next chapter of discovery is unfolding now, so as you read this, I am on this journey with you.

I GET ASKED, HOW DO YOU LIVE MORE LIKE SOUL?

By firstly understanding your human body and how it connects with your soul. You can't miss out the physical body. It is your tool after all, and your connected to it with every breath, never separated from it. Like the universe is infinitely connected, until you take your last breath. Because if you just jump into spirituality and ignore your own connection to your body, or don't face yourself totally, then the spiritual aspect of yourself is being used to hide the physical part, or to only see certain bits and ignore other parts, even though all these parts make all of you.

As you know this universe is transparent so hiding only works for so long, and your soul will encourage you to look at all your parts, not just the select few.

I ALSO GET ASKED, AM I A YOUNG SOUL OR AN OLD SOUL?

You are neither young nor old, as you're not defined by a number because you're infinite. Numbers and words were not always used in the physical reality. This evolved and got taught, to communicate in the physical. Souls communicate via sensing and connection; humans communicate what they select, not necessarily what they actually feel and mean.

All souls in this universe are from point zero. Point zero is where every soul is collectively together. No soul has left point zero. Why, we have a connection to everything. Look at it like being at home and video calling someone in another country. You haven't left home but you're communicating across many miles. The video is like how souls reflect here; some even understand it easier as a hologram energetically. As you can see, there are many ways of explaining the same thing.

We are all the same in the sense that we are all souls regardless of our experiences and travels across this universe.

During my work as a soul reader, I have come across souls who are ready to travel to the next universe as they have completed this one.

I will share more about my work towards the end of this book.

Once you remember you're a soul, you don't end up being too caught up with the physical. You view life from a bigger picture. What used to bother you doesn't so much anymore.

YOU CAN'T HACK THE NATURAL STATE

The soul is the soul it will always be regardless of how many lifetimes of different bodies that you have connected to in your past lives.

You may remember World War One and Two, or any past memory history moments.

You may remember being a different character in a previous life experience.

You are not your physical bodies. You are your soul, even though you may remember your past lives. It is like dress-up to the soul, like when children enjoy dressing up and playing out role play.

This is what experiencing life with a body is like for the soul.

If you have ever researched NDE experiencers, one thing struck me as a common theme. They weren't keen about coming back or connecting with the body that they had spaced out from.

I use the term *spaced out from* because they have not taken their last final breath.

The organic energy of any form is at the nucleus of itself.

If I showed you some seeds, then showed you how those seeds would look once they had grown. If this is something you have no experience of seeing for yourself, then it would be hard to believe that a small seed could grow into a tree or whatever the seed is.

To plant a seed a big hole is created, far bigger than the seed itself. The seed is put in the space and then covered up and buried with earth. Then watered, etc.

The seed is alone with itself, in its own space ready to connect with the space in which to grow.

Once the seed grows roots, those roots spread out to occupy the space.

Once germinated the seed is ready to sprout into a plant or a tree, etc.

To the physical eye, it looks like nothing is happening externally. Patience is required and trust.

The physical sees nothing for a while but continues to nurture and water the seed.

Eventually, the physical eye will see green shoots sprouting from the soil.

The seed gets stronger and grows into itself.

Nature shows us how to grow ourselves, with patience, trust and commitment.

Sometimes it takes years for the plant to bear fruit before it gets established. Some fruit matures, and some do not.

This year I got four lemons on my lemon tree. Three matured enough to eat, but one did not and became stuck at a limit of self-development even from the same tree.

There are many branches on one tree, all experiencing itself at different stages of growth.

Like we do, how our human bodies are as a baby are not the same as puberty or when we reach older maturity.

We look different as we grow.

I can look at flower beds and herb gardens and see how each individual seed is growing at its own rate.

It is given the conditions and space to freely be itself.

A sunflower doesn't look at a rose and decides I don't want to be a sunflower. I want to be a rose like my neighbour next to me.

Nature and animals recognise and accept that they are what they are and have no need or desire to change themselves.

When did humans stop allowing themselves to grow into who they organically are?

If you come across different tribes, they are not focused on the human body in the same way as the western world.

It boils down to priority. I am sure if the western world still had to hunt and gather to live, many of the things they used to worry about won't be important anymore.

Our basic survival and lifestyle are what directs what matters.

The connection between the soul and the human body used to be in pure acceptance and knowing.

This changed when souls stopped living as souls and started to learn and live as a physical human.

A BIT ABOUT OUR HISTORY

When earth's space got created it was just space. It didn't have its own signature frequency or vibration.

The first souls that arrived here on earth's space and lived in peace and harmony. The souls were uniquely themselves and blended in harmony and matched with the other souls that arrived here.

The earth's space gave them a backdrop like a blank canvas in which to express themselves, and to experience their totality infinite possibilities from the shopping mall of this universe to this space.

Liken it to being in a silent room and upon entering all you can hear is those already there, chatting because there is no background noise.

The first souls brought their personality and character to life here.

There was no fighting. They knew how to take the first breath, and in doing so connected with their chosen body.

They knew how to take their last breath, so they did not need illness or accidents in which to use as a plane ticket to exit earth.

They lived soul and their soul energy flowed beautifully in connection between the soul and the physical like a figure of eight as a visual example.

The body grew with no limits, and with no limits and expansive space, everything grew big.

The physical body grew around eighteen feet tall; trees and landscape matched in vastness. Everything was gigantic compared to how we view it now.

Like the saying a goldfish grows to its environment.

Humans have searched for the fountain of youth through the physical reality. Unable to find it, because in comparison to back then nothing lasts long, not even material goods.

Hence, the fast turnaround of manufacturing.

The fountain of youth is your soul.

Depending on your connection between the physical body and the soul, without the physical teachings getting in the way. The soul flowed freely through and around the physical body.

The first souls would connect with a body for as long as they wanted to; five hundred years was not uncommon. It saved having to keep letting go and coming back in which to complete an experience. This way it was done in one go.

Souls lived a peaceful harmony life, enjoying their soul abilities through the medium of a physical body. This is like water experiencing itself as boiling or cold or warm or freezing or even vapour.

Souls knew they were in control of the physical body via the breath.

This all changed when a select few of souls arrived and observed how earth's space didn't have its own signature frequency. They watched how souls lived in peace and harmony but noticed how the souls did not tune into a backdrop. They harmonised their own signature frequencies with each other and blended peacefully. This is how starlings fly by following the vibe of the resonance that match with each other. Tuning in to the same frequency, you can follow the flight path of energy while still being your unique self.

Space makes this possible. It's like listening to a choir singing in harmony. They know what note to sing, and they too are following a resonance to be in harmony.

These souls had an idea. They saw an opportunity in which to take over earth's space. They realised that their soul didn't have to match the backdrop of earth's space because it did not have its own frequency yet in which to match it.

They saw earth's space as empty space.

They decided they wanted to take control of it.

These souls started by ripping hearts out of the souls' bodies. This caused the soul to take their last breath.

This caused shock and fear and confusion. Souls had been used to being in control of their first and last breaths. To see this happening and bloodshed caused the originals souls to flee.

They spread far around the earth.

The feared souls went after them. It wasn't enough wanting bodies; they wanted the land too.

The new paradigm caused divisions.

The original souls lived peacefully in the now, as souls in this universe do.

The fear escalated across the land. Money and time got invented.

The more the fear station took over, the soul way of living stopped, until all what was left of the soul connection was the breath. Not even the heartbeat could be heard, just the taste of fear.

Word spread on how to navigate the new fear paradigm. Souls encouraged souls that arrived to live in the past or the future but discouraged them to avoid the now, as that is where the bad stuff happened.

Soul abilities stopped. Souls stopped using knowing and gut instinct.

To blend in and hide, souls learnt the fear paradigm way of life.

The soul connection weakened; the fear connection strengthened.

With the soul connection, weak the longevity with a body lessened.

Now bodies had a lifecycle of forty to a hundred years, if lucky.

The fear controllers knew that pure souls lived amongst the feared humans. They did everything they could in which to find them.

Pure souls hid in forests and stayed away from the main communities.

It took many centuries for the fear lifestyle to take hold. First, they had to wean soul off their soul connection, so they only remembered fear and the taught way of life.

With the absence of gut knowing and instinct, the fear controllers taught souls how to hijack their brains. They encouraged souls to bypass their gut and feelings and feared them into using the taught script of the mind.

First, rules got introduced followed by taxation and manipulation of bartering.

The body itself weakened and became fragile because the brain was no longer able to just do what it was intended for: communicate with itself along the spine.

Now, it had to use its energy for memory growth.

This caused many malfunctions within the brain and body.

Accidents occurred and disease grew from malfunction.

The pure soul way of life became a distant myth, covered in secrecy and fear.

Ghost stories got told to discourage souls from connecting to their soul.

The fear controllers knew that for the physical taught way of life to exist they needed the connection of the soul. Willing cooperation was necessary. They set life up in such a way that souls became grateful for what they got so they could feed their families. If they did not agree and toe the line, they had the consequences of slaughter or prison. Entertainment grew by word of mouth about such tortures. At first souls went to watch to see if the stories were true. Once they saw this for themselves, they became spectators to keep safe. In their minds they thought if they watched then at least it wasn't happening to them.

They drank alcohol to numb the shocking memory of what they had seen.

Life grew in this fearful way and carried on until 2018.

Even though prophecies were told throughout the centuries, the Mayan calendar is one many will remember about the end of the world on 21st December 2012.

Knowledge of the past wasn't always understood.

But they knew the old paradigm of fear would end and that a new paradigm would take over.

Going back to come forward requires souls to remember who they are.

Are you just a physical body? Or is there more to life than this? Maybe you have never questioned anything as long as the bills were paid.

BACK TO THE SELF

Points we have in common with one another.

We are a soul.

Our soul connected with our chosen physical body at our first breath.

We arrived only with our soul and nothing else, no clothes or bank balance.

We have our five senses for the physical and soul gut instinct, known as the sixth sense.

Up to 2018, the taught way of life has rubbed off on us.

Post 2018, we are encouraged to let go of this way of life back to our organic soul selves.

In the past we have been encouraged to not pay much attention to ourselves. To be distracted with time keeping and schedules. To fear or doubt the future while not realising now is where it all is happening.

Pre-2000, we were encouraged to use our brains. Now, we are encouraged to let technology do the work for us.

We are increasingly seeing how supermarkets are changing into self-serve only.

The negative has been followed and any positive doubted.

Confusion in life has caused self-doubt in so many areas.

The relationship with the self was once so strong that deals would be made by word alone, no back up in writing was necessary, as the vocal word was enough.

When did this change?

When did we stop accepting ourselves?

How has the connection to the self been ignored or devalued.

Over the next four years between 2024 and 2028, life will change so our priorities change in depth and meaning, which will create quality.

Working out who we really are for ourselves.

The fake way of life is over, the illusion of reality is over, and the taught way of life is over.

You will be encouraged to listen to yourself.

Do you take your word for it?

GUIDANCE

Guidance has always been around and always will be. The reason being is because you're a soul in this infinite universe of infinite possibilities.

You arrived here with soul backup.

The physical is unable to sever the connection of the soul with this universe.

Space connects you to everything. This is why space is around you no matter where you go.

You will always be met with space of this universe.

The energy grid of this universe isn't seen with human eyes, as the physical is a different reality. The energy of this universe is seen with the soul.

Whatever you need will cross your path in aligned connection.

Depending on what you have set for yourself on your soul map, the physical path is not the same as the soul path.

You will be given all the space you need to experience your chosen soul map, not limited to your present physical body choice. Why, you can have many body choices but still follow the same soul map over many centuries.

Your soul map doesn't change because of your physical body or if you're distracted with it. Your soul map waits for your soul attention not your physical reaction.

THE PHYSICAL BODY

The human body is our main distraction from ourselves.

To the soul, it's not so much about how it looks, etc., but more about if it serves my purpose.

Your purpose being what you select before you arrive here on your soul map.

The soul has no agenda, only to connect and complete what it has chosen to experience.

The physical body for some souls is a challenge in itself, before even experiencing what's on their map.

It's one thing connecting with your chosen body, it's another thing settling in and being comfortable with it.

Matching up is how this universe works, and the soul and the physical script don't match in energy and vibration. This inner knowing from the soul gets lost in translation via the physical.

The physical being external in view compared with internal feeling of the soul, liken it to the soul not being in play when living from the external taught script of memory. The soul enters standby mode when not in play.

You can act your life without your heart or soul being present or involved.

The memory bypasses connection in autopilot reaction.

To truly live is to not live in memory.

If you choose to live in memory, then you won't have access to more and be limited to the script. Living like this is like ignoring your reason for being here to your soul.

The way life has been structured up to 2018 won't be enough anymore, because memory is weakening.

Souls are letting go of their mind to use their soul connection. During this transfer it may seem like humans are losing their minds. In a way they are as the old way of a scripted life that won't work in this new paradigm of soul energy.

If you're noticing that the script doesn't fulfil you anymore, then you're ready for your own self-discovery.

To remember who you really are before the taught, scripted-way lifestyle.

What are your values or your moral compass? Do you even have a moral compass?

Or do you not give it your energy?

Do you give anything your energy? Or is your life viewed as a job and to-do lists for the day while following what's in your diary.

Do you even enjoy your life? When was the last time you felt free and full of life and laughed because you felt it?

ENTERTAINMENT

Humans over centuries have gotten used to being entertained. New souls that arrive here and grow up during childhood will use their imagination and find a way to entertain themselves.

Adult responsibilities sidetrack us that wealth is happiness, but if this was true then why do we not see wealthy humans happy and content. Nothing fills the space of self-connection.

Why?

Because the external physical reality is a different reality to your soul.

You have access to your own two stations: your physical side of you and your soul side. The physical will not compensate for your soul.

They are not the same.

Your physical energy is connected to the physical reality of matter, your soul energy is connected to this total universe.

As soon as we arrived here pre-2018, we were encouraged to focus on the physical reality and ignore the soul, one apart from the connection with it via breathing.

Entertainment softens the blow of hard work, a reward via many tools of the physical trade.

Eating, watching films/shows, holidays, rides at the theme park, walks out in nature, quite a lot of things to choose from.

EATING and LIVING

Growing up back in the 1970s and 80s, if you were hungry you had to wait for dinner or supper, etc.

The high street had a variety of shops. Woolworth's was a go-to favourite. This shop was amazing. It had a variety of stock for all age groups and interests.

In our high street back then we had a chippy, a portion of chips in newspaper, a warming and filling treat after a day out; a wimpy; and an Indian restaurant. No coffee shops or bottles of water in hand. If we were thirsty when out and about, we drank from the public water fountains.

No mobile phones or tech, just the red telephone box that wasn't fun to wait for if it was already being used. If you saw piles of coins stacked, you would look for another telephone box or wait until you got home to use the house phone.

We had amazing sweet shops. You got a bag of sweets for a few pence. Wow, writing this I must sound old.

But that is how it was back then. Quality was still present in retail and customer service as a valued part of the shopping experience.

You had to be able to add up in your head if you worked the tills.

Pay was cash in a brown envelope at the end of the week.

To manage housekeeping, pay packets got divided into different envelopes. I even remember our television was on pay-as-you-go and you saved your fifty pence to watch TV.

As each century passes, I am sure each generation has a story to tell on how life was back then compared to now.

Like anything, you have your advantages and disadvantages.

TASTE AND SMELL

I remember everything tasting and smelling better.

When the roast was cooked, you smelt the dripping and flavours.

Unless taste buds dampen as you age, but food had flavour naturally.

Now, you add flavour.

Quality does not make you rich quick.

The throwaway lifestyle and quick turnaround of high demand grew profits and waistlines, and the medical industry was relied on more than home remedies.

Self-responsibility was slipping through our fingers without realising it for an easy life.

Clothes used to be mended and darned. Shoes were not thrown away until holes appeared.

Having one wardrobe with your Sunday best and a couple of choices to cover winter and summer.

Simplicity at its finest.

When did this change?

The cost of living and throwaway products.

Maybe even after the war when women were needed for skilled work.

I don't know when exactly but cost of living would be the obvious reason.

Plus, for some it would have been a choice.

EARLY 1980s AS A TEENAGER

I remember hearing the word yuppie. Those who had money bought a Porsche car to show they had money. They often worked in banking or the stock exchange, I think.

Looking through the local gazette, there were plenty of jobs to choose from.

Interviews were in person.

People smoked in restaurants and on trains. You planned to meet up in-person if you didn't want to call them on the phone. You trusted they would stick to the plans.

You still had your everyday problems, human-to-human relations, and managing to pay your bills, like in every era. Money comes and goes. You have moments in your life when you have more than enough, and you have moments where you barely have two coins to rub together and rely on debt to survive.

That's life.

Food wasn't really used as entertainment unless you were on a date.

Takeout food was limited and was a once-a-week treat, especially on a Friday night when you queued for fish and chips. Eating out has become part of daily life whether hungry or not.

Back in the eighties, supermarkets mainly sold the weekly shop. Popping in and buying a sandwich wasn't a trend.

If your place of work didn't offer lunch or a canteen, then you made packed lunch. There weren't many options like now. You did see cafes around busy seaside towns or busy shopping centres, not so much on high streets.

If you were hungry while out it was usually a bag of chips or sweets from the sweet shop.

Sweets got weighed and you chose how much you wanted.

We didn't have sell-by dates on food. We had to use our noses and tastebuds to work out if the food was off.

Trust me, you knew straight away if it was fresh or not.

Crisps didn't have weights on the side of the packets. Opening crisps back then you had to be careful because they were filled to the top.

A bag lasted you ages.

Portion sizes are much bigger compared with back then. A grab bag or sharing bag is eaten as a treat now. These sizes weren't available then.

Diet trends have come and gone.

As a child I was only interested in flavour and whether I enjoyed it or not and if it filled me up.

Teenage years changed this simply because of self-conscious body image, etc., together with added words or opinions and comments.

SIMPLICITY AT ITS FINEST

From my teenage years to now, I have seen most diets, of all types.

I have tried many over the years.

My conclusion now for myself.

It's not so much about the diet, but the energy connection towards the food.

Each diet has baffled me, especially with access to online researching. The library isn't the only source of information. So much more information is available from all walks of life.

Why is it that you find so many versions of the same diet? Is this confusing or what? Why if they work are they altered?

They often don't match up.

Is it the humble food anyway?

I look at what people ate and looked like after World War Two.

Homemade cooking of pies and potatoes and veg, cakes and crumbles with custard. Sugar was added to cooking. Fat and lard. Sprinkled sugar on toast was often enjoyed.

All the foods eaten that is classed as bad and yet they were trim around the waist.

I know there is not one-way-fits-all because we are unique, why the placebo effect happens.

So, does it come back to our connection with food and not so much the food itself?

FOLLOW THE ENERGY

If you're reading this, then you will remember your childhood.

I remember mine and my relationship with food was simple until I reached teenage years.

So much choice compared to back then. Maybe this is a factor for wider waistlines.

Eating when not hungry too.

Eating for entertainment.

Eating choices for an easy life.

Getting back to words, words come with a delivery of your energy, so therefore what is spoken has a frequency transfer that alters the outcome of an experience.

(Taken from a Google search)

Japanese researcher Dr. Masaru Emoto conducted experiments that explored the effect of words and emotions on water. Emoto's experiments involved exposing water to different words, pictures, or music, and then freezing it to examine the ice crystal's structure. He claimed that water's physical structure could be changed by emotional energies and vibrations.

Emoto's findings included:

Positive words, water exposed to positive words and intentions formed symmetrical, beautiful crystalline structures when frozen.

Negative words, water exposed to negative words and intentions formed disorganised asymmetrical structures.

Water from different sources, produced different ice structures. For example, water from a mountain stream formed beautifully shaped geometric designs, while water from polluted sources created distorted ice structures.

Rice experiment – Emoto also conducted a rice experiment that demonstrated the power of positive and negative words. He found that speaking negatively to rice in water caused decay, while speaking positively allowed it to thrive.

THE HUMAN BODY

(Google search)

The US Geological Survey (USGS) says up to 60% of the human adult body is water. According to Mitchell and others (1945), the brain and heart are composed of 73% water, and the lungs are about 83% water. The skin contains 64% water, muscles and kidneys are 79%, and even the bones are watery: 31%.

We are made up of a lot of water.

How do you treat you each day with words?

Obviously, I am just sharing my own rabbit hole that I have gone down of self-discovery. I am not trying to teach you anything, but I can guide you back to yourself so that you start asking questions, which will take you down your own rabbit hole of self-discovery. This is the reason why I am sharing. And this is why you picked this book up, to encourage yourself to ask your own questions.

Asking questions guides you to discover more about yourself, not just the physical side of reality but your soul side too.

I am not writing this book to answer your questions but so you find the answers to your questions inside of you.

You do not have to wait until you take your last breath to be reacquainted with your soul.

You're connected to it now and it is the sole reason why you're here, having your experiences that you call life (okay, pardon the soul pun).

To me, the soul has been ignored for far too long and often tarnished over the centuries.

If I can get the soul word highlighted in a sentence I will, because I want to big it up, so your soul gets your attention.

The physical has taken the spotlight for far too long.

Getting back to energy and our connection with food.

Souls back in history had a stronger self-connection in all senses.

Food was survival as the human body needs food for cell regeneration.

Water to replenish the cells.

Your body signals when it is thirsty and when it is hungry or tired.

The connection to our senses has been dumbed down with words.

When did we need so many words? And often words made things complicated.

Together with pictures, they can often have many different meanings. We go back to being spoilt for choice.

Obviously, no one is spoilt. We do live in an infinite universe, but what it boils down to is can we handle choice in harmony without causing disharmony and distortion?

Humans in the past read lots and listened to many words via radio, and yes, still do some more than others.

Life online has speeded things up. Small video clips have taken words by surprise and only a few words are highlighted.

Often watching things online, it is hard to know what is real and what isn't.

We either take it all in or back off and start to research within ourselves to find our own truth.

IS IT THE FOOD'S FAULT FOR OUR QUALITY OF HEALTH?

Following the energy and knowing that the first element of frequency in the language of this universe holds the key.

Or should I say the door open to more.

If we are living in a soul infinite reality, where everything is energy, then our connection to our life is what alters it.

Life isn't one size fits all.

We are unique. Even twins aren't the same; they have differences.

So, what changes our body?

A variety of factors depending on the alignment of your connection.

It is not a one-word answer.

Food has been around for centuries, longer than a hundred years, but within this period bodies have changed a lot.

When life was basic and simple, work was often the job in-hand, literally. It took skill, concentration and energy, due to the quality and detail of the task.

Products and goods were handmade.

Not just machine made.

There wasn't much standing around to think of other words.

Commitment and craft and energy were applied.

At the end of a working day tired and hungry, the family sat down to eat.

Home socialising consisted of musical instruments or handmade games, reading and listening to the radio and later the television.

The newspaper would be read to keep up to scratch about local and world news.

Life became more complicated with more access of choice and demand for excess.

Production wasn't about quality but became more about quantity.

The more home lifestyles changed to adapt for an easier life it made it more complicated and distorted, changing from fear driven to stress driven.

With each year passing vocabulary has grown, our memories have been saturated with negative words.

Have you ever paid a compliment to someone only for them to reply with a negative response? It is easier to complain in life rather than appreciate and compliment.

You still find quality business and handmade products and customer care as a valued service.

I have equally seen lack of care and morals and a "I can't be bothered" attitude.

Attitudes such as these show the connection is obviously missing to the job itself and the only reason for being there is the money.

Energy is important in quality work; otherwise, it is like receiving an empty box without any contents, but the packaging looks good.

I am here. Aren't I enough?

You can't miss someone with energy as they will have a sparkle in their eye or a genuine, warm smile that is not painted on like part of the dress code.

Organic energy is golden.

If you come across those with energy embrace them, as it reflects that they are in touch with their soul.

You can tell those who are lifeless and not present and functioning day-to-day.

It takes experience to master your soul energy together with the physical body because the interference from the physical memory gets more airtime and disrupts your natural rhythm.

Not anymore.

Soul energy is taking over. This is why I am sharing what I have discovered over fifty-seven years so you can look back on your years with a different open view.

If you have ever asked the question, is there more to life than this?

Then now you will see, yes, there is more to life than the past physical script of memory.

Souls were not meant to connect with a physical body for an experience, to become soul dormant and live a life of limitation to the point of such self-physical destruction and self-loathing.

Loathing is a word. I wondered whether to write it or not, but if it got your attention like it did me as I wrote it, so yes, for this alone it's staying.

I could have chosen any word that is the opposite of self-love. It doesn't really matter to be honest, sticking to the facts here. I have observed many conversations of self-attack.

Picking at how we look or at our skin or teeth any part of the body.

Why has this been so ingrained as acceptable?

Because if something wasn't picture-perfect as portrayed in magazines you needed a better lifestyle. If you looked a certain way or lived a certain lifestyle or became famous, it meant living happy ever after. The same went for marriage. When I watched films, people often lived happily ever after if they got married. I believed the films back then, but after a few marriages I soon realised marriage didn't give you a happy ever after, connection to who you are did.

But, and a big but, if your relationship with yourself is in self-attack mode then the relationship will suffer being attacked.

A peaceful self-connection and settled self will start off a settled relationship with another.

So, if two people meet who are not self-settled then the relationship will be in for a rocky ride.

It's not to say they can't weather the storm and grow towards a calmer life. They can usually live a calm life if the fighting doesn't escalate from the self and one attacks the other.

A sentence my youngest daughter said to me recently is this, "Why would I want to hurt the one I love?" So true, but we do.

It's not in an ideal world. It's a choice of our own making, between memory, habit, and laziness towards change.

If the journey over the years has been tiresome, it is not always easy to find your own way when it feels like you have gotten yourself into your own emotional maze.

Reaction is not a solution, understanding yourself is.

When do we get a chance to work out who we really are without the physical getting in the way?

If you're too deep or intense or not living like everyone else then something is wrong, or is it?

Being infinite is unique so every word works in which to describe the soul.

It is both of every opposite.

What makes infinite work without spinning you out of control is your connection in the moment, without getting memory involved.

The memory is like a third party that is not required but you get accustomed to it.

The memory makes a heavy load and slows the journey down.

Often what the physical doesn't understand is treated with medication in the hope of it going away.

This happened in my teenage years.

Just to fill you in, if you haven't read my previous books, I was sent for sleep tests to see why I saw dead people. Being psychic wasn't an option, so a medical solution was opted for.

I was put on medication that made me ill. Luckily, my guide had my back and told me to stop taking them.

The situation was never mentioned again, as if it never happened.

I had heard how some psychics in the past had been medicated and put into mental asylums.

Seeing the dead was confused with having multiple personalities amongst other things.

I am not encouraging you to stop your medication. This is just how it worked out on my path.

When you have a chance to listen to yourself, then you don't have other people's opinions or words to take into consideration.

It is often enough dealing with your own memory without the overload of someone else's.

Odds are you're not going to match someone else, because you're infinite and unique. If, on occasions, you are on the same page it won't be totally. You will still see how different you are, and your differences will surface.

It doesn't mean anything is wrong. The difference highlighted is reminding you that you're both unique.

We can blend and harmonise with others, but this isn't the same as being a carbon copy.

You are you and there is only one of you in this universe.

MAINTENANCE

After we connect with the physical body, how does our soul maintain it?

The soul's energy flows within the space of the body tissue via the breath.

The physical breath is viewed as just oxygen on the physical side of matter, but each inhale and exhale occur because of the energy of the soul. Without it, it would not work independently.

The soul is the power source to the physical body.

If you have ever used a muscle stimulator, the current runs from the device and into your body making the muscle spasm and move.

This is like what the soul's energy does as a power source, so your body works.

Breath is first for energy flow transfer.

Then we get the physical element of our physical body. The cells need food and drink for moisture to stay hydrated.

The body gets tired easily and will need rest to repair itself and grow.

Anything past these basic elements comes into physical experience.

MOVEMENT

Our first basic movement is breathing and the muscle of the heart contracts so the blood flows carrying the nutrients around the body.

Walking comes much later to humans compared with other animals in the wild.

The human body is out of balance to start with when learning to walk. Often, it is clumsy and falls over.

Once balance is mastered it then becomes about coordination.

Our eyes and hearing aid these skills.

In those first two years of learning to use the body, the abilities of what it can do comes to light.

I was a premature baby, so my eyes didn't get developed very well. One eye was weaker than the other. Around two years old I was given glasses to wear.

If you ever watched the milky bar kid adverts in the seventies and eighties, they looked like those.

Metal round ones, the arms on them you could bend to fit around the ears.

INDEPENDENCE

I became independent from an early age.

Those first fourteen years were about survival and learning to adapt to each new situation and circumstance that I found myself in.

When I became an orphan, my once settled life uprooted me literally from myself, like a plant being uprooted and repotted.

I couldn't settle again in life because of lots of movement and self-responsibility, whether for myself or others.

I could not relax. Life kept me on guard as soon as I left the familiarity of my family to a life in the care system until I left at eighteen.

I grew up fast in self-awareness of doing things for myself.

By four I was dressing myself and making my own bed in the children's home with folded hospital corners.

It wasn't a case of look what I could or could not do. To survive I had to be able to hold my own.

Practically, I managed to keep up.

We walked everywhere. I soon got used to walking at speed to keep up with everyone, being the youngest when I first arrived at the children's home.

ROUTINE

The homes run like clockwork on scheduled, staffed timetable. Having so many kids to look after it was a job not a home, yet everyone made it a home with their energy.

It was a practical home that served our needs.

Regardless of our histories or backgrounds of how we ended up there, none of this mattered.

We lived together and just wanted to get on and have fun as kids do.

We knew that our pasts were the reasons why we were not able to live with our families.

We accepted each other and nurtured each other, adopting each other like a family.

We laughed and we played. It was a welcome relief to have some childhood fun after facing adult situations and circumstances.

Facing adults and their lives was like being a passenger on their journeys, unable to avoid the collisions that crashed into them and then feeling the impact and often blamed for their inability to face and own their lives. This is why passengers often take the blame, as it's easier to observe the whole situation compared to the one leading it.

I learnt quickly how to manage it. It was to face it and take it. It may last years or months, but each month is a week, and each week is a day, and each day is minutes and seconds, etc.

This is how I dealt with it, in the moment. I counted my way through the challenges and pain.

As a child I had a thick skin that protected my feelings inside, enabling me to store my feelings up for later, when I wasn't so distracted from myself.

I spent those first years living day-to-day and zoning out with any painful bits that hit a nerve, and instead focused on the fun bits that made me laugh.

If it got too much, I would say to myself, ya gotta laugh ain't ya? Yes, I had a cockney twang.

I guess it doesn't matter where you live growing up or what circumstances you find yourself in. Anything past the self, if it doesn't match up with you it will clash with you.

I used to think I had just picked a short straw, and you're only in the care system if you come from a troubled life.

As a child I was observant and I had an ability to tune in to others, but as I entered adult life it became more about my personal life.

This zoomed my life closer into my personal space and I then realised family outside the homes came with their own limited obstacles.

THERE MUST BE MORE TO LIFE THAN THIS

As I turned the page into each new year, my life became a domino of events that mirrored the previous year. I said to myself often, surely there must be more to life than this?

Have you ever asked yourself this question?

Well, there is more to life than this!

There is a big world out there past this physical bubble, or should I say there is a big universe around you which is your actual reality.

If you don't want your physical bubble to be burst, then put this book down and stop reading it.

But if you want to be guided back to your true self then keep reading. Forget the mind, I am not trying to convince you of anything. I am sharing my reality. It isn't the same as yours. This is fact because we are infinitely unique souls. We will never be the same. But what does match between you and me is that we are an infinite soul connected to our physical body via the breath.

LEAVING SCHOOL AND FACING ADULTHOOD AGAIN PERSONALLY

My birthday being in the month of August I was one of the youngest in my year, so when I left school, I was still fifteen. I didn't turn sixteen until after I had left, compared to some that had already turned sixteen or closer to seventeen.

You must choose what you want to do when you leave for work. I didn't have a clue, not being academic and more practical. Nothing about my skillset stood out for a job.

I loved caring about others. I wanted to be a nurse but didn't know why.

Being unsure of a career path, I enrolled at college to do a city and guild's course in community care.

My college timetable didn't always have full days, which meant on those days I could go home early.

The year course soon came and went, and I had to choose what I wanted to do for a job.

I did want to train as a nurse, but I was too young to be accepted. To work on the wards, you had to be eighteen for insurance reasons. Becoming a nurse was not a choice as I had another year or so before turning eighteen.

Upon leaving college I got a job as a care assistant in a care home for the elderly.

It was tough emotionally.

YOUR CHOICE TO FOLLOW THE SELF OR NOT

There is always something to follow in the physical and always something to blame other than the self.

You can be a leader or just tag along. The choices we make reflect how we hold our own.

You have the option to follow other humans, timetables, expectations and people pleasing, or go against the waves and follow your own soul path.

The physical offers limited choice of repeat. Throw time in the mix and the calendar gives you the illusion of more.

Change your limited repeated options up by using time and dates, convincing how choice gives the illusion of freedom of choice, from the physical script menu of course.

What choice do we have? This sentence is often heard to succumb to a situation you would not have personally chosen.

Why do we suck it up? Because everyone else does.

Why do we feel we have no choice?

In fear of being rejected or isolated and alone.

Souls are social and love being in the mix with others. It doesn't matter how you mix, whether with nature or animals or other humans, you're still not alone.

Even if you sit in your home, you're not alone if you listen to the radio or watch television. Even if you sit in silence, you are connecting with universe around you.

To escape the timetable of routine we find ways to escape.

Some I have already touched on previously, but I will highlight some more from a different angle.

ESCAPISM IS NOT ENTERTAINMENT

Covers everything from shows, the stage, human-to-human interaction, sport, challenges, fighting, circus, food, radio, TV, music, and technology expanding into virtual reality.

A physical reality created from a mix of visualisation, imagination, magician's magic, mentalists, spirituality, reading, sex, drugs and food to name but a few.

To gain access you sign up to work to spend or hold onto your money.

The physical bubble started off basic.

The human-to-human trade of bartering to share goods.

The bigger the trades grew into family business and investment, the basic needs of feeding the family weren't the reason to work anymore – it was about becoming rich. Volume took over from quality control.

Money took over from abilities.

The focus went from craft to what brings in the most money. Then the rich got bored, so they needed more things to entertain them. Then these toys got shared to bring in more money and so the cycle continues.

The more the physical experiences the physical, the enjoyment bubble bursts and the quicker the boredom sets in with feelings of lack due to dissatisfaction, resulting in wanting more because what you have is not enough.

The physical way to more is excess in saturation not contentment.

The physical is always hungry for more without reaching fulfilment because the first element of frequency of the language of this universe is missing. Connection to the self, bypassed with buying goods to fill the void.

Have you ever felt that something is missing? I know I did when I was growing up.

Connection brings fulfilment, enjoyment, fun, pleasure. Without connection, it feels like virtual reality as if here but not. Connection is what makes it real.

You don't need to escape anything, and you don't need to be entertained.

You have everything you need in you to be fulfilled and satisfied.

Sharing and observing others and their gifts and skills is in appreciation.

Entertainment fills time out, time out from working.

You can equally not work and not be entertained because you're content with peace and quiet.

The universe is projecting and reflecting constantly in a flow and rhythm that's calm and peaceful.

The physical is noisy with confusion, miscommunication, and distorted meanings, often lacking in element number four commitment and continuity to keep going without giving up. Connection element number one holds the journey together. Giving up on you is like not being in play and switching you off on standby.

Then when life slows down the question is asked, why is nothing happening?

Always look to the root of the situation, your own self connection. It will always reflect your answer.

If you are not connected to yourself in all areas, then some areas may be moving forward – say, in a career – but personal relationships are not.

Holding our own is the ability to communicate what we want.

We each have the responsibility of our own reality, hence the saying, each to their own.

We have our own path in life. Even if you join groups or classes, your position within the class is what matters. What you get out of anything is down to your meaning for being there.

INHALE-EXHALE IN EVERYTHING

We can inhale deeply and exhale slowly. We can shallow breathe in stealth mode. We can hold our breath. We can barely whisper and can shout loud and clear.

Our body is like a balloon expanding and deflating depending on what we consume or let go off.

Both physically and emotionally and energetically, mentally in memory, not excluding food.

Food is in everything; energy is food even in thought.

BALANCE AND BOUNDARIES ARE NOT HABITS

We create boundaries to keep our connection with ourselves intact and to guide us to stay balanced and in harmony.

Boundaries are not seen as healthy and have more to do with protection.

It is understandable why it is viewed this way when boundaries are used to fence around where we live.

The physical reality lives within boundaries. The soul lives within space.

Boundaries are used as a gauge to keep a steady flow making life more manageable.

If we overdo anything in any direction, it stops the steady flow. You don't need rules for this. You just know by how you feel.

This is where element number two of feeling is applied.

If we are closed off from our feelings then often the gauge of balance and boundaries are not applied, and we use the default setting of the brain and memory instead.

If we are fully dialled in to our feelings by using our instinct, we are aware more of our personal limits.

The physical reality can feel like an emotional roller coaster, feeling either up or down or all or nothing or get the feeling that not much is going on at all.

Our balance and connection and need to feel in control often stems with food. Food is an easy weapon or tool as it is our basic need for survival. It is easier to control food than it is other humans. Our feelings can throw us off balance if we are overstimulated and get flooded with emotions. Our instinct is to want to move on from feeling out of control.

Food can be used as a substitute for the lack of connection we feel within ourselves and to those around us.

Connection is the first element of frequency so if we lack connection we will feel out of control.

Too many choices often throw us off.

Cutting back makes it feel more manageable, but is it?

It's still hard to stick to indefinitely because cutting back on anything you know something is missing. And souls don't like to miss out on anything because they know they are infinite and not less than infinite. To cut back is to cut back on being total. It is wise to use connection for a balanced harmony sustainable life as totality can flow in all directions. When listening to the self, you know your own limits of satisfaction.

DAMNED IF I DO, DAMNED IF I DON'T

If we only had ourselves to see to and kept ourselves to ourselves without added words and stimulus of differing opinions, we would not worry about half of what we do worry about.

The road to a clearer self-path is one that is organised, like when we sort and wash our clothes.

You may have a mixed load of clothes belonging to different members who you share life with.

But you know which garments belong to who.

To sort ourselves out and get back on our soul path, first our physical load needs sorting.

You may be surprised to read that your life doesn't just consist of your energy, if you have lived alongside the physical script up to 2018.

We often share where we live with others where we work. Name tags and labels are used so we know who owns what. Names on doors and walls and even ceilings help send us in some sort of direction.

On a personal note, it's our personal space that gets my attention the most. As we can visit others and places around us. But our personal space is where we actually live from no matter where we are.

When we first connect with our physical body with the first breath, our personal space only has our signature frequency over it.

Others visit our space in our crib, introducing their frequency to us.

Their energy is what we connect with first. If we are compatible with their energy, we enjoy the interaction. If we don't feel comfortable and they're not familiar to us, we will cry to let them know.

Babies cry for many reasons as a guide to let humans know what the soul wants past the physical needs of the body.

Our soul brings our character and personality with us and this shines through once we are more aquatinted with the physical body, dependent on what we have selected on our soul maps.

At first our social circle consists of immediate family members and or carers.

If circumstances are favourable, we get the chance to focus on ourselves and learn more about what the physical body can do.

At first it is very physical: eating, drinking, sleeping, crawling and walking and then playing.

What happens next is where it gets more interesting.

THE MIND RECORDING MEMORY

If your soul needs to remember something that benefits the soul path, then it will be stored, but it won't find it necessary to store daily events if it doesn't benefit the soul.

If it is stored, then it goes into the memory and stays there if replayed. Whether short or long term, it is still memory.

The soul knows everything, so it doesn't matter that the physical forgets a lot even in stored memory.

The soul is like your personal assistant.

The reason why stored memory gets forgotten or the details weaken is because the memory isn't being replayed.

If a memory isn't replayed it no longer needs to be stored and the soul fades from memory until you're ready to let go of it.

Your soul doesn't need the brain, as it uses instinct that is embedded in the soul. The soul masters the physical art of practical movement, balance and fine motor skills of the hands.

The soul starts off our journey here. In the past, up to 2018, souls took approximately twelve years to learn the script of the physical dos and don'ts.

By age seven the character of the soul is revealed enough that sets the soul's backdrop for the path ahead, covering both the physical reality and soul reality.

Physically, the soul masters the physical body enough by age four. The rest of the years is learning more words and other skills set out by the schooling system.

WE START WITH THE SOUL AND END WITH THE SOUL – THIS IS THE PHYSICAL BIT IN BETWEEN

The physical journey consists of what we copy and replay back. We watch facial expressions as a baby and through repetition we learn a language and how to communicate with others.

We are shown the world around us via reading books and exercise books.

We learn through play with the toys that are offered to us, mirrored on roles that we see day-to-day.

This scripted version is handed down from generation to generation, century after century up to 2018, making sure the script outlives our physical bodies and continues.

IN PLAIN SIGHT

The script isn't a secret. It is in plain sight, blindsided because everyone else is following it, so humans are following humans not the actual script. That's why it's been followed for centuries. Souls stick together, the herd mentality, safer in numbers. By joining forces, it made souls feel safer when facing the fears inflicted on them, regardless of if they were threats spoken without action. Time itself caused souls to live in fear of what could happen.

A self-inflicted script because humans follow other humans.

Mixing amongst other humans is what distracts us from noticing it.

Once it is pointed out or highlighted, you can't unsee it.

It's so obvious once you know souls that are connected more with their soul will have a hunch and will know that the script doesn't match or resonate with their soul.

You may hear such souls say, "I feel like an alien here," "I don't fit in here," or "I don't feel like I should be here."

Yes, you should be here and congratulations that the script didn't rub off on you totally.

Well done for sticking with and following your soul and not falling for the script.

The systems set up around the script impacted everyday needs, such as food and fuel for warmth and a roof over your head.

Time and money got invented, another thing added to learn. If you could not read or write or do maths, this made it hard to follow for some, which resulted in theft.

Those who understood joined the system so they could survive and thrive, as was told for the good of all.

The introduction of money created the urgency for an education. With each century that passed, the fear system made sure there was something extra to learn.

If you want to live in the physical you must follow the systems, even if it doesn't sit with you.

Some souls have chosen to take their money and skills, go off grid and be self-sufficient, enabling them to take back their freedom.

GOING BACK TO COME FORWARD – IT'S NOT NEW, IT'S CENTURIES OLD

The first souls to arrive on earth roamed the land freely. They hunted and lived in harmony amongst their community.

They did not need passports or money so they could feed their families. This changed as soon as some souls created the script.

Some tribes are still living like the first souls that arrived in their own space and way of life, with little interaction with the western script.

How did they get everyone to follow the script and give up the peaceful soul way of life?

FEAR AND FIGHTING

Souls come in peace. How to be fearful and fight is taught via words and stories and pictures. These symbols started off as warning signs and soon turned into maps.

In the end everyone copied for an easy life, in exchange of food for goods.

Inventions of new tools to make farming and agriculture easier, inventions in engineering creating vehicles, boats and planes to travel via land sea and air.

Electrical engineering created telecommunications and light bulbs in which to see.

WITH THESE INVENTIONS CAME DEPENDENCY

The more you have the more you don't want to go backwards but is it possible to go backwards and forwards at the same time without realising it if distracted.

Of course, because the universe provides opposites, not one or the other.

When I was a child, we turned the television channels over by walking over to the television set and changing it manually. We didn't have remotes to change the channels without moving from your seat.

Who would want to keep getting up if you don't have to?

With each new invention in one hand, it makes life easier, but on the other it brings with it a diluted version of the self.

Technological advancements are amazing. To think, in the last forty years, we can now video call our friends, when forty years ago we were still putting pen to paper and communicating by sending letters.

Life has altered and evolved over the years. Some say technology of what we know so far has always been here, recycled and brought to use in different centuries. Unless we can rely on the history books of what we are taught about history, only our souls know the whole story, but do we listen?

WHAT MAKES A TEACHER? IS ANYTHING REALLY TAUGHT OR DOES IT TRIGGER OUR KNOWING?

A teacher in the physical sense is one that teaches subjects from the curriculum that has been outlined by the Department for Education (DfE).

A teacher in the soul sense, is someone that encourages another to grow from themselves (self-growth).

Anything that is taught physically, through the eyes of the soul, isn't really taught. It is copied and memorised.

"Repeat after me, children," was often wrung around classrooms back in the day.

WHEN DO BODIES STOP GROWING?

When we feed newborn babies, they direct the parents/carers when they are hungry.

They cry when the nappy needs changing or if they are tired.

If the new baby soul hasn't been taught these things, how does it automatically know?

It knows by how comfortable it feels.

If the body isn't comfortable then it knows what it needs.

Being COMFORTABLE is a valuable gauge of guidance.

When a baby rolls over it may have encouragement to keep going.

When a baby decides to crawl, it will find its own way.

When a baby decides it is ready to walk regardless of age, it will.

We think we teach them, but I would say we more support and encourage them.

I have had four daughters, so I have some experience with mine.

I can't speak for anyone else, but this is how it feels to me.

The brain communicates with the body through electrical and chemical signals sent by neurons, which are nerve cells.

These cells carry messages between the brain, spinal cord, and the rest of the body.

There are different types of neurons, sensory, motor, and interneurons.

Sensory neurons carry information from the senses to the brain, and motor neurons carry messages from the brain to the muscles, controlling movements such as walking and talking. Interneurons connect sensory and motor neurons.

This is the basic rundown of the brain's function with the physical body.

If the brain or spinal cord gets damaged, then these signal pathways become affected causing loss of movement and functionality.

Often, it is said that the body stops growing after puberty or any age between fourteen and eighteen, or for some it is twenty, or longer if they have gigantism.

I am not a biologist or a doctor or a specialist in anatomy and physiology.

But on a basic level, our skin and hair and nails are constantly regenerating.

The eyeball lenses, the cornea stay the same size from birth to death because of the absence of a blood supply, while the ears and nose continues to grow.

Teeth are the only body part that cannot repair themselves.

The brain is a painless organ.

The neurons of the central nervous system live as long as the body does. The nerve cells you're born with stay with you until death unless in a severe accident.

The internal organs keep growing with you until they stop around puberty.

The size reaches a limit, while other parts regenerate.

WHY DO WE NOT LOOK THE SAME IN AGE?

We are unique, because the soul is the fountain of youth if you use your soul more and keep your connection with yourself flowing. Odds are you're not going to age drastically even if you have had a colourful, challenging life.

You can meet someone who has had a tough life and yet still look so youthful. You can also meet someone who has had life handed to them on a plate and yet have aged quickly.

There is not one rule fits all. It depends on the integral relationship going on between the physical and soul itself.

Our body will need physical maintenance in which to cell regenerate, etc.

But if there are limited amounts of soul energy running through it, regardless of food, water or rest, then it's like running a car on fumes, unless adrenalin kicks in.

Not much attention is paid to the power of the soul connection.

The soul connection via the breath alone can still guide us if it catches our attention.

This is often observed during extreme stress and/or fear. The soul will space out from the physical body. At this point, the consciousness of the soul flows through the soul, leaving the physical body hanging by its breath. At this moment, the soul has the chance to view the physical body from the soul's perspective. Some have reported this as a near-death experience while on the operating table and saw their physical body from the view of the ceiling. The soul isn't confined to the body, and this is experienced more if the body shuts down when asleep.

When the soul experiences itself, it will remember that the physical can touch physical, but it cannot touch the soul.

If during the waking day, a soul is not using much soul energy, then it will be reliant more on external resources rather than internal soul connection.

Fitting in with the infrastructure and others is vital, because the soul is not being accessed only the physical supplies.

The physical body can burn out and stop and it can keep going when exhausted by using adrenaline.

The physical body is given space to experience itself unless we are going to implode, by falling apart within. Anything that comes from within sets the soul in motion as backup.

Think of your soul like your own bodyguard.

WHERE DOES ALL YOUR ENERGY GO?

On you? Or others? Or both or neither?

A plant when growing is aware of their own space and other plants around them. But their energy goes into maintaining their root and growth.

Connection is connection to everything, which is why we turn to something.

It is teamwork in this universe, why we lean towards something if we are making decisions or choices.

Our selection of variety sometimes makes it harder to choose.

We either go with what we know from memory, or chance something new even though our gut deep down may be sending us red flags or white flags, or the green light or red for stop.

Sometimes doing nothing and not rushing or forcing change is where you're at on your path.

This inaction can be taken in many ways. Disinterest or dragging your heels or not as serious with your intentions, the list can go on.

So, what do we do when we are at a crossroads in life, or we have no clue of what we want or where we are heading?

You're spinning out in your thoughts going round in circles only to be in the same situation or cycle or position that you disliked years ago.

Why do we put ourselves through years of repeats and moan while doing so without changing it?

Not knowing and not having the connection with the self enough to drive your life out of reverse into forward.

It will always come back to self-connection.

YOU are your doorway to your life. If you don't want to face you, you're avoiding the door you need to access what you want.

Then you become your own elephant in the room, keeping busy to pretend it's not there, or concentrate on what makes others happy so they don't highlight the elephant in the room.

This is the classic juggling your life, the yo-yo of run so you don't catch up with yourself.

At times our soul does catch up with our physical selves and gives us a soul wedgie, as I call it.

DISTRACTIONS USED TO AVOID SEEING OURSELVES

When you come face-to-face with yourself, you cannot deny it or miss it.

Self-reflection is powerful.

But often we give our energy to those we connect with and take the blame whether it belongs to us or not. We can often find ourselves in a no-win situation, a stalemate of agree to disagree is the only conclusion if you're in a situation where you are damned if you do and damned if you don't.

Do you take care of yourself and take care of your life or continue going round in circles?

Souls are clever. They can be whatever they want to be in the physical reality. The script has taught them how to cheat and lie to themselves and others. They can convince themselves that the lie is the truth. Those observing it will believe it for so long under the physical umbrella, but the soul will not accept anything that isn't truth. If a lie upsets the energy of your soul map, then the vibration of the soul will see through the lie. When others stop listening and don't take you seriously anymore then you know they have had enough of your self-avoiding ways.

Often, when these moments happen, the soul that has not been facing themselves will be fast-tracked up to speed of the realities of the situation. They will be holding onto their life by a thread, because change is happening now, and time or excuses can't stop it. It doesn't matter whether you react in anger or like it or not, at this stage opinions won't cause a ripple effect of repeat. Those who have shared their life and waited for change to happen are ready to move on by themselves, not able to wait for any more excuses.

We have the choice to either change with them, or we are left to pick up the pieces and face ourselves because we may have ignored ourselves for long enough.

If you find that others move on, they haven't left you. They have removed themselves from a stuck and repeat environment. By letting go they give you more space to yourself to work out what you want. Freedom to live how you choose and freedom for themselves to achieve more than the present situation was able to offer. This is not personal. It is about self-responsibility with element number one the self.

Our soul has every eventuality covered on our soul map. There is nothing the physical can dish up that the soul isn't already prepared for.

Before you arrive here, you have gone over your soul path and all the physical possibilities why life isn't too unfamiliar. You will notice words such as déjà vu because at that moment it is remembered.

You have already played out energetically what you are living.

You are connected to your own soul energy supply. If you use it, you feel it. If you don't then you will be alerted of it when phenomena experiences happen.

Your soul will try and get your attention during your waking day and during sleep, because the soul never sleeps.

Your energy flows from your soul and expands out and back to the self, encasing your infinite space.

This is like the inhale and exhale of the physical breath because the soul will always choose to match up with the physical.

You can ignore your physical self, you can even ignore your soul, but it's impossible to ignore space. It's around you as you go about your day.

Space is this universe. Have you ever sat next to a stranger and notice you feel more comfortable if there is space between you. The little bit of space reminds you of how comfortable you feel in this universe.

INVADING YOUR SPACE

Space is important not just to store your belongings but so you can breathe and hear your inner voice.

If your life is just noisy with limited space to catch up with yourself, then you're going to feel frazzled energetically.

Moments of peace may only happen when you're asleep. Although you may feel rested, it is like you're not conscious of some peace and quiet.

You may grab some me moments when you go to the bathroom or have a bath or shower or go for a drive or a walk on your own. Even walking to do errands can feel wonderful if you're able to zone out from external noise.

If you struggle to switch, then you're still working on self-connection.

If you're juggling a busy life and the demands of others but have no problems with switching off when you're finished, then your connection with yourself is fine. It's more self-management and schedules.

If you find you have a balance between work and a sense of self, and fit you in for some you quality self-interests, then you have created your foundation and are aware of what works for you and what doesn't.

EMPATHS

Being an empathetic soul is wonderful but can be a burden as well. Empathetic souls don't need to be first in the queue.

They remember they are souls and following their soul map to support others through the physical maze.

Up to 2018 empaths have been the bridge between the past and the future.

Visiting other souls who are stuck in their past or floating in the future, that's not happened yet.

Empaths encourage souls to let go of the past and move into the now and guide future souls to settle rather than hanging around.

There are different types of empath experiences depending on the empath's soul map.

Some souls are experiencing sharing from the self in the deep end, which leads me to element number two, pulse sharing from the self.

The power of connection rolls into the next two elements until you reach element number four vibration, completion that oversees the other three elements. This is how the language of this universe covers everything. It is such a simple clever language that the physical will not be able to manipulate it.

CHAPTER TWO – PULSE sharing from the physical self

(Element number two)

Mastering the self so you can hold your own is enough in itself but adding emotions and feelings into the mix while sharing with others makes it even more challenging.

The connection to the self matches up with element number four vibration completion. These two elements are like bookends for the other two.

To put it more simply as a metaphor, if the four elements were a sandwich, element one and element four are like two slices of bread and element number two and three are the filling creating content of eventful experiences.

Put them together, they each interweave creating variety and self-mastery.

This is why before we arrive here. We create our soul map and highlight the elements we want to master while here.

Space around us is what makes the universe transparent.

Why are we in this universe? To master ourselves.

Everything and everyone are seen and heard and noticed. No soul is left out, because of the connection with your soul, which is your connection with this universe, a direct link.

Your soul is what makes this universe expand. Remember inhale and exhale. This universe does the same with space around your experiences. The more you experience the more this universe expands.

Connection will never be separation. Separation doesn't exist in this universe. What humans see as separation, the soul sees as expanded space.

Space in the physical reality is seen as dividing things up. The soul sees it as the potential to experience more.

GETTING BACK TO FEELINGS
WHY DO WE EVEN NEED FEELINGS ANYWAY?

The soul has everything covered like I said. The soul is the energy behind this universe.

If one sense does not work in the physical, the soul will use something else as it always has a backup when senses become dormant.

Why does the soul always have a backup available? The soul being infinite, it doesn't run out of ideas.

When the first souls arrived here before the fear taught script, souls didn't need to feel in the way we know through tears and laughter or pain.

Feelings to a soul is one of flowing energy in connection. A soul feels it totally or not.

When souls transferred from living like a soul to living as a taught human, the senses used changed.

The physically taught humans lost touch with the connection of the soul abilities, these abilities got stored inside the gut nucleus of the soul.

(I am describing how the physical would relate to it. Translating soul is like different languages. Sometimes there are no translatable words to explain it, which is why metaphors come in handy).

Feelings to the soul are an internal flow of continuity and movement. Feelings to the physical are felt via touch and a responsive reaction.

SWITCHING ON AND OFF

Souls do not switch off from feeling connection. Humans switch off and on depending on if interested.

The human body became like a television screen often used to cover up true feelings.

Feelings got lost in translation causing frustration of not being seen or heard.

The volume of sound got turned up in compensation to override others and action got more expressive to stand out from the crowd.

Feelings start off here as noise. When a baby feels cold or hungry or sleepy, it will make a sound to alert those who are caring for them.

Communicating how we feel isn't easy, when sound can be ignored.

Listening is a skill in itself, as we can listen with intention but drift off if something else gets our attention.

We can listen but not listen and not actually hear a word that is said or hear words and not even understand a word of it.

Humans think they hide behind a human body, but it is space they are daydreaming in.

Communicating is hit and miss, missing the point or the facts and not even touching on the truth.

Memory has come in handy to bridge the gap when bluffing or blagging, pulling words off and making them sound convincing. When did we become great actors? Dramatising isn't just for drama kings and queens.

THE WORLD DOES NOT PHYSICALLY REVOLVE AROUND YOU, ONLY IN CONNECTION

Growing up around religion, I was taught to love thy neighbour as thyself and to put them before myself. I believed what I was told and did exactly as the vicar instructed and turned the other cheek.

Wow, it didn't serve me well at college. During an argument, I got a right hook right across my cheek, not to escalate it with a returning punch. Instead, I turned the other cheek and got another punch, I wasn't about to stand around for more, so I just walked away.

The crowd watching was waiting for it turn into a boxing match. What opinions others had of me at that moment I don't know. It wasn't a life-or-death situation. It just ended as quick as it happened.

I felt embarrassed more than anything that I had taken the vicar's advice instead of standing up for myself, because I wanted to set a good example like the bible had said.

Looking back now forty-one years later, I now realise those words of wisdom don't match this universe, purely because of how the language of this universe works.

Element number one is the doorway to everything. You have responsibility to the self to have your own back and look after yourself, not just take what others dish out because they are out of control with themselves. Especially, when we have no excuse because we have within us everything we need to communicate peacefully with each other.

The issue is mastering ourselves enough to be able to do so. The taught way of life has made it so complicated and time-consuming, so we don't have much energy for ourselves.

No wonder why we are like fireworks being set off when something triggers a reaction.

Reaction isn't communicating. Reactions don't mean you actually feel it or think it or realise you're acting a certain way. Memory is everywhere in the body, not just the mind. You hear of muscle memory.

Of course, no one wants to fall out with others and more so with those we have a physical personal connection with. We are not going to always be on the same page, and like driving at times, we crash into one another.

Especially, if everyone is just making noise and not actually hearing themselves or others in the process.

I can handle a lot and can take a punch and take words that have been fired at me. What matters to me is that my conscience is flowing. My conscience is my soul gut flowing through me.

It is like a flowing river of information that flows through every cell of me that I can pick up and use to navigate while here, liken it to a soul satnav.

Humans get lost in the mind and, therefore, dealing with feelings can feel overstimulating.

Yet to get to element number three wave for actioning your life, you must pass element number one and two first.

Humans think they can skip on some elements, forgetting because of connection everything coexists. Nothing gets deleted in this universe; it just keeps playing within itself.

Humans think they can blindly go through life in an autopilot way, ignoring this and that, but this pattern and cycle will only go on for so long. (Element number four oversees everything. If change is needed, then element number four steps in.)

To the soul this is like standing behind your own front door of element number one and opening and shutting it constantly and not actually moving through it.

It will feel like you're busy in action of being open and then shutting yourself off, in relation to on and off and stop and start in a yo-yo fashion.

If you have ever experienced this with another person, it is so frustrating as you don't know where you stand with them. They want you in their life and then not, sure but not sure, feel it today but maybe not tomorrow.

The it could and it might or maybe happen but not today. Let's see tomorrow, but tomorrow never comes, rings loud and clear. One thing you will know for sure upon hearing this is it's not a sure thing. Odds are it won't happen, but the yo-yo will. You either hang around hanging by every word clinging to hope or give up and move on.

The taught way of life created the fifty-fifty foundation so humans would struggle to commit to anything or feel confident within themselves to make decisions. If they didn't feel confident enough, they would hold back letting others take the lead instead. The taught way of life encourages inconsistency, hesitancy, doubt, etc. as it is the opposite to being a soul.

The only way humans would commit to anything is by those who have a strong sense and connection with themselves and a willingness to lead. It is why leaders are appointed for those who do not have a sense of self and would rather follow dictators.

The taught way wants you to live by the script not your soul and, therefore, wants you to avoid being reminded of who you really are.

A soul.

Being stuck in life is a human taught cycle of memory, repeating the same habits on a loop until you pause and pay attention to yourself, because you're wondering why you're not getting anywhere. When you have had enough, then you stop to observe your life because you know you no longer want another day of the same memory different day.

I am sure this sounds familiar.

Now you have your own attention, because following others causes limitation of self-expression.

This doesn't mean you can't share your life with others.

You can have both yourself and enjoy others company as you do yourself.

A soul will support and encourage another not hold on to another and hold them back.

CHOOSE ONE

Humans are taught if you choose or select one thing you can't have more, you're greedy or selfish or not leaving enough for others.

Sharing has nothing to do with greed but everything to do with being self-responsible. Need occurs when we are not applying our own energy to our own life. Humans think others can do it for them, forgetting they are a different frequency to you. You are your own station; others can't pretend to be you for you as you cannot be them for them.

This is why nothing can be copied, and why no one can blame another. What you choose to do on your path will have your frequency all over it. Some call it a vibe or a hunch. You can be a passenger in someone else's scene and feel the effects of their scene, but you still chose to be a passenger.

You will not be responsible for the events in the scene because you're the passenger and not the driving energy of the scene, so your frequency will go as far as choosing to be there.

Souls that want to find out the truth will tune in and follow the energy as our signature frequencies are on everything, which leads back to ourselves.

This is how I do my work around the world. Each soul that crosses my path for a soul reading, a connection happens instantly as soon as they start communicating with me. To do their soul reading, I tune into their soul signature frequency that is connected to the pieces of their soul map and physical realities. Their soul plays the relevant pieces to me.

Humans have called me many names – psychic, freak, shaman, angel, and medium – but truth is we are all psychic because we are soul. I just happen to use my soul more than the physical.

Connecting with your own energy doesn't need utensils, just an ability to be aware of yourself.

There are so many reasons why we hear opinions and judgements, but these words alone don't mean anything without the full story. And you don't get the full picture in the physically taught script. The soul is where you find all the pieces pieced together.

If I did a soul reading on the physical side alone, the reading would not be clear or reliable because the information comes from the soul. If the physical side is holding anything back and being selective with what they share, then there will be a lot of missing details.

This is why I work soul to soul and avoid the physical totally. It is not a reliable source of information.

The soul is infinite. It can have as big and expansive experiences as it can handle.

Some souls have bigger spatial appetites than others. Maybe this is why we come in different shapes and sizes.

Again, it's not one-size-fits-all.

Yet as a child I remember the sheer joy of choosing many different sweets at the pick 'n' mix counter.

We arrive with an array of variety and uniqueness experiencing what we have chosen to experience from this universe shopping mall that already exists.

Like I have already said, there is nothing new in this universe, just more ways in which to experience it.

Like you can buy different outfits and style them up or down, etc.

Knowing total infinite knowing isn't the same as experiencing it.

Why we have created the space of this universe, we know it before we experience it. Liken it to picking a sweet to eat from a chocolate box, you have had the same one before, but you still enjoy having it again.

The physical way of life is mirrored on some of this universe, but it has been tweaked over the centuries to fit the taught narrative rather than the freedom of self-expression. Humans are open to trying anything different but only once if it is not enjoyed. You may buy a cookbook, and you look at the recipes and select what interests you to recreate it.

You're not copying it in your reality, you're experiencing it in your reality.

Copying is if you take the recipe and say you created the content and ideas when you know you didn't.

Recreating the dish is sharing your appreciation of the recipe, but you would not be the creator of the recipe. It's just your dish that you made by following the recipe.

This is why souls in this universe do not need safes or storage cupboards to hold what belongs to them. They also do not need certificates or patents or proof that their creativity belongs to them.

Because the language of this universe has this covered with element number one connection to the self.

BILLIONS ARE NOT THE INFINITE TOTALITY

As I have already mentioned previously, follow the energy. What comes from your energy lasts here past your physical body's death.

How is this possible if your physical body no longer exists?

Because of your impacting soul, your soul is energy and never dies, like the phantom limb still exists past the removal of the limb.

Your soul is your character and personality. When we share our energy, we share our character and personality, which is impacting and leaves a lasting impression.

You can meet a soul for one second and you can't get them out of your mind. You can be around a taught human for years and be bored out of your skull.

Impacting others is infectious when it comes from your soul. The human body can be ignored because it does not contain your character and personality.

Physical-to-physical contact can be dead on your feet. Have you ever been in a room where it has no atmosphere and lacks warmth? You can meet up with people and be greeted with an empty stare. We can switch between the station of our soul self and the station of the physical self. Blowing hot and cold, if you have ever experienced this? Now, you know why. It is how that person is transmitting themselves, but from what side?

Your soul energy is your own unique frequency, liken it to your signature.

See how the taught way of life has been mirrored on this universe, because to exist in this universe it must match in connection with element number one. The taught way of life uses your physical signature of your name.

You didn't come with a name; you came with your soul energy. You could say your soul is your name, but humans cannot read frequency they have forgotten.

I have been called many names and many labels, so who or which one am I? Do any of the names define me? No, they don't. Names are just a physical heading in which to be physically recognised so we can be told apart.

When energy isn't being used then labels and headings and names are needed.

A soul will recognise another soul by their energy. A taught human will recognise another human via look and name.

(Being a soul reader, I work and live soul to soul. I don't remember names, which is why I call everyone my loves because it's my way of addressing their souls.)

102

This reminds me of the front cover of a magazine. If the front cover is stunning enough and picture perfect, then we will look at what's inside.

Beauty is in the eye of the beholder, so they say.

Why does the physical have to name everything? Because it is branded like a business.

Your signature in the physical is your written commitment regardless of how you feel towards what you're signing. You may put your signature to things out of desperation or if needs must.

Necessity over choice and feeling. I have often impulse bought. If I feel a connection to it, then it won't be regretted.

The soul has no regrets because the soul does not put price tags or labels on things. The focus is on the meaning and enjoyment.

Taught humans are encouraged to copy and have the latest trends. If you don't you fall behind in society. The taught way of life makes sure we stay herded by what we are told we need.

GOING BACK TO COME FORWARD IN CONNECTION

Over the last six years in our house, we have gone back to come forward.

We don't have a microwave, we don't have an iron, and we don't have a tumble dryer. That's not to say we haven't had these gadgets in the past.

They made life easy with a big family.

The reason why we gave up on a microwave is to have more space on the kitchen work top. As it turned out we ended up not missing it and enjoyed using saucepans and the hob to heat things up.

When our tumble dryer broke, I looked at ways to save electricity. I remember seeing a Sheila Maid and thought I would love to try it out.

We invested and got one. Five years on we have never looked back. We were amazed how quickly the clothes dried compared with floor airers. Most probably because heat rises. We added a crank to make it easier to pull the clothes up to the ceiling.

As for having no iron, once our children left school, I just hung clothes up to dry and once dried put them away crease free.

There is a backstory reason too. When I was a single parent, I had to work many jobs to make ends meet. I had the bright idea of doing ironing from home once the kids were in bed. To cut a long story short, the clothes I often received to iron was often the stiffly creased kind. It took me hours. Once the kids were in bed, I would start ironing and often not finish until midnight.

Doing this for a year on top of my own washing put me off ironing for life.

After I finished this enterprise, I only ironed what was necessary.

Recently, I have come across clips that people have shared on different online platforms of what life was like in the 1950s.

I was amazed to watch how advanced they were. I saw adapted wheels on a car to make parking easier. Kitchens fitted in a way to hold a well-stocked kitchen without needing storage jars. Fridges far more advanced than the ones we use now.

Why did these items stop being produced?

Especially as these were made to last for many years.

Yep, you guessed it, money.

Money is the reason why the gadgets we used for our homes are not made to last. They stripped back on invention and creativity to simplify the item so they could mass produce it instead.

Making items basic so they did what they said on the tin.

What has all this got to do with feelings you're most probably wondering. Nostalgia isn't feelings.

Well, to sell anything you need to have your attention sparked. We have already established that sound alone can be switched off. Manufacturers would have to make sure they got your attention.

With sound not being reliable, they turned to vision and image. This was more reliable because seeing is believing.

To hit emotions, it had to be impacting and relatable.

The sure way was with sex appeal.

Those that have participated in sex will know it touches feelings like no other.

Sex appeal in image and using real human bodies made it more desirable.

Adverts used this approach which turned heads. Soon everyone was rushing out to buy what was advertised because of who was in the advert. Mirroring again is a sure way of following trends.

By using the human form, which is instantly relatable because we all have them, we want to mirror the life the human in the magazine or advert is showing us.

Especially if your life at present feels gloomy in comparison, sell it to me because I want my life to be like that and not my current one.

SELL QUICK AND SELL FAST

Life sped up in all areas. Life became about selling rather than about connection.

When I was in my early twenties, I would often hear my friends say, "Oh, it's Friday. I am on a promise."

"What do you mean?" I asked. "A promise?"

"Oh, I promised my husband sex tonight if he treated me to some new shoes."

Relationships became a shop of bartering in exchange of wants and desires.

This way of communicating did fade out I guess when women had less time to themselves, especially when the family units started to split up because of the pressures and demands.

The taught way of life and systems changed the rules and felt unstable with living standards.

The cost of living was going up and down like a yo-yo. When you're on the up, you overspend out of a false sense of security, even encouraged to spend only for this high only to fall flat when interest rates rise.

"Oh. you should plan for this," they may say, but how when you don't know what's coming next until you're in it.

If you have ever struggled then you know it isn't always easy to manage, especially when you have children to provide for.

When you have up times, you want to grab it by the horns and enjoy it as much as you can while it lasts, in case it doesn't come round again.

The ups and downs are in everything, with us, with goods, with life, and just to throw it in because it's an English thing to do, and the weather.

When it rains it rains, but when it shines it's marvellous.

Feelings are needed if connection is off. Feelings are our safety net to ensure that we keep turning up and keep showing up for another day.

We think events and others are the cause of our woes, but are they really?

It's actually our feelings.

Because of the four elements of frequency, when you are in any action, you will have your feelings and yourself involved too.

It does not matter if there is a delay in catching up with our feelings they are still involved.

This is why the past can impact us after the event more than when it happened.

It's us catching up with it.

Just being present in life aligns you in the centre of your life. Humans think if they are in a queue they are not first. If you stand amongst a crowd that you're not seen. If alone in your room that you're out of the loop.

Yet, in truth from your soul's perspective, you are always at the centre of your reality. Whether you notice you or not, listen or not, or just switch off, you will always be the centre, and your soul self will wait until you're ready to notice yourself before physically moving you along on your path.

This is why you can think of someone, and they call you, or you bump into them. Being in the centre of your reality means that everyone associated with your reality will be able to see you and hear you.

Liken it to them standing in a ring around you. Any communication from you is heard by those who it is associated with.

If there is no need to physically be in touch then they won't cross your path, but if they can aid your path in life, they will cross your path.

Where there is connection feeling follows.

Whether you have loved or liked or hated an experience, to the soul it's still valuable content.

Reactions guides us by encouraging us to make different choices, but often humans don't pick up the meaning, holding on to situations as if playing bat and ball, making it personal when it isn't and continuing in the hopes of changing the game. But it doesn't change until the self-connection is acknowledged. Making anything personal in fear reflects the self, but if you know yourself enough under element number one then you will find you won't take element number two or three personally. If you do take it personally, then it's a gentle reminder that your connection to yourself is having a little shine up.

STICKS AND STONES WILL BREAK MY BONES BUT WORDS WILL NEVER HURT ME

What happens in the physical stays in the physical. Remember the two realities. Because of space they stay unique to themselves.

This universe pairs energy up like magnets that connect when attracted but equally they can repel if the polarity doesn't match.

We do the same. This makes sure there isn't anything random slipping through the net.

Plus, it stops physical manipulation, causing a domino effect of catastrophic happenings.

You may look at life around you and the history of the earth and view both personal and global events as catastrophic. I will explain further why all is not as it seems.

Everything in your life matches up even if your view of it on the physical surface is of the opinion that no one in their right mind would choose this happening to them.

But humans forget that it isn't just the physical at play here. Each human is a soul too.

The soul energy makes up your total life directing your physical reality, even if you're not aware of it, because your too focused on the one side of the physical fence.

If your body was like a sock and you noticed a hole on the sole, then you may say it's catastrophic. But to the soul that space of a hole is soul energy of the sock exiting.

Like my previous experience of getting punched in the face, I am not going to deny that it hurt. It did physically but also my sixteen-year-old dignity felt bruised too, because I would be viewed as weak and a coward and none of them knew my history of what I had survived.

Feeling less than yourself is like deflating the energy from yourself if you were a balloon. You don't want to be less than your totality.

Humans forget that totality is everything, not just when you're flying at your best and winning at life. (It includes also when you feel like you're not winning at life.)

When you feel weak and on the floor, you're still your total best. When you're hurt and fall to your knees, and when you're sad and crying, life feels overwhelming.

Throw any human experience at me and the answer will still be the same: you are being your total best.

Humans grade things in value, in price and with self-worth.

The physical does not have enough money to purchase you. Have you ever stopped to ponder this view?

If you're an infinite soul, and your soul is infinitely everything that is created in this universe before the physical experiences it, then how can the physical purchase what your soul already knows?

Money hasn't been around forever, time hasn't been around forever, and your belongings on earth haven't been around forever, only in energy. You, your soul, has been around infinitely and will never decay or wear out.

The physical cannot destroy what the physical cannot physically touch, hence the example of the phantom limb.

My first awareness of energy to do with phantom limbs was at sixteen when I worked as a care assistant in the care home for the elderly.

I walked behind a staff member who was pushing a man in a wheelchair. They had their backs to me. I hadn't been working there long, and the other staff member asked me to go to the laundry room to fetch a towel and to meet her back in the bathroom.

I got the towel and walked into the bathroom where the gentleman was already undressed and ready to get in the bath.

Staff asked me to hold the man under his armpit while she held the other side so we both could lower him into the bath.

I could not help but notice that he had lost both of his legs. I had never seen an amputee before.

His character and personality impacted me and made me feel at ease instantly.

He looked up at me and handed me his flannel and with a big smile on his face he asked me to wash his feet.

Stunned by his words, I felt like a deer staring at headlights unable to move.

The gentleman said I still feel my feet you know!

I was fascinated and he went on to explain how his legs feel to him and about how he missed his wife and how he loved to nestle his head in her large breasts.

I didn't feel shy one bit. His openness and confident character lit up the room. I only met him that one time, but I never forgot him. His energy I could relate to totally.

Since this first introduction to the phantom limb, I have come across it where others have felt the same with their missing body parts. The energy is still active and alive. It happens with any body part, not just legs.

I am sure I have even heard that they are given medication to help with phantom limb feelings.

The physical body can take a lot, and you can remove a lot and still have a fairly, what is termed, normal life, such as without one of your lungs, a kidney, your spleen, appendix, gallbladder, adenoids, tonsils, plus some of your lymph nodes, the fibula bones from each leg and six of your ribs.

The physical needs the energy of the soul. Behind each cell is an energy source, primarily soul mixed with physical adrenaline.

Soul energy is never cut off. The physical limb can be amputated and the physical energy supply severed.

Cells obtain energy from food molecules and sunlight through a series of reactions within the physical body. The energy of the soul flows through the body via the breath even while asleep.

Physical body breakdown does not stop you from having a life. It may not feel as enjoyable if you're living with complications within the body.

The nerves of the body hurt when they are touched. Not all parts of the body have nerve endings or senses pain. I found out this week from my daughter that her dentist filed between her teeth to make more room for reshaping. Listening intently, I didn't have a chance to ask if it hurt. She continued to explain that she didn't feel anything. Her dentist had already reassured her that it would not hurt, because it's like cutting your nails, only it's enamel and not nail.

This makes sense; otherwise, flossing the teeth would be painful.

The brain doesn't feel pain, the spinal cord, the middle ear and hair and nails.

Neurotransmitters are important to keep the communication flowing in the cells of the body, to enable movement, sensations, and information about the environment.

The internal functioning of the physical circuit board.

This is why words can hurt just as much as being hit hard.

Words carry information and we digest the energy of the words said. The energy impacts us if it touches a nerve even in feelings.

YOU ARE YOU, SO WHY DO WE SPLIT OURSELUES IN TWO

Sharing from the self isn't about splitting yourself in two or three or four. The best example I can give is a fruit bowl. Buying fruit from the shops you will see that the fruit is displayed individually by the fruit names. It isn't thrown together and mixed up, although it's the fruit section.

Then why is it humans, when thrown together, lose themselves in the mix?

We have a body, but we are unique if you spot the differences between us. You will not find another you. Even if bodies are altered in any way, they are still their unique selves.

(Google searched ashes after cremation)

According to the website Cremation Solutions, the human body is primarily composed of water, carbon and bone.

Even after cremation each person's ashes are unique, due to how they have lived their life. The cremation process destroys all traces of organic, carbon-based matter and all bodily fluids evaporate and escape through the cremator's exhaust. No organic matter remains after cremation, the only thing remaining of the human body after cremation is part of the skeletal structure and occasionally small amounts of salts and minerals.

What is ash composed of?

After cremation the bone fragments are cooled and passed through a magnetic field to extract any lingering pieces of metal that remain, such as tooth fillings or surgical implants or casket parts. Pacemakers are removed prior to cremation because they can be explosive. The remaining bone is crushed and reduced to a dense sand of ash. This generates a uniform pale grey to dark grey powder which is similar in appearance to coarse sand.

The unique habits and life experiences, including environmentally lived by humans while here, leave a distinct elemental fingerprint on their skeleton which is present in their ashes after cremation.

Where is your character and personality gone?

Even though cremated ash under the microscope is unique, to the naked eye it all looks the same. It doesn't matter what size you were or colour of your skin or hair, etc. None of these things matter after cremation.

Our experience with our physical body is a short journey, some longer than others. You choose your body that you want to experience your choices with.

Why would you not want to enjoy what you have chosen? Don't you trust your soul to choose wisely? Your soul chose your body because it matched your soul map. Why would you want to only focus on the body when you have your chosen events on your soul map waiting for you to connect with?

Your internal body communicates with itself so you can get on with your soul map.

This obsession with the human body has become a distraction and has turned the body into a business rather than an aid for your experiences. This changed the view of acceptance to finding fault in search of perfection in perfection in ideal rather than how it uniquely is.

Connecting with the human body if challenging is because the soul has chosen the experience to master the elements of their soul map.

Altering the body when bored with it will not lead to internal satisfaction, as the procedure passes resulting back to feeling bored. Souls can be what they want to be. What defines us is the connection with ourselves and the ability to express ourselves in a comfortable happy manner.

How happy are you? Do you feel the quality of your happiness?

You may have heard, "What a happy soul," but you don't hear, "What a happy physical." You also hear, "Wow, they are the life and soul of the party." You don't hear, "Wow, they are the life and physical of the party."

When the soul is mentioned in sentences no one bats an eyelid, in the sense no one questions why are you bring the word soul into it when you're being physical.

Because deep down we all talk soul even if it's in the odd sentence context.

Souls are happy continually being themselves. Souls don't have to try and be happy or go and find happiness because they are being it organically.

HAPPILY EVER AFTER

If only this was the case, wouldn't it make life magical? The big guarantee that life will be forever happy without connection.

If you follow your soul, you are. Sadly, if you follow the physically taught reality, this is an instant guarantee of feeling unhappy if you don't bring your own soul energy to life.

You may have achieved so much and purchased your ideal life, thinking that it should automatically make you happy.

But does it? If you stop for one moment, how much attention do you give to the things in your life?

Yes, you can have many items but how much energy of appreciation do your items get?

When it's fresh and new, it gets all your attention, and you can't put it down because you love it so much. Then what happens? You outgrow it and not so interested in it anymore.

We commit to purchasing things in the search of finding everlasting happiness in everyday physical life, without the commitment from ourselves.

Coming across glimpses and moments of happiness, depending on your self-happiness status and involvement. Your self-happiness status will define how happy or miserable your day ahead will be.

You may have heard the sentence, "I woke up the wrong side of the bed," or "I have woken up in a foul mood."

Your internal conversations are what you hear first before anyone else can drown you out. It's the foundation that holds up your day.

It doesn't matter what side of you is chatting, your soul side or physical side, only you can master yourself.

Every second of your day starts with you first before sharing with others. Why? Because of your memory bank of stored words playing inside of your head constantly.

The soul doesn't sleep or switch off, and the physical side unless mastered will repeat your own thoughts and the thoughts that you have received, but often mixing other people's thoughts as your own.

This relationship with yourself is a collaboration between your physical self and your soul self before you even come in to contact with another soul.

Humans blame others for the state of play in their life, but if they remembered that before anyone else outside of yourself shares anything with you, you are at your door greeting them first.

Makes sense because element number one the self is before element number two sharing from the self with others.

You are what faces you constantly in every situation and circumstance, why others are not to blame.

Team you either blocks others or entertains them. Your bodyguard of you won't let anyone else take your place, because of space around each frequency.

If this simple understanding were to be remembered, then self-responsibility would override blame.

I often hear physical humans say, oh, I will be happy when I get my hair done, or when I go on holiday or buy some new cloths or when I buy my home. The list is endless.

Why is it that these things once received don't bring everlasting happiness?

Because happiness isn't a thing that can be bought. Happiness is the energy that reflects from you to the things you buy. If you're not happy, then whatever you have in your life will not bring you happiness.

Remember how this universe works in matching and pairing up.

Whatever is in your life in any form matches up with your energy.

Do you even pay attention to the words you use to describe your eventful days?

WORDS ARE YOUR ENERGY TRANSLATED IN ENERGY

I have observed many conversations, the ones I have had with myself between my soul and my physical self. To listening to the words of others.

The reason why I listen is to understand the meaning of the conversation.

Often words are said out of habit or to gain attention.

We focus on attention to detail on body presentation but forget to pay attention to how we address ourselves with our words.

Communication in the physical makes the flow short-lived due to lack of stability with element number one, the self.

It is so changeable it makes it hard to form a solid connection, which is why tools come in handy to bridge the gap.

TAKE AWAY EVERYTHING WHAT DO WE HAVE?
JUST US!

If we only had ourselves and nothing else but just space and one another, how would life be?

How would we get on?

Imagine it for a moment, no clocks, no schedules or to do lists. No toys or gadgets or stuff, just us.

No clutter or need for banks or the systems that make up our infrastructure.

We would have our character and personality, but no memory bank of words. We would live in the moment with no preconceived ideals.

We would feel accepted and comfortable with ourselves and others because we know we have everything we need within us.

We would be the same in the sense. Souls having a spatial experience within ourselves. There would be no competition, physically speaking, because we would know our path is unique to us.

No external noise to distract us.

Now, it would be about inner comfort.

We would allow our unique characters to shine without FOMO (fear of missing out) – getting in the way because FOMO would not exist to the soul because unique is not the same.

We would meet in alignment and vibe with the atmosphere.

Enjoyment would be the reason why we are here.

Waking up happy because we can be ourselves rather than trying to be a version that we are not.

It is easy to see why children have temper tantrums, because the energy is off.

If humans encouraged other humans to be themselves even though they are different, they would know they are not any threat and not trying to copy or impersonate them.

Feeling threatened in any way is the reason why humans fight.

When you don't feel threatened, you thrive.

You will find humans need each other but souls do not because souls support without needing to take over.

Communication that isn't flowing will create obstacles even when the intentions are loving.

The taught way does not multitask very well.

Humans can juggle jobs and think this is the art of multitasking in action.

Multitasking is the ability to listen to yourself and others and share in a self-responsible way without losing yourself in others.

Element number two sharing from the self comes before element number three action work jobs.

This is the art of multitasking, paying attention to yourself while listening to others.

The only way not to lose yourself where others are concerned is by having a solid sense and awareness of yourself while holding your own.

Facing the total physical self is the hardest challenge through the physical taught view because it doesn't make much sense to the soul.

It is why so much energy goes into picking at others in the hope it affects them and not you. It affects yourself first as you come before others. If you don't see you, others won't see you. Walking around in the dark and guessing your way through life bumping into things as you go.

Throwing your weight around is throwing your energy around with no direction.

However, it is said it's not fun!

You shine the light on your life, by connecting to yourself and guiding yourself when mixing with others. If you're switched off from you, then your life is switched off because of you.

Face it, there is only you in your reality even when mixing with others. Your reflection shines back at you from their soul window.

You can try and focus on what they are doing, but that will be in action, not your meaning.

You bring the meaning to your life.

Observe for one moment, a personal relationship.

You like someone new, and you both decide to go on a date to get to know one another.

After the date your friends will ask, what they are like and how did it go?

The rundown will be what they look like, what the interests are, what their social status is, etc. Did you feel a connection?

Yes, sharing in sex is an action as you do not need to be present in essence, just physical body.

If you drank too much to calm your nerves, then maybe the first time isn't even remembered.

You can be physically present but not soul felt.

There but not, humans can love but not feel in love.

We read the room, the atmosphere, the vibe from each other before entering.

We buy things to make an impression, but it's our energy that really does this for us.

Okay, what matters to you counts big time; this is your meaningful content. The ticking of the boxes.

Not the grade.

Boundaries are created by what matters to us, our depth and meaning. If one soul is tidy but another is not, this is a reflection of their soul map not a physical trait.

Your soul map shines in your life guiding you back to yourself through everything.

You think you can hide but to your soul you can't.

How a date goes or continues depends on so many layers of the self, the reason and meaning is the main foundation of what happens next.

YOU RUB OFF ON ME

Have you ever met someone for the first time, and they impact you because they are different to anyone else that you have met so far?

You spend a lot of time together and find yourself picking up their words or ways, mirroring one another.

Our journey on earth starts with ourselves, but I bet by the time a soul exists if they have not paid much attention to themselves, they won't be completely themselves by the time they leave here.

The physical reality makes sure we get wrapped up in other people's demands, expectations and even conflicts.

What actually energetically belongs to you? Have you stopped to even see for yourself, or haven't you realised you're carrying the responsibility of others that doesn't even belong to you.

What belongs to you is what stems from your energy.

It is easy to mimic others especially if they look like they have their life together and it seems they are having more fun. We want what we don't have yet, and if someone else has what you're waiting for this reminder makes life feel miserable making you want it even more. You can't stop thinking about it. You think if I have what I want then I will be happy, RIGHT?

Nope, it doesn't mean that at all.

So many factors within you goes into what makes you feel happy.

If you're mastering element number one, you may feel independent and holding your own and got your life mapped out how you want it feeling in control. But then when it comes to personal relationships you don't feel in control and so they fizzle out and don't last. If your relationship with yourself is on form, how come having relationships don't always match?

It's because we are uniquely different and rub off on one another by clashing with our differences rather than working with them. Often seeing our differences as something wrong because it means we are not on the same page.

You are on the same page because you're in this situation together, what is really going on is self-avoidance. Personal relationships create reflection. Mixing with other souls gives us a chance to view ourselves. If the other souls are not clear, then our reflection is not clear and rubs us up the wrong way. We try to overcome this by people pleasing, which doesn't work for either of you.

Why?

Because by people pleasing, we are actually trying to please ourselves to avoid disharmony. We come first, remember. So, it may seem on the surface people pleasing, but the deep-down reason and meaning is for our own benefit and self-preservation, even if it is to avoid confrontation. Avoidance is still the common key.

By facing ourselves we have the confidence to face others no matter what.

We think if we meet the demands expected in relationships that we will have our happy ever after, again, this doesn't work because action comes after connection.

Managing relationships where a connection is missing will feel more like a job than a loving relationship, without getting rewards or pay.

Relationships change us because they rub off on us. If you're given the space to be yourself then the relationship will shine your character as you work together. If something is missing within yourself, then the relationship will be required to fill the gap of what's missing in self-connection, element number one.

If a relationship is purely for sharing but not for self-altering, then a relationship can expand and grow in love and understanding and not seen as a self-sabotage attack or threat.

This is why some relationships grow, and others go round in circles, repeating what they are stuck on, which is often the self.

Sharing in relationships is the ability to get over the self without losing your connection with the self.

If you need to control others, then you have not settled into your own space within you, trusting yourself enough to be content with just being you when mixing with others.

Yes, you are enough for you, because you are what started your journey here. If when sharing your life with others makes you feel inadequate, then you are listening to them more than yourself.

You know you more than anyone because of space around each of you.

Others can view you, but they will never walk in your shoes.

Your life is made for you and only your signature frequency puts your stamp on it.

I CAN ONLY IMAGINE WHAT ITS LIKE FOR YOU

Exactly!

When we experience what is perceived as the same thing as someone else, your experience will not be the same.

Why our take on things is different.

If humans understood the magic of space, then variety would not be taken personally or seriously, but as spatial happenings.

Really humans know this because of their soul. They will ask what is happening today, not what is personal today.

You may get asked what is your personal take on something, meaning what is your unique view of the situation.

Words have got lost in translated meaning.

Our feelings are as unique as us. Some souls have high pain thresholds while some may find a papercut enough. Some souls feel no pain literally at all within the body. We can feel the pain of feelings with emotion without being touched.

Experiencing our reality is not one-sided or black or white.

It involves many senses and reflexes from both the physical and soul.

But like I shared at the beginning, the physical does not exist without the soul. If you ignore your soul, then your reality will be a one-sided reflection of limitation.

BUT I WANT MORE WITHOUT INVOLVING MYSELF

Humans want a lot and want to know the truth but without minimal effort. What this really means, from the soul perspective, is not putting your energy into more and wanting to be spoon-fed.

Human reality it seems is enough to just be present with a physical body without much else happening.

Tired bodies are everywhere, whether physical, mental, emotional, or plain just over it. Without connection, interest flatlines.

There are lots of things available to numb the pain in all areas of life.

It may help to start with but it's never enough why more is needed by upping the intake.

What is missing is not intake, but the connection to us is not flowing in sharing and action. Life may feel overwhelming or underwhelming, stuck behind our own barricade pile up of energy.

What is not faced will pile up like washing, only to feel overwhelmed until we face it.

What you process and understand in your life will either become a pathway or a dead end.

If you're feeling tired with life, then stop looking at others and listen to you. By doing so is like doing a three-point turn out of this rut.

Okay, you may not know where you're heading yet and in what direction, but at least you're on the move.

Once you move then you will be guided what direction to go in by the prompts around you.

Avoid the brain you will only find the past and memory there to follow your path know how you feel.

Connect back to you if you have been out of touch with yourself for a bit.

Connecting back with yourself and giving you your energy will open the doors so you can share yourself with others in action and plans.

You bring all what's missing in your life back into play just by connecting with yourself.

Liken it to your front door key. The key is you and when you open your front door you gain access to the rooms in your home.

Your soul is your universal home. When you are connected with yourself you gain access to this universe.

If you forget your key, you will feel locked out.

This is why element number one comes first.

The physical has a time and date on it, even down to the physical body.

The soul is infinite and only needs the space in which to flow.

If you have stored or pent-up energy, then it will have a knock-on effect within your physical body.

Sometimes, all the physical body needs to feel in harmony is to use some of its stored energy.

Some souls have more soul energy stored rather than physical energy; some souls have more physical energy stored rather than soul energy.

This is why we see a variety of situations happening in life, depending on where the energy is coming from.

You may apply your energy towards yourself and your relationship with your body. This alone may start off as self-maintenance but then becomes an adapted lifestyle and job.

You may even become known more for what you apply your energy to than who you really wanted to be. What started off as a good idea may take us away from our purpose in life because the money or attention was appealing.

All paths in the physical lead back to ourselves. No soul avoids this, whether sooner or later.

Time may seem on our side or our age and money, but day-the-day of self-realisation catches up with us all.

"You can fool some of the people all of the time, and all of the people some of the time, but you cannot fool all of the people all of the time."

—Abraham Lincoln

This quote explains how difficult it is to get on with others in the taught, physical reality. It makes sense why element number one is first and element number two follows.

Mastering the self isn't selfish, neither is using your energy for yourself.

This is being self-responsible.

But it is often argued that if you go on ahead your leaving others behind, but maybe they are equally holding you back.

There is no right or wrong here; both have meaning and value depending on your soul map details.

To the view of some it may seem you're giving up on your life to aid another, but to your soul that soul is actually benefiting your soul path.

The physical has a limited way of viewing situations especially when it is summed up like a wrong or right maths equation.

Life is often viewed by how it should look on paper.

We are told what to expect before we even get there, the taught reality needs everything preplanned. The soul doesn't because it knows all the outcomes.

To keep the taught life going in a conveyor belt fashion, the physical does not want unpredictability or spontaneity.

Follow the script or else you will remember who you really are.

Humans think they have freedom but on reflection this is written by what is preempted.

It's the cycle of the human body and what to expect at school, at puberty, in relationships, work and home. The only thing that is not pre-known is death. Little is remembered about the facts of the soul.

Freedom is feeling comfortable to follow your own guidance in the now without the need for a plan.

Remember, when you are connected with yourself you have access to totally everything. When you are not connected with yourself and let others guide your life, then you only have access to the taught script.

Why it is followed by those who are not self-connected.

PREGNANCY

When couples get pregnant, they are told what to expect with each trimester. Once the child is born, they are told how to look after it with instructions on how often to feed it, as if a machine.

We doubt our abilities if we don't match up to the instructions, thinking we won't know how to communicate with them without it.

Yet, we know the power of motherly instinct when applied.

We ask gingerly when growing up do you get this or feel this, wanting reassurance that it's not just you experiencing whatever it is with the physical body.

Do you promise me you have had the same experience too?

We are insecure when it comes to the physical body, a taught way which doesn't come natural to us, together with being unique isn't going match up the soul and the physical body together.

This division isn't separation or division but expanded space between the two. Being spaced out from yourself doesn't allow for connection to happen. Liken it to holding two magnets near each other but with a big space between them – they stay in their unique space. Move them closer then connection or repulsion occurs.

You are like two magnets in one, either connecting or repelling yourself, between the physical side of you and your soul side of you.

This universe works in pairs, and your body is a pairing of your choosing that matches your soul.

But if you don't recognise this pairing, you're going to repel it rather than connect and use it.

Have you ever watched a child playing happily on their own, in their own little world, playing out life that they see around them with the toys that they have?

They may use their imaginations and play for hours, reading, colouring, construction, being creative and totally absorbed in expressing themselves. To humans, it's just playing.

What is actually going on is the soul has connected with their chosen body and using it to express itself through the toys provided.

Connection is play in action.

If a child just stares or shows no interest, then the connection between the soul and their physical body is still being established. Remember, self-connection comes first before sharing in any action.

You can try and teach it all you like, but without connection nothing much can happen.

BIG KIDS IN A SMALL SPACE

Childhood, it seems is a privilege and doesn't last long. Why is this when childhood is where the magic is?

Adulting is the term used in which fun stops and responsibilities take over.

Childhood is where souls have the ability to be totally absorbed in their own space without feeling guilty for doing so. They reflect self-responsibility doing what they want within the safety perimeters of play.

Kids will be kids because they are allowed to be and given the space to do so, obviously dependent on the foundations of the adults around them.

Why does the fountain of youth stop?

Because we stop being ourselves and stop feeling comfortable with who we are.

The views and opinions of others swallow us up.

Yet, our journey starts off as fun because we are not self-image focused. We are self-energy focused. To our soul our image is our energy, and we apply it as a child with every step we take together with vocal sounds. Children have so much energy because of the connection to their soul.

As we become switched off from ourselves and become more obsessed with what others are doing. This slows down our energy flow, making us as adults tired.

The fountain of youth is flexible in energy.

Space is what changes as the body grows.

We outgrow our clothes, our furniture, and eat you out of house and home.

Children are like sponges soaking reality up, never full up and always hungry for more.

Depending on the environment, and even if situations are not favourable, the main thing a child will turn to is to find fun, past food and water and shelter.

Sounds like the animal kingdom. Their babies are doing the same, eating, sleeping and having fun.

It's hard work for the carers, providing food for the children as well as feeding themselves.

One mouth to feed is often enough; providing for others takes our attention away from ourselves.

Making ends meet when produce is scarce is stressful.

If it is plentiful, our energy is preserved because it is not about surviving and more to do with enjoyment. Different situations bring with it a different set of skills.

Around World War Two, families were rationed. Neighbours clubbed together, often swapping different rationing coupons with each other.

They had a sense of community spirit. They didn't so much fear one another as they had bigger fears to worry about – the bombs that fell.

They were encouraged to grow their own vegetables and to have allotments.

Families became self-sufficient in skills such as cooking, sewing, knitting and dressmaking as nothing was thrown away. If it could be reused or mended it was. The impact of rationing made the focus about quality, so items bought for the home, such as fridges and cookers, lasted around twenty-five years.

Families might have had to save for such luxuries, but once bought they didn't have to buy them again for a long time.

The quality of skills run life, from within the homes to outside of it. Toys were handcrafted and engineered after work to make gifts for birthdays and Christmas.

Every family was in the same position and situation. No-one was better off than anyone else, materially speaking. Obviously, if you were not green-fingered or able to sew, etc., then you would be reliant on community generosity and maybe you offered your services in other ways, such as child minding or cleaning in exchange for goods.

Bartering has been around for centuries, an exchange of energy of what we apply from ourselves to serve the self before another.

You may view this differently and say I am doing this to serve others who are in need. Yes, they may be in physical material need, but the exchange served your abilities of sharing first.

If another soul wasn't in need in the physical, then there would be no need for sharing.

To make it easier to understand, let's remove the word need, as this confuses the meaning and reason.

When another would like to support a soul, they will step up to offer their skills.

This enables the soul to experience sharing with others.

I have often used our hands as an example to explain the art of sharing. We give in one hand and receive in the other.

It looks like one or the other is going on, but both are happening at once.

You are receiving the experience of sharing the self as others receive your offering.

So actually, the focus is on you than rather them.

In every situation you will find the opposite of it. This is why it's not a one-way view of right or wrong; it is an infinite view at once. If you pick the nice bits from an experience to avoid the not nice parts, just focusing on the nice bits does not delete or remove the bits you don't like. They are still present whether you focus on them or not.

Everything is playing in this universe at once, regardless of what we are focusing on.

If you focus on number one out of a hundred, number one doesn't cancel out the other ninety-nine numbers.

They exist as the one does.

Humans focus on one-thing-at-a-time thinking. This is the only thing that exists. This focus helps them manage less rather than more. Meanwhile, the soul is connected automatically to infinitely everything in this universe and will bring more into play to encourage them to view a bigger picture.

If you want to blame anything, blame your breath for this one.

Of course, if you want to use blame that is.

But as you know blame leads us back to ourselves.

Hence, the infinity loop goes in one direction to itself in a loop.

What you focus on is maybe what you can physically see, but it won't be all that there is.

Just because you can't see it, it doesn't mean that it doesn't exist.

Souls that arrive here are what the physical would call psychic.

What this actually means is that they are running on their soul energy and not learnt the taught physical script yet.

Their connection via their breath gives these souls total access in this universe.

This access in space closes in the more the taught script is used.

It takes a soul, old school pre-2018, roughly twelve years to learn the taught script.

Post-2018 souls that arrive here won't play by the script.

You may even have noticed this yourself, this year in 2025, that children are harder to teach and not listening.

It is because they are hardwired to their soul and not interested in the teachings of the taught script.

They will want to be themselves organically and grow uniquely with the skills they brought with them. But these skills won't be like the curriculum.

This will cause the script issues.

Over the next four years, souls will turn the tables on the script.

The soul is the powerhouse and no fight is necessary because of connection alone.

Whatever souls connect with will become their reality.

Some will try to keep the script going but the numbers of followers will go down drastically.

New schools will arise that will benefit the soul's growth.

Liken it to planting seeds in the garden. The seeds are given their own space in which to flourish.

The systems up to 2018 have denied you your space to be you.

Crushing your roots hanging on to the script for dear life.

Like I shared earlier, if you don't want the scripted physical bubble to burst then stop reading this book.

I appreciate you reading up to now. It shows you're interested in you. But I am not sharing my take on this universe to burst your bubble.

I am not even saying that the taught physical reality hasn't existed. It has but not to serve your soul. It has served distortion.

You know that sound you hear between tuned-in stations? It sounds like static noise.

Static does not translate clearly or show a clear picture.

It's distorted for a reason to stop you from transmitting yourself clearly, knowing if self-connection is missing you will need something to take its place. And what has taken its place in your reality over centuries is the taught script.

Souls arrived eager over the centuries with their soul maps with the intention of following their soul path, only to forget it when they arrive because of the magic of space around each frequency.

Together with being distracted with learning, learning should go as far as mastering the human body, but the script took it further to include everything in life.

Without a connection you won't remember what your soul brought with you.

This is why souls are prepared what to expect and taught about the script as soon as the body is born so the soul connects with it.

You are prepared for the birth and how to look after the child before you hold them in your arms.

You have a mental plan of action.

The script has fed you on what to do and not what to do. Even mapping out graphs to see if your child matches up with what is set as a satisfactory gauge. Nothing unique about that.

A spoonful of stress from the get-go is what it gives you.

Anxiety often through the roof, even if subconsciously speaking. How your energy feels will tell you if you feel comfortable and confident. If you're not feeling this connection, then you are not going to feel your abilities from the get-go.

You have instinct and a connection to the body you have given birth to because your soul energy flowed through every cell of it.

You know it inside out. If you have the space to let instinct kick in, then you would not need to follow any scripts and graphs. I have had four children over an eleven-year gap. What the script told me to do with my first said wasn't right with my second and third and so on. It changed with each pregnancy.

Follow the money not the energy in everything.

Things are changed that make money. Keeping on powdered milk makes more money on top of weaning food.

In my humble observation from my experience, the script I followed with my first was that you wean them at three months. They can have cow's milk from six months.

Now it's different.

I am not saying what is right or wrong. Neither allow a mother's instinct to kick in.

The script tells you it's there to help and support you, but does it?

Your body does all the work to make sure the body grows, ready for the waiting soul to connect with it.

Your soul energy flows through the placenta and the umbilical cord and into the new body that is growing, making sure it is in working order. Think of it like taking a flat balloon from the packet and exhaling into it to expand it. This is what your soul does to the body growing. This is why you feel the movements inside of you as an indication that your soul has a connection with it.

The soul waiting to connect with it at the birth will visit it during the pregnancy.

At the birth itself, the soul watches the process. It is a physical-to-physical happening.

The physical body only experiences the birth. The soul-to-soul connection between the soul waiting and the soul of the mother is communicating on the side. The mother's soul will know when to stop breathing through the umbilical cord, as the soul waiting is ready to connect with their first breath. This transfer can happen during labour itself or after the birth of the body. If a body comes out crying, then you know the transfer between the souls happened during labour. If the body comes out silent and not working, then the connection of the waiting soul has not happened yet. Once the waiting soul takes the first breath then the new body will work.

Then the first cry and movements are seen much to relief of everyone present.

The waiting soul knows how to take the first breath and does not need to be taught how to do it.

It comes naturally to souls.

It's why we breathe constantly without consciously thinking about it.

You trust yourself to breathe, so you can trust yourself with everything else.

LEFT TO OUR OWN DEVISES, WE ARE FINE

Element number two sharing from the self throws a spanner in the works of element number one the self.

It is not easy to juggle the self while accommodating others.

Why is that?

Because humans have forgotten who their souls really are.

They view themselves through the looking glass of taught human expectations, opinions and judgements and grades of worthiness.

They believe they are their human bodies even though they do not work on their own without the soul energy.

The soul has no need for grading because everything is experience.

The soul will see the totality of each soul even if the opposite is being expressed.

Humans only see what they think they are seeing or assuming is the case.

What makes up every event is an accumulation of many pieces that forms the meaning of why you are involved or sharing in an event with others.

You bring your soul energy together with your physical energy to events that you have chosen as others are doing the same. Imagine a bunch of different balloons being held as an analogy.

What you experience, while in the mix with others, depends how you hold your own and react to others while in their company.

The reaction you reflect is often blamed on others, but in truth this is a reflection of your own relationship with yourself.

We are fine tuning ourselves constantly. It's why it is hard to keep the flow managed and why this fluctuation in energy causes ups and downs.

How we react to anything is like throwing a stone in the sea that causes a ripple effect.

From the human perspective we react to others, but from the soul perspective, subtly just before that reaction, something else was going on that humans miss with themselves.

How you felt within yourself in your reality makes all the difference to how we react or handle others when we mix with them.

Example: I may put pressure on myself to complete a project that I have set for myself. My soul is happy getting on with it, but my physical side may feel bad for not being available and not meeting the expectations or demands energetically that has previously been set out in my physical memory routine.

In my head, what I think others expect and want from me.

Our memories subtly play back to us, and we use this information before we even engage in human-to-human sharing. We may react to others that may seem out of character from memory.

It is not personal in the sense of a malfunction in our reflection and character. It is more to do with juggling space to freely be ourselves, without the demands of the past physical memory that are running in the background getting in our way, and in the way it does.

I JUST WANT TO BE FREE

This has nothing to do with cost or money but everything to do with energy. You can have a high-powered job and be busy from morning to night and still feel free to be you.

To be free is to feel your own space around yourself, rather than the infringement of others placed on you.

If you have sat next to a physical stranger, if there is a slither of space between you and them, this makes you feel more comfortable. This is because this universe is space, and upon feeling the connection of that slither of space you're reminded of how it feels in this universe. It feels comfortable.

We have boundaries around our homes to enjoy our own spaces in the garden. But why is it if we want our own space within ourselves viewed as isolation, rejection, and judged as not being very sociable?

Being sociable is often too much stimulation. A lot of frequencies are playing around you constantly. This is like being in your home and turning on every appliance and gadget on full volume and living amongst it.

It is noisy and not always constructive noise.

A soul will search for some peace and quiet.

You will know when you want to find your own space is when you migrate to quiet rather than needing noise.

Humans can find silence deafening because it means you don't want to listen to yourself.

Migrating to external noise is a sure way of avoiding connecting with yourself.

It is wonderful how the soul has this covered, considering the soul never sleeps, but the physical body does need sleep to switch off and recharge.

If you're running on soul, you will be flowing in your peaceful space of yourself. If you're running on physical, then you will be stretched to your limits.

Each soul does catch up with itself even if it is during sleep, just the physical doesn't remember when they wake up.

Being connected to a physical body doesn't make you less soul, it just gives you an extra frequency to play with while you're here. Your physical frequency works through your soul frequency, this is why your soul frequency can switch between stations constantly and subtly.

You are never just in one station totally because you are connected to the physical one by the breath alone that runs through your soul like a split screen.

FAMILY UNIT

You don't bring your kids up because you want to be part of a scripted organisation called the family. You bring your kids up because you love them and want to support their growth unconditionally.

The family unit comes with expected ties.

Even birds encourage their young to flee the nest.

Humans want to belong to others rather than being encouraged to belong to themselves.

As parents and carers, we share our love and show that we are not too old for a cuddle.

Until teenagers show us that cuddling isn't cool.

Parents/carers back off to respect the teenagers' boundaries and space.

Only to be reminded when they become adults of why you don't cuddle them like you used too. They forget that the teenage them told you it wasn't cool. It is easy to blame others when we don't piece all the pieces together that tell a story of why it has turned out this way.

We oversee our parts we played only focusing on what others are doing.

It is not one-sided for anyone, and this is evident once we are ready to view the bigger picture and not just the comments section.

FAMILY LOOKS EASY TO YOU, BUT IS IT BEHIND CLOSED DOORS?

It is easy to assume everyone else is playing happy families when you don't see behind closed doors.

Family life growing up in the early seventies and eighties was tucked away in some file or at the bottom of a drawer inside of a photo album or a love letter, or the secrets inside of a diary or hidden deep down in your feelings.

No one said much about family life, just the basics of the birds and the bees and to get married to have kids and to have a good job so you can buy a home.

Settling down was expected young. If you weren't married or pregnant by twenty-one, then you were scared of being left on the shelf.

This was the subliminal message that I picked up anyway.

As soon as you grew past puberty, it was "Oh, what's your job and are you in a relationship?"

Pairing up again to make sure the next generation follows in the footsteps of the previous, so the script continues.

If everyone spread out from the family nest by focusing on their own unique gifts instead of the hand-me-downs of the script, then life as we have known it would be very different.

LIFE INSIDE A GOLDFISH BOWL

And I thought these were just for fish. I never knew I would see the day when humans did it to themselves. Don't get me wrong. This universe is transparent, but the difference is in truth.

Family life is not just a private family affair anymore – a private life, forget it. Anything shared isn't in confidence anymore because we share it with a third party, the internet. Any secrets past our private homes are shared across the wide web platforms. Everyone knows your business and if they don't it is there to find out by someone who has heard it.

Back in the eighties before this third-party reality, we lived our best life in real time, not recorded to watch later.

The only thing watched that was yesterday's news was the news itself.

But family life was more up to date and a lot would be going on because of our emotions.

We respected our own privacy and the privacy of others on the whole, unless you were nosey or got paid to find out more.

Invading people's privacy didn't happen. I guess it was easy back then because no one shared or talked much. Whatever happened in your reality, you kept it to yourself and got on with it.

The stiff upper lip they used to say before the war.

Back then you were seen but not heard.

Now you're seen and still not heard. So not much has changed in a hundred years apart from becoming more tech visible.

Back in the day, it was your trodden footsteps. Now it's your online presence.

TECHNOLOGY

Technology is amazing if you're tech-minded, and I am not tech savvy. I still rely on hard copy, pen and paper.

I use gadgets and I am using one to write this book as its quicker to send the manuscript to my publisher. Being in the UK by post would take much longer.

Technology has sped our life up so much that we don't have the time and space to listen to others let alone ourselves.

This is like being squeezed to get every last drop of energy out of us, and then we wonder why we feel burnt out.

With anything in life what you get in one hand you lose in the other, especially if the connection to the self is missing. The external world will prop you up like scaffolding rather than your internal energy of your soul.

Bigger houses, bigger cars, more tech in every room, we are overloaded with downloads.

Yep, you see it like me. The script has grown past the self and become AI.

Chat bots of artificial intelligence, it's funny the choice of words used. Artificial and virtual both sum up a reality that doesn't feel real. Why? Because it is viewed and not created through our energy.

I loved watching the television in my teenage years once I had access to it more, disappearing into the scripted film or series.

But I would not want my life just to consist of watching life. What would be the point of being here? But this is exactly what is subtly going on.

Children are given phones to watch rather than amusing themselves with toys.

When I watched the happy scenes on the television, I wanted their happiness, and it took me away from my sadness I felt in my life.

But it didn't lead me back to myself. It led me up the garden path, as they used to say, of an ideal reality that didn't exist. A kiss on the cheek does not make a happy ever after because of the chores and bills. They missed this in the films.

SETTING US UP FOR LIFE

Usually, the first thing that is focused on is money. Do some errands to earn some pocket money. Have a nest egg for a rainy day or save your pennies as the pounds look after themselves.

If you work hard enough and invest your money in property, you will be set up for life, secure in the knowing that you have something to pass down in your will for your children. Peace of mind knowing that your hard work doesn't just benefit yourself by having a secure roof over your head it benefits the next generation with helping them up the step ladder of independence and self-sufficiency too.

The message is loud and clear: work hard and you too can have peace of mind.

Hard work and working all the hours life sends, going without to make the dream possible is worth it, isn't it?

The more new tech arrived, the more it upset the apple cart of old-style ethics.

The fast-paced way of life with each passing year didn't set the next generation up. It set them up to fail in debt.

Previous generations saved for what they had and if they couldn't afford it, they didn't get it and made do with what they had.

The memory of making do faded fast. With the eighties came bigger options and more money.

Wondering what club to go to next, families started to travel more and have holidays abroad, and timeshares became available to live the dream abroad.

Guaranteed holidays for the family sounded like a dream come true.

LIFESTYLES AND TRENDS COME AND GO

In the past, pop groups set the stage for different fashion styles. It gave teenagers a chance to express themselves.

You had the teddy boys, the mods, the punks and soul boys among many.

Icons adorned many teenage bedrooms, and music was the sound blaring from shops as well as homes, and by those carrying their music down the street.

Nothing stopped the sound of music.

Surround sound for the living room to fully immerse yourself in what was playing, either records or the television.

When the nineties arrived, it was like someone had turned off the music as the party of fun times were over.

Interest rates went through the roof, and the yuppy era faded as quick as it arrived.

Families struggled to pay their bills. Many gave up and handed the keys back to the building societies.

The struggle became real. Debt became a lifeline of juggled hope.

Obviously, these years relate to my era. I guess many different eras would say the same happened for them, where they remember feeling on top of their world and then not.

What these memories reflect is that life doesn't stop still for anyone. You either keep up or not.

Life never went back to those fun styles again. Over the years shops changed too. The high street stopped the music and switched to online selling.

Human-to-human contact slipped away and was replaced with online chat.

The next fashion trend stopped and suddenly the shops stocked all the styles that had ever been.

Technology and fun games emerged first from the mobile and into our homes with graphics no one had seen before.

The virtual world became our reality by the 2000s.

As soon as one new gadget is mastered another one would be revealed.

I am still waiting for holographic displays. I am surprised these are not used and projected into our homes making traditional televisions and screens obsolete.

Back at school before I left the seniors, office jobs were the go-for jobs and becoming telephonists.

Within a year, it was IT (information technology).

If you were more tech-minded, this suited you. It was where the money is apart from the obvious, stocks and shares, a doctor or solicitor.

Any other jobs got you buy, but not the promise of having the dream lifestyle.

Being more practical, the tech options for me were out of my league.

I wasn't really interested in chasing after money, as money had made my childhood miserable by others who chased it.

MONEY GROWS ON TREES, DOESN'T IT?

I was first introduced to money at a cost to myself. Money exchanged hands to look after me in return upon my mother's death.

An agreement kept for six months until the money ran out.

My mum's house was ransacked rather than shared out fairly. One member of the family took it all, creating ill feelings between everyone.

A time was agreed to meet but they chose to arrive a few hours early and taking me with them, their credit card agreement.

The pain that was inflicted on me showed me that it doesn't matter how much money you have. It doesn't make you happy.

It can either bring out the best in you or bring out the worst or even both.

Money to me from this experience was to avoid it or avoid fighting over it because it causes misery.

This made me turn to my energy and to rely on using this as my exchange instead.

I SEE YOU, DO YOU?

Growing up in pain showed me what I wanted, fun, love and laughter.

Even though I didn't have these organic comforts without a price tag on my head, I still held it as my guiding light.

Even when I was fostered money was highlighted, especially when I left school as I had to make up for what would be lost in money for my care.

Everyone has to survive and pay the bills, and it is the main reason for getting up each day.

Even if you hate your job or love it or like it, just think of the money at the end of the week.

Turning up to a job you dislike is soul destroying.

It sucks the energy out of you.

Humans became more miserable the less they could be totally themselves.

Money being the main driving force instead of enjoyment and pleasure.

Technology softened this blow giving families an outlet to enter a virtual reality that they felt involved in and could control.

CONTROL THE CONTROLLER

Some controllers were easy to manage on consoles than others, staring at the screen trying to remember to blink.

Frustrations ran high when competing with others.

Whether one player or two, playing was more fun even when challenging as it was still better than work.

Combat games became popular bringing back fighting and winning.

It's not real. It's only a game, isn't it?

Sharing in anything rubs off on us because of element number two.

Energy either attracts or repels, benefiting us in either expansion or down the rabbit hole of need and obsession.

Not all the time though.

Space between sessions makes playing games acceptable. I have been at work all day, so this is my reward.

The attention to detail was once human-to-human interest, replaced by an avatar that looks nothing like you.

Souls can be anything they want to be, so makes sense this is available in the game world.

Do you have control over the game, or does the game have power over you?

Or do we just get sucked in to whatever gets our attention.

Once upon a time it was sex, drugs and rock 'n' roll, money and things and now technology.

WHAT DO THE SMITHS OR JONESES HAVE?

I used to hear this remark when I was a teenager. I didn't really get it, but it was neighbourly competition to have the next best gadget before anyone else.

This soon faded when technology was not just for the rich but available for everyone.

Debt made this possible.

Past standards of lower, middle or high class went out of the window.

Old class system related to politics and voted according to what lifestyle class they fell into.

Why?

To preserve and keep the lifestyle that they had been accustomed to.

The black market became the deep dark web.

This is nothing new in society. If you don't rank in any of the classes, then you create your own.

Often with violence to get what you want.

ILLEGAL HAPPENINGS

This is often a label put on the wrong'uns, the people that steal and take things without paying for them.

I found myself in this position at four years old when I was living at the children's home.

I went out to the shops with a bunch of the older kids from the homes as it was called. This was short for children's home.

The older kids decided to steal some sweets from the shops but got caught.

The police were called. They bundled us into police cars and drove us back to the children's home.

I remember staff standing us in a line while we waited for the policeman to turn up, our heads going down as the line went from eldest to youngest, the youngest being myself.

I was closest to the door and saw the policeman position his hat on his head before entering the room.

He told us all off. I zoned out as I hadn't really understood or followed what had been happening. Yes, I had followed them and got caught with them, but I was in my little world not theirs.

The policeman left and the mood in the room was sombre. Punishments had been dished out and served.

Something I will never forget, not because of the wrongdoing but because this experience highlighted to me, that you can be in the same scene as another but have different experiences.

If you look back in history, there has always been illegal goings on. Some are just more highlighted than others.

Some are so well-known that they get celebrity status.

But if we are honest with ourselves, it's happening everywhere.

SCAPEGOAT OR COVER UP?

Growing up I was what is termed as the black sheep of the family, the kid and or the adult that doesn't fit in anywhere.

My name didn't fit, my face didn't fit, my status didn't fit, my abilities didn't fit.

The list of inadequacies grew with me.

Once labelled, if you can't beat it, you join it and become it anyway.

I will admit I had a colourful life, one that I wasn't always proud of, but it is where I remembered everything of who I really am.

On the face of things, my life matched my glasses, my eyes being boss-eyed where one turned in. I tilted my head and grew a fringe to cover it up.

It's not just me. Cover ups have been going on for centuries. There is so much that you think you know but actually don't.

Even the military have case files that are black ops.

The fact is we don't know everything until we start asking questions and searching for answers.

But this upsets the apple cart. I don't want change, so let's turn a blind eye or the other cheek.

Some things are in plain sight and some things are in plain sight and still invisible.

Pay attention to what you're doing and ignore what so and so is doing. Being a nosey neighbour was called being a peeping tom. Words and sentences spread the word subtly and sublimely, so the public created the script without even realising it.

Clever is as clever does.

Growing up I heard sentences such as "Why can't you be more like your friend?" or "Why don't you stop copying your friend and be more like yourself?"

I would be myself if I had the chance to know who me was, but the script does not give me the space or chance to find out.

SLEEP TIGHT, MAKE SURE THE BEDBUGS DON'T BITE

Sweet dreams, if the day wasn't hectic enough to dodge words and actions and feelings while mixing and hanging out with others, nighttime didn't make it any easier.

Most kids learn while at school. Fo me, my learning happened at the universal school of this universe.

From four years old after finding my mum dead, my guide Ramini took me under his wing – well, actually under his arm. He wasn't an angel.

The first few years he communicated with me via internal dialogue. I was aware of his presence, but I didn't see him visually. This came later.

I guess he didn't need to make himself known when I could hear him and understand what my thoughts were and what were his. No different to talking to any person you have a conversation with.

You know who is who by the tone.

We each have our own unique tone that we are recognised by, often referred to as your vibe.

It was lovely having him by my side because he didn't hurt me and actually listened to me.

An internal friend that no one in the physical saw, it was like my inner reality secret.

146

I adapted to visiting the physical taught reality but making my inner reality my home, my space where I belonged and felt loved and more importantly understood.

The more I settled into my inner home, the less I enjoyed visiting the taught reality.

Before I left the care system, I briefly opened the file to my history, which sent my feelings exploding into the air.

Being reminded constantly that I didn't belong anywhere and stood out like a sore thumb, so I turned to what made me happy.

Any human that showed me attention and made me laugh I felt a connection with. It didn't matter what they looked like, or even if they actually loved me. I didn't need to be loved as I felt this from my internal universe. I guess I wanted to be seen and heard and valued more so I felt part of this taught reality.

No matter how I tried, and if I bent over backwards, it always turned out the same of not being enough. I was wanted for my abilities and for my ability to be able to take a lot when I was needed to be someone's punchbag. I stood my ground and took it all.

But this receptive cycle wasn't fun, and I wanted fun.

It was made easier when I was introduced to alcohol. Wow, I could not feel a thing. I could join in with this horrible reality and not feel a thing. It numbed the pain wonderfully, until it wore off.

It was fun while it lasted, until the spinning room appeared followed with throwing up.

I soon understood why balance is important to pace it, so I could manage how I felt.

Drink came hand in hand with going out. Everyone was doing it, so it made it okay.

It's not just me as many a teenager was doing it.

My first boyfriend introduced me to sex in the adult context. The first time you usually remember but alcohol wiped my memory.

Sex seemed a big deal, like a taboo subject, only highlighting contraception and how to protect yourself from catching anything.

Adulting comes with many clauses.

Death is not talked about either, so facing my parents' deaths was dealt with the same as kids were, seen and not heard.

Get over it, enough time has gone now, drop it and move on.

The one thing lacking here is not so much my parents but the lack of understanding how things work.

I mean, who wants to be in pain or feel sad morning, noon and night. I know I didn't.

But I couldn't drop it not because of the death word, but because I didn't understand all of it.

When I understand something then I can drop it.

PAY ATTENTION

The five senses of the physical body are the reason why everyone is fighting to be heard and seen, why statements and declarations are written.

We give in one hand and take away with another, leaving an empty hole waiting to be filled with something.

Yes, it is waiting to be filled with ourselves because this is what is missing.

Growing up I was in survival mode, which gave me little drive to pay attention in class, especially if I didn't get it or understand the subject matter.

I got through the classes with my friends. We made light of the fact that the whole school knew who was in the dunce's class and who wasn't.

Try harder then maybe you can go up a class.

This never happened and after a few years being with the same faces in the same class made it easier to get on.

Being in the same boat helps in any situation.

Safety in numbers because it is harder to stand out amongst many.

It is easier if you have an extrovert in the class who gets all the attention.

If you're willing to put yourself on the line and face the consequences for doing so, this depends on the meaning behind the actions.

Is it for the greater good of yourself or others?

If you're sticking up for others, then others leave you alone. If you stick up for yourself, then others take sides.

If the sides outweigh the other, then the majority takes the lead over the minority.

SCHOOL'S OUT

I experienced the immoral compass of school attitudes when my children went to school.

(Remember, I am just sharing a true experience).

I will explain what happened next in a shortened version.

My third daughter was close to leaving junior school with a few months left.

Roughly eight children wrote a letter together to their class form teacher. Out of the eight children one included my daughter.

My daughter told me that they didn't like getting changed for PE (physical education) in front of the male teacher. They didn't like how he stared at them.

The head teacher called the parents of the children into the school for a meeting.

The head teacher told us that the police had been called to deal with the matter because the children had written the word pervert in the letter.

This one word escalated the problem and the children's reason for writing the letter was dismissed and ignored because of this one word.

The police arrived at the school telling the eight children off for using such implicative language.

The eight children were in tears and punished with isolation and made to write lines. It didn't matter that they felt violated for wanting their privacy when changing for PE.

Not being heard or understood without words getting in the way isn't easy in the taught reality script. But it is okay because everyone is doing it and so it makes it okay.

I spoke to the parents involved asking them to join me in making a complaint to support the children.

No one was interested, the attitude being what's the point? We are the minority; they are the majority.

I was on my own with this one.

Being a minority didn't bother me. What bothered me is the children feeling listened to and supported. If I can't support and stand by the side of my child, then who can?

I felt alone but I soon found out that I actually wasn't.

My heart guided me to follow and stand by what I morally believed in.

I had little sleep for the next few weeks. I wrote statements and made enough copies to send out to every teacher and department at once.

I phoned the education authority and even social services.

The following Monday morning, I knew everyone in each department would receive the statements of events at once.

Okay, I found out after that I hadn't dealt with it how the school wanted because I wasn't aware. By addressing the situation to the teacher then the deputy head and then the head mistress before the governing board, I just addressed them all at once.

By Wednesday people from the education authority descended on to the school, and the school was pulled to threads, not because of the event itself but because they had not put in place a visual board of contact names and faces available for parents.

Ironically dealing with the situation from my gut turned out beneficial. The school should have had names and faces of teachers and governors easily seen for parents, so they know who to address. The fact they did not provide this information made the system of addressing each teacher in rank null and void.

The next week these issues where rectified, with faces and names now seen on the wall by the front office.

The head teacher got sacked, and the children got a room in which to dress for PE with dignity.

Oh, I forgot to tell you, one night during it I had a knock at my front door. It was eleven p.m. at night.

Two people from the governing board were telling me to drop the case, because I was the minority not the majority, physically speaking.

However threatening they tried to be with words used, I just shut the door and continued.

I guess my secret inner world comes in handy because they can't see what I can see, this universe.

They may have had each other's physical back, but the energy of this universe had mine.

Plus, my deceased dad turned up. During the stress of the situation my daughter regressed. I cheered her up as much as I could, but the heavy load took its toll on me too.

When I had finished putting the statements inside many brown envelopes, with the last stamp applied, I scooped them up in my arms to take them to the post office.

I opened my front door and saw my dad sitting in the driver's seat of my car. He was smiling at me while holding brown envelopes like me.

As I shut my front door, I felt the warm glow inside and smiled the biggest smile. My dad may have left my car by the time I reached it, but I loved the message he left for me.

At this point I knew this situation was over and everything was going to be okay.

The next week many parents came up to us and congratulated us for standing up for the children.

I turned to my daughter, and I said, "We did it." I gave her a big hug while saying, "Never forget I will always listen to you and stand by your side. Nothing is too much trouble for me when it comes to you."

It doesn't make me any better than anyone else. I just had the strength to follow my gut rather than fear of the mind.

When you use your connection, you don't stand alone because this universe stands with you.

The other reason why I did it is for the next set of kids that would be starting the school.

Setting a foundation that encourages growth. Being told is not learning, but being listened to is. As adults can learn from children too when you forget who you are.

I AM POWERFUL AND THE BOSS – DON'T YOU KNOW WHO I AM?

What makes someone so powerful?

A status a heading a title?

Many tools are used in which to get to the top of the game.

Sex, money, lie, cheat, deceive, twist or bend the rules, and turn a blind eye and sweep it under the carpet. Your secret is safe with me.

Just don't utter a word.

This works if everyone is on board.

Corruption is in all walks of life.

What I see as titles is another way of saving your own skin.

Saving our positions in society or holding on to a marriage, holding others to ransom are all forms of using others for our own neglect of holding our own.

Yes, you read it correctly.

Others are used to prop us up, when we can't or won't, energetically speaking.

Well, let me put it this way, a happy together soul will not need to subject such behaviour to another.

A together soul has their energy in check.

What would be the point if they have their life managed in a self-responsible way.

Those in position can do such things by abusing their position and status. It's down to their own self attitude.

In a nutshell, it is their choice. Okay, you could say they were forced to; otherwise, they would lose their job.

Money came before morals. The threat of loss is often said in words, which is enough to force compliance.

The imagination can run away with us and make it a lot worse than what it actually is.

Follow the energy that will give you the facts, as it will have the creator's signature energy all over it.

Peel the layers off. It comes back to the self. To feel the need to control another is to feel out of control yourself.

Remember, the first element of connection to the self. We are not singled out, just if we get found out.

How long you can get away with anything depends on many factors, mainly who is listening and who is following you and for what reason.

If calling you out makes their life come crashing down, then they will want to keep it under the radar as well. If calling you out promotes their life, then obviously the self comes before you.

YOU'RE NOT HARD DONE BY

"Stop feeling sorry for yourself and brush yourself down and pick yourself back up."

"Hold your head high and get back on your bike to continue your path."

We have heard these lines said to us on our journey, words of denial or words of encouragement.

This depends on the narrative.

If words are used so you skim over your reality, then piecing it together will have to wait. Just pile the pieces up as you will get round to it another day.

ARGUING

Arguing over the point is pointless unless you're on the same page, and if you're on the same page then there is nothing to argue about.

Arguing occurs when you don't feel heard, making points to self-validate and preserve.

Each soul will have their own point of view, because they are in this universe like you having their own unique infinite experience. Look around you. Every soul is doing the same. There are no grades or high scores or status.

Why?

Because you are this universe. You created the backdrop, the infinite knowing of possibilities.

This is why no soul is wrong or right as everything is present and known.

It would be like saying to a child as it tips out the pieces of a jigsaw puzzle onto the table, pick up the right pieces and don't touch the wrong ones.

The child would look at you confused knowing that all the pieces of the puzzle make up the total picture of the jigsaw puzzle.

If you left pieces out, the picture would not get completed.

Knowing the language of this universe, the four elements of frequency, element number four vibration/completion overlooks the other three elements making sure completion is reached.

In every piece of this universe, completion is guaranteed eventually. It takes as long as you.

If you try to delete or ignore or dodge or hide anything, you know you can't anyway from the transparency of this universe, and you know you're only trying to hide it from yourself.

Here comes another analogy: Say a child is holding a small toy and wants you to guess what hand they are holding it in, when their hands are behind their back. Then the child will pass the toy behind their back between their hands until they decide which hand they will hide it in.

Once decided, they will ask you to guess what hand it is in. If you already know this game. You know how to work it out. You concentrate on the movement of the hands rather than being behind their back.

If you're bigger than the child, then their smaller size may give the game away because it is easier to see, and their back isn't hiding it very well.

This concept happens between the physical and the soul.

The taught physical souls have forgotten that everything is seen and not hidden.

The soul that remembers works out what has been forgotten.

The soul loves to share past the self, resulting in getting imprisoned or burnt at the stake in history of course of the past.

And so, the cycle continues through the centuries.

Souls that have arrived on earth either hidden behind their physical bodies or continued to be their soul self.

Those that chose to hide think that they outwit the four elements of frequency because they are following the script.

Buying and selling and throwing words around to impress even if they are not understood, makes it more convincing. You know the instruction manuals and Ts and Cs. We scan and pass them quickly so we can play with the new item.

Why is everything made out to be so confusing when seeing this universe in transparency is simple?

Because the taught script does not want you to remember more than them or to give the hiding game away.

Hide behind the physical veil and we will hide this universe from you.

UNDERCOVER MEMORY

The stored script had one problem: it could not exist independently without the soul.

The soul's energy when connected to itself runs through the physical and soul memories, not just the selected physical ones.

This is why you have random dreams and meet people you know in the dream but don't know them in this reality when you wake up.

Remember, the universe deletes nothing, so every memory both physical and soul is accessible when the soul uses its connection.

It's why the script will want you focused on the taught reality to stop you switching to your soul.

The physical script will encourage you to pick one of anything, or you can have a slice or two, but not too much.

As long as you stay away from your soul knowing.

Knowing or choosing one thing from many is difficult, resulting in you wanting to come back for more.

A failproof system in how to get you buying into more of what the script provides.

Have some money and put the rest in the bank and we will look after the rest for you.

Buy a house but land registry will keep hold of the deeds.

You hold half or half of a half of what you have, depending on how you share it around.

Sadly, the script lets your physical body grow while stunting your growth of self-responsibility.

When did you lose the ability to look after yourself?

You can look after your stuff yourself, if you can purchase it, you can look after it surely.

But it takes the stress out of it if someone looks after it for me. Saves me the worry.

REALLY?

Is it so!

Until something happens of course, then all hell lets loose.

You may invest into schemes that have a wonderful, hopeful return. Often, sadly, it is not worth the paper it is written on, even in writing if the rules change in this taught script.

Oh, that was then but isn't now, the get out clause.

Keeping you confused and on your toes while being distracted by what you can purchase next.

Gold and silver were once king, then cheque books and cards and now online banking, crypto.

What's next?

It doesn't matter what playing pieces are added to the game. It keeps you busy, so you stay hidden, so you don't work out the bigger picture.

Knowing the truth bursts the bubble. You know what that feels like, when you were told what you believed isn't actually real.

TOOTH FAIRY AND FATHER CHRISTMAS

As a kid when Christmas came round, I wasn't worried about what toys I got, if I got something as I wanted to be included and not left out.

When I had children of my own, I wanted them to feel the magic in my soul, but I only had the tools in the physical reality to create the magic for them.

Feeling the magic is a wonderful experience when you can take part and put your energy into it.

This is the magic of being connected and involved.

Over the years I have seen the magic overshadowed because children didn't get what they asked for, believing that Father Christmas can bring them whatever they want.

The buildup and the hype making it feel so real and believable.

There is magic in this universe, but it's not a made-up story.

You are the magic of this universe when you connect.

You can bring anything to life and be whatever you want to be.

Within the guidelines of your self-created soul map and chosen highlighted elements.

This is why what you experience on earth is tailor-made to match you. If you don't like what is on your plate, then you are not directing it or following what is on your soul map.

If you can't remember what it is on your map, then you will follow in the footsteps of others.

If you leave your life up to others to dictate, you're setting yourself up to be miserable because if you don't have a say in your life in energy, then you're not connected and a visitor in your own creation.

That's like putting the energy in to buying a house only not to enjoy living in it because you forgot you bought it.

I TOLD YOU AND TELL YOU TIME AND TIME AGAIN

We get it. Time and word telling is what makes the script repeat itself.

This universe doesn't tell you what to do because you know it yourself.

I told you it is a self-reflective sentence because it starts with I.

Yes, yourself.

You are telling yourself what you told the other person. They are just listening.

If a soul is offering guidance to help support another on their path, then the I will be switched to you. You would be wise to make this choice or if I were you, I would do this.

As you can see everything is visible in plain sight if we are not blinded by words flying around.

Words that are used in understanding are very useful, when the self is in alignment and not all over the place.

Self-stability is the foundation of continuity.

You know the souls you meet that you can depend on and rely on because their guidance and support is sound.

These souls don't change themselves because life has changed. They keep being them even if it means going it alone.

You are not going to want a bull in a china shop. You will want those who can hold their own.

I TRUST YOU

You know what I previously shared to do with the letter I. Yes, we are talking about the self.

But do we trust ourselves?

Obviously not, if we require others to manage our lifestyles for us.

If you're old enough to buy it, then you're old enough to look after it has been told.

But we don't look after ourselves totally, do we?

We do what everyone else is doing, getting money in one hand and dishing it out the next. Crosses your hand for five minutes.

Back in the past, it was known that people put money under the mattress.

This was okay until it went missing.

The fear of losing your money is why we trust the banks with it.

Banks back then were more for holding your savings, because the bills were managed from indoors.

Online banking didn't exist then.

As previously covered, many an envelope paid a different bill.

Whatever money was left after the bills were paid allowed for a treat at the end of the week or saved up for a summer holiday.

Something to look forward to in the future but not right now.

Not much has changed. The banks don't just hold onto our savings. They now hold on to our debt too.

THEN, NOW, PAST, PRESENT AND FUTURE

These words bring the reason, not necessarily the meaning.

We just can't wait for anything, can we? We want it all now.

Why are we like this?

Does it mean I am greedy or impatient or selfish or self-absorbed?

You're none of them and all of them purely because of being an infinite soul that covers everything.

Meaning all these possibilities exist in this universe, but did you really select any of them?

Or were they put on you from someone else.

Humans are good at dumping things on anyone if it means they don't have to carry it or look at it, or worse, deal with it.

Quick fact to get to the point.

There is no trick question or big secret.

Now is then and the past, present and future.

Whatever you experienced then was once your now and what you experience in the future will still be in your now.

What these words have in common is the word next.

What comes next covers content in the now.

Your soul can be in many places at once but describing where isn't easy when dealing with words that have a present tense to them.

In a nutshell, it comes back to what is your meaning for doing your next thing now.

Even if you have many things lined up to do that takes you over a few days, it's not because of the days of how long it takes, but the event itself that continues for a while.

If we took the batteries out of the clocks and unplugged every gadget, we would soon lose track of the days, months and years.

You would still be you now regardless of sunlight and moonlight, as the energy reflects this.

Daytime and nighttime come from the original sayings of sunlight and moonlight.

Before this, it most probably was something like eat boar for daylight and shut eye for nighttime.

Words come and go and so does the reason for saying them in which to describe what you're doing now. Your meaning is what brings the purpose of being here alive with your connection.

Your energy is what you thrive on, denying yourself is like turning your phone off, or worse, losing it.

WAKE UP

We don't fear falling asleep because you know you're going to wake up, because you're in control of your breathing. If you put your breathing in someone else's hands, then you worry if you will wake up, say like when you book-in to have an operation.

Maybe this is why kissing is so personal because it's the closest souls get via the soul breath.

Even if a soul passes in their sleep, they do not fear it because they already know it is coming.

Remember, the soul knows everything already.

Psychics are not understood, because they are using connection and not sticking to the repeated words of the script.

THERE IS NOTHING TO FEAR BUT FEAR ITSELF

The first thing we fear once we become more self-aware is not the shadows on the wall at night but how we will fit in here.

What is fear? It is not a physical object. Like a magician, we conjure it up in our mind.

We fear ourselves above anything else. Self-presentation, our look, our abilities, the list is endless. We fear we are not enough for others, when in fact we should be focusing on how we are enough for ourselves already.

You chose you after all.

You will not be someone else's enough, because simply put, you are not them.

That is like cutting a triangle and a square out of the same piece of paper and expecting them to pair up. It's not going to happen because they are uniquely different.

When humans are comfortable with being unique, then they will no longer focus on changing how it looks and equally will no longer fear themselves.

You don't see animals changing themselves unless the form is already meant to, a caterpillar and butterfly as an example.

You don't see your flowers and trees in the garden using scissors to alter themselves. They just get on with being who or whatever they are in their space.

Animals don't talk taught languages because they follow the sounds of this universe.

Some animals and creatures have the ability to see and hear what humans cannot. They have a range within their frequency that our bodies or our gadgets do not.

SHOCKING

This may surprise you to read that you have not just been your physical body form.

You have been all the genders there has been. This is why you feel something you're not.

You have been all skin tones and heights and all shapes and sizes over the centuries.

Everything is within your soul energy reflected here.

Shamans of the past have touched on what I am sharing here.

Shape-shifting.

Remember how words get lost in translation.

What this means is that you have been more than the physical form.

Those that are green-fingered will have known what it is like to be a plant or a tree and so will continue feeling this connection even though they are experiencing being a human body.

Some may feel drawn to the sea and sea creatures, because they remember the connection to their past.

You cannot delete the history of energy and self-expression. It is continually playing.

You don't lose touch with your past life because you have physically forgotten it while here now.

Your history stays with you.

Remember, follow the energy.

In this universe you can be whatever you want to be.

This lifetime you have chosen your physical body to have an experience with.

You can be a bird, any animal, a rug or a cup.

WAIT a minute ....

Stop here. Are you saying that everything we touch here is a soul having an experience?

Yes, this is correct.

Just because they don't have internal organs doesn't mean they are any less a soul.

Look at your clothes you have worn over the years. They often get holes in them. But where are the holes from the clothes? Why do you not see the pieces that have fallen from the garment on the floor?

Why is the missing piece of garment not seen and why does it leave a hole?

The hole appears when part of the soul that has connected with the garment passes, leaving the space which looks like a hole to humans where the material once was. The hole was once occupied by the soul reflecting its energy.

Why do you think humans fall in love with items?

It's because they have a connection at some level with them.

Some souls may have not actually experienced an item but supported another soul with their energy.

Some souls piggyback off other souls.

I will share about the soul in part two.

But before getting back to the physical, just a quick note, this is why the soul can take or leave the body and not be consumed with it.

Because whatever the soul chooses to experience it never takes the place of the soul, no different to when humans wear clothes. It doesn't take the place of the human body.

What you see in me I see in you, because we can experience whatever we want within ourselves. This is how we relate soul to soul and recognise one another.

Because we know this universe totally, so what anyone else is choosing to experience will be recognised by everyone because they chose it from the already-stocked shopping mall of this universe.

Nothing is new. What is new is your take on it.

Example: If I give a colouring book to one child, they may colour neatly within the picture. I may give the same colouring book to a different child and they just scribble all over the pages.

This is not about ability. This is about action, which leads me into element number three wave, action.

CHAPTER THREE – WAVE, action, work, jobs from the physical perspective

(Element number three)

Mastering the self covers the four elements of frequency and it includes the senses that comes with the human body.

The human body has the five senses to aid functionality because it does not have soul gut instinct.

DO YOU MEASURE UP?

Why do humans weigh babies? Surely, they can see they are working. Then what does weight or height have to do with it?

Who knows? Maybe it has in the eyes of doctors.

But through the eyes of my soul, it doesn't make sense to me.

When I have bought natural vegetables, they come in all funny shapes and sizes.

What is the obsession with everything being the same size and weight within certain guidelines?

Human bodies are organic matter, no different to what we grow in the soil.

When humans stop picking at it, they will then see what the soul can do with it.

This is not possible yet until souls stop using the script.

If you had to be a certain size, shape or weight, you would have arrived with your own unique tape measure.

You don't for a reason so you can be yourself.

Humans, way back when before things were taught, did not weigh anything. They just ate until full and shared life together, accepting that variety comes in handy.

It makes sense when you view it from a different angle.

Like giraffes eat from tall trees. Tall trees are still accessible for ants because they can crawl up them, but not so easy for humans unless you climb.

VARIETY WORKS FOR A REASON

Maybe we need different sizes, so everything is shared organically without the need to fight. Taking it in turns because we would be hungry at different times day and night.

After all some animals are carnivores and some are herbivores, and some are nocturnal, and some are not.

This organic inbuilt knowing makes sure each soul knows what to connect with without trying.

This would make more sense to why some humans like savoury and some sweet.

Sharing in the table of life is mapped out for us already within our knowing and taste buds.

This is why humans that follow the script struggle with it, because it doesn't always match up with your soul map menu.

Maybe this is why diets don't work.

I CAN'T GET MY CHILDREN TO EAT ANYTHING

Each soul that arrives here will know what they like and when they will want it. It is very hard to force anything on another. If they succumb it looks like you forced them. You didn't. They just gave in because they can.

They have chosen to eat it out of feeling hemmed in to making a decision or a choice.

They might not like what they are given to eat but they know it won't affect them unless they get a reaction from it.

If they get a reaction, then it's not on their chosen menu of choice that they brought with them.

Variety is the spice of life but equally too many spices can ruin the dish.

It is balance.

Souls once they know they like something they stick with it. Humans that haven't a clue of what they like may be seen as picky eaters.

It comes back down to connection. Does this food spark your interest from your menu? If not, then this alone would put a soul off, not because of the food itself.

Remember, this universe pairs up.

The human body will not starve itself because the physical senses match up with physical food available and then to your soul menu that you brought with you.

YOUR PERSONAL MENU

Yes, you arrive totally with everything you need for your soul path ahead.

Before you connected with your physical body, you scanned the energy of it and knew ahead what your experiences would be like if you connected with it.

You know what foods you like and what ones you don't like.

This is why you soon get to know what foods babies like, as they spit it out or vomit what they don't.

We dictate our own reality.

We may come with our own menus of choice, but we don't come with a diet.

How to manage what you eat is simple.

Eat if hungry and drink if thirsty and sleep if tired.

It's exactly what babies do.

No time limits needed.

If they are hungry, they let you know.

When did this simple way of self-managing stop?

When everyone else started to share how they self-managed.

They may say this works for me so it will work for you.

Hmm, I doubt it unless you feel a connection with it.

There is no magic wand only connection.

We have been saturated with information overload. If we are not listening to ourselves and matching the food of choice with our own menus, then it's not going to work for you.

Don't blame the diet or the food and look more closely at your own map.

Before you become an adult, you should roughly know your own menu.

I wasn't a lover of fruit. I loved potatoes cooked any which way and starches and fibres like baked beans, with protein.

I didn't have a sweet tooth; I liked more savoury foods.

Funnily enough the food of choice at the children's home and at school matched my pallet beautifully. The jam on the semolina I either scooped out or just didn't inhale it too closely.

FOOD BAD, FOOD GOOD

Food is just food. It doesn't matter if it is meat or vegetables or fruit, etc. Food gets eaten and food gets digested and then we go to the toilet.

We confuse the energy of what we are eating as digesting the history of the food, forgetting because of space around each frequency that this is not the case.

The history of the food background stays with the food itself. What we pick up reflects our own energy.

You can pick up anything to eat and not even be aware of actually eating it, or it didn't even touch the sides.

Like if you pick up any instrument it does not play on its own. Your connection with it is what makes it play in your reality.

Any object in life whether an object or instrument or food, allows us to play our own tune with it. If our connection with it does not offer our tune within us to play, then it will do nothing for us.

We are here to play our own tune, when we match up with our choices we flow through those choices. If we don't match up, we can't play our tune.

Food gets blamed for being just food, yet what alters the experience is how we put our connection and our tune of ourselves to it.

This is our actual experience.

You can call food all the names and headings under the sun. It will still come back to the self of how you connect with it and how your energy vibes with it.

Our bodies are like walking tea bags. We keep inside what we require and squeeze out what we don't.

This is why you have senses throughout the body alerting you to what is hot or cold, sweet or

sour, and when your stomach is full and how the energy within you feels.

Your brain does a great job communicating with your body parts if aligned. Your soul does a great job communicating with the cells of the body with sharing what's on your menu for the day from your soul map.

This is why you get the fancies.

Remember, follow the energy with everything.

Humans see things at face value of how it is presented and packaged.

Humans have seen food in a basic way of I am hungry so I will grab that and eat it, with a I-don't-care-what-it-is approach.

And food is seen in a micro way of analysing it as if under a microscope.

Your soul has no preference to how you relate to food physically because to the soul it is how it connects with your energy.

Liken it to this as an example.

Follow the music.

I have a piano keyboard. I can touch any note, and it will make a sound. Some notes will sound in harmony, and some may sound off, depending on how I interact with it, not how it interacts with me.

The notes themselves are not off just how they are played together.

Everything has a note to it like a musical instrument.

We have our main note and tone called our vibe. It is our soul's frequency that is playing constantly.

Our soul map and the contents we selected will have their own notes too but will be already in blended harmony.

If you pick an item of food and the frequency does not match your menu, then it will taste off to you.

You may wonder why it is one person likes one thing, and another doesn't. It's not the food or the taste buds. It's the frequency match between them.

(Google search)

According to Verywell Health, taste buds work by detecting chemicals in food and drinks and then sending that information to the brain as a taste signal.

The brain interprets the electrical signal from the taste bud as a particular flavour.

Taste buds are replaced regularly, the body replaces taste receptor cells every ten days or so. However, as people age some taste cells don't get replaced.

The brain combines taste signals with smell signals to determine flavour.

As I keep saying strip it back and follow the energy.

Behind everything is a frequency, a tone, a signature frequency, and they either match or they don't.

It is not personal to the said item.

It always comes back to the self. What we pick up and what we connect with, does it give us the space to experience our internal soul map that is stocked with our pre-selective choices that we arrived here with?

If what you pick up and connect with does not give us the opportunity to apply our soul map contents, then we stop experiencing and enter standby mode.

This is why we can feel involved and equally not involved. It has nothing to do with status or if your face fits. It all comes back to if can you play your own tunes, your vibe and create your own take on things.

Food is a form like you. It will have its own experience in its own reality.

Each soul has been accounted for it doesn't matter what the form is.

Each soul knows what they are doing and nothing is by mistake.

Organic matter, regardless of what it is, doesn't have an eternal stamp on it in the physical material sense.

It will continue until it has served its purpose.

No doctor can preserve anything in working order organically.

Life cycles in organic material is unique to the soul itself.

Another true example, I have a lemon tree this summer I had four lemons grow on it.

Three of them I was able to pick to use and eat, one did not ripen and reached a point of growth, which it has stayed at.

Same tree, all unique lemons with their own select lifecycle.

There is no good or bad of anything. If your frequencies within you can flow with whatever you connect with then it will enjoy it.

If your energy can't flow with what you connect with, you will feel it and not enjoy it.

This universe is not complicated once frequency pairing is understood.

Humans don't look at the energy behind anything. They just see the heading name or label or instructions of what it should be known for.

There are billions of souls here with a different take on things, so taking other's opinions as gospel won't work for you unless it matches up with you.

This is why element number one runs through everything.

The connection of the self doesn't worry about what others are doing. Notice what matches up with your frequency.

If you enjoy it, then go for it. If you don't, then your taste buds and body will soon tell you.

Your varied diet is on your menu that you brought with you and will not match the menus of others around you.

Yes, we eat the same food choices but as you know not everyone has the same experience.

We are unique for a reason, so we have our own unique experiences.

This is why following others will work for so long, but to the soul it will be like stopping for a break. It won't aid your journey unless it matches your map.

Your soul sends subtle messages through your physical body to guide you on your path. You either pick them up and trust them or doubt them and ignore them.

Your soul map is a bit like having your own underground train map. Your map will take you on your own journey and as you travel you will meet up with what matches you.

This is why others cross our paths at certain moments.

Humans take selection personally from an opinion point of view. Your soul knows the physical is not the reason why you are where you are now, it is because of your energy driving you.

Forget times dates and years. The reason why you connect with others is not because of how long you're in contact. It is because by being together you can play out your own choices.

In a nutshell, whatever you do here, be it eating drinking sleeping and action, what defines your life experience, is not what you do but how you connect with it.

YOUR ATTITUDE

Attitude is another word for your energy and vibe. How you feel in any moment is a reflection on how your soul is playing through the physical tools available.

Humans see themselves as separate to the things in their life, but the things you see on the shelves of the shops are being themselves. What changes is how you interact, gel or vibe with it. If you do not connect with it, then the item is still being itself regardless of whether you interact with it or not. You may see food items as raw one minute and cooked the next, but the item is still being itself whether cooked or not.

Same if you stand out in the sun. You are you regardless of whether you are burnt by it or not. Everything here is a passing experience created by our take on things.

We can view experiences one way, either our way or your way. What this will show you is that all ways are happening at the same time in anyone's reality.

The magic of space gives everyone their reality in their way with their vibe.

You are in control of everything in your life because your element number one in you directs your element number two in you and your element number three overseen by element number four.

Your soul has everything covered and taken care of every minute detail, which is why no soul is ever lost. They may just not be using their connection.

OUR BODY PARTS ARE THE SAME

If our basic body parts are the same, then why do we have different tastes and experiences if we are using the same tools and buying the same stuff?

Because of our soul maps and not because of the body parts or the items.

Humans see objects and forget their connection and energy is what brings them their material reality.

Using space to separate ourselves so we don't take responsibility for our choices.

It is totally down to your character and personality together with the content of your soul map, and your chosen highlighted four elements of frequency the language of this universe that defines your life experiences here.

It is down to you and no-one else.

Everyone you see around you is a passenger in your reality, same as you are a passenger to them.

Example: If you're a passenger in the back of a car and the driver has an accident, you cannot be blamed for the accident unless you physically grabbed the steering wheel, of course, and played your part in it. But if you were just sitting there, then it is down to the driver. You will, of course, be a witness in the physical sense and an observer in the soul sense.

If it is argued who did what, just follow the energy as each action you make will have both your physical and soul frequency connected to it.

You cannot rub out your signature frequency – remember, the phantom limb. You can destroy physical evidence, but you cannot destroy the energy that comes with it.

This is why the truth comes out in the end, even if it is years or centuries later.

I WILL SAVE YOU

Follow me and I will save you.

The physical thinks it needs saving because it doesn't want to die, but what it means to the soul is I will support you.

To save anything is to preserve it. Organic matter does deteriorate if there is little soul energy running through it and purely reliant mainly on the flow of the physical energy supply.

Do you remember what it has felt like when you're buzzing about something, when you're over the moon and very happy, ecstatic even?

What makes you actually feel like this?

You may show it in an action by jumping up and down for joy. Forget the event that is going on as it could have been anything that was happening. Pick any event winning the lottery or winning a house or a car or a holiday or you receive an award for your work, etc.

As you can see it's not so much the event, even though you can feel buzzing when any of them happen.

What is actually going on behind the scenes is that you have hit your own self jackpot.

This is when your selected four elements are in alignment together with a chosen choice on your soul map, when these align you will atomically feel buzzing.

It's you, your own soul alignment, that is causing you to feel what you feel, the tools you used made it happen that particular time. But you don't have to repeat the same sequence as you have infinite opportunities for it to happen again if you follow your soul map.

You don't need saving because you're an infinite soul that does not ever die.

You wake up every morning and put on different clothes. It doesn't mean you died because you have chosen a different outfit.

This is the same for your soul, just because you connect with many bodies it doesn't mean that you die in doing so.

Like you wake up and go to sleep and wake up, you are continuing where you left off. The soul does the same when choosing another body to connect with.

The reason why you never die is because you are not your physical body, but you are your soul energy.

Because of space around each frequency of each soul, you are in your own bubble if you like.

Yes, you can see everyone else in this universe because space isn't a brick wall.

It is space.

You never bump into space because you are part of space, and it accommodates you as you create yourself in it.

Space creates your experiences with you as it expands within and without you.

If you look at your skin, you have pores. If you look at your cells, there is space between them called intercellular space.

You have space between eyelashes, between your nail bed and your skin and between each hair follicle. Space is everywhere.

Space is what the soul uses in which to connect matter together, in connection of expansion or contraction.

Inhale and exhale the body uses energy to interact to create movement.

Piecing together the elements of frequency reflects how your life is a unique intricate connection that makes up the material of your life. This is why blame, wrong, right, good, bad, grades, or opinions won't cut it alone.

By choosing one word to describe it will miss out the other words that can describe it also.

Humans see one way; the soul sees all ways.

Many views are seen in one scene.

Example: Humans may run a bath and say I had a lovely soak in the tub. What created the scene for it to be enjoyable or not depends on your mood first. Then you run hot and cold water, you may add different scents to the bath. Does the atmosphere within the bathroom and outside the bathroom match your mood?

Some days you may want to have fun and have a splash about with the kids, or if you're tired or hungry you may want peace and quiet and have a long soak, or a quick dip as you can't wait too long to eat.

The senses add to what you're doing in any event.

Children may make a noise, and it ruffles your atmosphere. You want to be quiet, so you shout out, "Please be quiet!" Other days you may zone out and it doesn't bother you.

It is not what the kids are doing or not doing or how they are behaving. It is whether they match you in that given moment.

This is what is going on for everyone, which creates the waves of ups and downs in the physical reality.

No one is doing anything wrong. They are just being them, but do we pair up, between ourselves soul to soul, physical to physical. It's nothing to do with situation but everything to do with the energy.

Others annoy us for many reasons, they may ....

Get on our nerves.

Frustrate us.

Make us wait.

Make us feel inpatient.

Bored.

The list is endless so odds are at some point we will rub others the wrong way.

It's not wrong. It's just our tone playing in that moment doesn't match in harmony with their tone that is playing.

You may have noticed you go through phases when you can listen to certain styles of music on a loop or read or chat with others for hours, and then you want to retreat and be on your own.

Nothing is wrong. You just know you want to be in your own space.

You are you and I am me.

I am me and you are you.

It is as simple as that.

If we gave the space to others that we have with ourselves without feeling threatened by it, then no one would have the need for opinions or judgments. Souls would understand that we occupy our own spaces within us like we occupy our own homes in the physical.

When someone decides to go home after work or a night out, it's not taken personally.

So why is it if we want to have some space to ourselves it is taken personally?

Your internal space is your soul home, your physical address is your physical home, both your spaces of residency.

If you can have more than one address in the physical and manage them then these two spaces won't be a cause for concern.

SCRIPTS ARE FOR ACTORS

Are they though? When did we start living roles in our life?

Maybe when we were introduced to the dress-up box at playgroup.

What would you like to be today? You can be anything but yourself while you are choosing.

From a young age, innocently and subtly, we are introduced to other versions of ourselves.

If we are not being our organic self that reflects who we really are, with our character and personality and content of pre-choice, then we are acting out from the script and taking on a role that we have learnt to become.

Humans used to laugh if someone was putting on a telephone voice which didn't sound like them when they got off the phone.

Our memories provide us with the script that we adapt to in our character.

Are you today who you were as a child in character?

It doesn't matter how you behaved what would have shone are your morals and ethics.

Obviously, it's challenging managing a physical body when your used to being soul energy.

Who are we?

What we project from ourselves?

Blaming others for what you select to project is like blaming a lightbulb for shining the light.

Like any appliance, it needs a power source.

You will select between your physical self and your soul how you want to project yourself, either your authentic self or your adapted, scripted version.

I have heard myself say it to myself. I don't feel this situation allows me to be me.

I remember back in the 1980s when we had a careers officer giving us advice about how to present ourselves for interviews to help with securing a job.

Jobs will expect you to have a certain dress code and to not have out-there fashion choices or styles. This didn't go down to well with the punks, etc.

We have our own style but are not encouraged to be our style unless your career matches it.

Pupils would respond, but how is this fair? If I am well-mannered and doing the job asked of me, why does it matter how I dress or look? Can't they see past this?

No, it's not how it is.

Each business will have their own standards and rules for you to follow.

So, does this mean I can't always be myself?

It depends in what context.

IN WHAT CONTEXT

From the physical point of view, there are limited ways of looking at things but to the soul it is infinite.

The physical will set out rules for you to follow and tell you how to behave and live.

The soul will align you with external choices that match up with who you are if you listen.

If safety is an issue, then obviously a dress code is for your benefit.

When we first start school, we are taught the alphabet and colours and numbers.

We are taught those things at face value, meaning red is red and yellow is yellow, like the sun, etc.

We are not taught that colours are wrong or right, just that they are neutral unless to describe our mood.

When did colours start to be an issue?

As children we are taught in an innocent way.

As we grow and the vocabulary grows with us then we get the rules of what we can say, when and where.

What was acceptable to say in one era isn't in another. The words are changed depending on our reason not meaning.

Humans have a problem with words even though these words have often been around longer than them.

Our physical self decides if words are appropriate or not, not necessarily if they serve our purpose and meaning to our soul.

What isn't acceptable to one human will be acceptable to another, because souls recognise that all words play their part.

If we rubbed out words and rubbed out letters and numbers, then it would be replaced with a new script that has been created.

Liken it to before decimalisation in 1971, the UK sterling was divided into pounds, shillings and pence.

One pound was made up of 240 pence, with twelve pence (12d the d, stands for the Latin denarius, a Roman coin) to the shilling and twenty shillings to the pound.

A bob was slang for a shilling, why we still say let's count your bobs or I will give you some bobs.

Old language interacts with the new, if even subliminally or occasionally in memory.

When decimalisation came in a new system was learnt, the old pound kept its old value and name, but the shilling was abolished, and the pound was divided into a hundred new pence abbreviated with the letter p. The new coins featured the word new, but in due course this was dropped.

Change has occurred throughout the centuries in the curriculum, our vocabulary and styles of writing.

Nothing stays the same, because we have so much available in this universe shopping mall to choose from.

When major changes occur it is because we collectively are causing them, not in action alone but in our energy that drives the action, but not the passenger.

We may think we learn new behavioural lifestyles, but we start them off within us.

Souls are communicating with this universe constantly.

Humans in the past said prayers nightly after a meal or before bed to show their appreciation.

Giving thanks it was often called.

The soul is breaking free from the script, which is why we are seeing labels breaking down.

You can see both sides of the coin here.

What humans struggle with is making room for many lifestyles, especially when a new one is adopted. It upsets the apple cart of the previous.

All should be able to coexist.

You don't see the letter H in the alphabet falling out with the letter G.

Or you don't see the number two being offended by number one.

You don't see pink being upset that red isn't pink.

Infinitely everything exists, like a well-stocked store cupboard, that we can select what we want to experience in the safety of our own unique soul space bubble. That is our own reality.

So, it should not matter what you call your body or what name you adopt, as you know from birth you don't stick to the one on your birth certificate as your title is added, or slang words. As a child you have no say in the matter, but as an adult you have the choice of how you want to be known.

To your soul, your signature frequency stays the infinite same, having no need to make alterations as it serves all your reality experiences.

You have the choice of who you are, and how you present yourself in your life, visually, feeling, action and connection.

Let's own it. We adopt and select what we want to experience that stems from ourselves.

You are not your physical bodies. You are not your names or status or your rank or title. You have picked these up on your journey because you have selected them.

If you had not been taught that letters create words or numbers or colours, you would not know what prejudice is. Prejudice to humans occurs when words are used in which to have an opinion without experience.

This universe to the soul is purely experience, which is why prejudice is viewed as pointless.

When something is not understood, then we select words of right or wrong or like or hate in which to describe something from a limited point of view.

If we are not our physical bodies or words and titles, then how can you be prejudiced to it if no one is it. That's like all the pupils being offended by the alphabet because they cannot relate to it, purely because they are not the alphabet.

Anything that has been manifested has energy behind it, you can rub out words, but you cannot rub out the energy of it. This is why trends come and go and so do styles, because they never get deleted. What changes is whether they are picked up to use or not. If we do choose to use something such as the alphabet, then it is our connection with it that makes your own story to tell from experience.

Prejudice is an understanding from a view that either stems from ourselves or from what is shared in influence.

As I have shared earlier in the book, you can see another human as white, but are they genetically?

If we went back before time and before money and scripts of right or wrong in opinions and judgments, then you would still be you experiencing what you have brought with you in your soul suitcase within yourself.

When you exit here, you won't be holding on to money or the colours of the rainbow or the words in a dictionary or a book, only your version of your experience.

You will hold what has meaning that has reflected who you authentically are not defined by letters or numbers or colours alone.

Humans use tools in which to create movement within choices. This creates a ripple effect like the waves of the sea that ebb and flow, if the energy of the soul is not being applied.

Like the sea comes in and goes out, what stems from us will lead back to us. What matters to you in depth and meaning in your reality is your responsibility towards yourself and not what you have copied to pass the time of day to please another.

You have a life review before you get here, while you are here and when you leave this earth.

Your soul guides you and those that can see your soul map will guide you too.

If you feel comfortable and enjoy your choices because they match you, then you are living your life in your authentic reflection mirrored on you and nothing else.

Then you are an inspiration to others, encouraging them to connect with their authentic self without the script getting in the way or being offended for doing so.

The old scripts are out. We are in a new paradigm, and it is your own responsibility now to create your own reality founded on you and you alone.

ACTION, WORK, JOBS, MOVEMENT

It is easy to see why this element can overshadow you.

It is more distracting than words because it is often visually impacting. Seeing is believing, isn't it?

Not always if there is a slight of hand as if by magic.

The television started without sound the silent movies added subtitles.

Words used to guide the narrative.

Sound brings in feeling and impacts from within.

Without sound to an action, we put our own experience to it.

A sad scene makes us cry, a happy scene makes us laugh, and a scary movie makes us fearful.

It's not actually making you feel these things. The actors don't move out of the screen and physically touch you.

What touches you is you yourself.

How the scene impacts you is what you select from your senses, both physical and soul.

You create your reaction to it because you are absorbed in your energy while watching it.

Bingo connection to yourself pairs up all your senses to what you're viewing.

Viewing or watching will either get your attention resulting in how invested you are in it.

You gauge the level of your commitment to watching it, by how much it stimulates your senses.

Reflection faces you in everything you do. Why some will see the joke, or some won't, why some find it funny, and others don't.

Our reaction to things isn't down to the joke itself or the external event. It's down to what's watching it, what brings it out of you.

We can use action to avoid blame. We can lie and make up an alibi to get out of being in a situation.

When I was a child, watching was more to do with watching my own behaviour and how I spoke when I mixed with others.

Before being introduced to someone, they would tell me to be careful with what I would chat about as they get offended easily. Don't mention the mole on the face, don't look at them a certain way and definitely don't tell them the truth. Promise me you will keep quiet.

I would be sworn to secrecy before meeting them, as I did speak my mind, or should I say soul.

This didn't give me the chance to innocently meet another and get to know their soul. The physical body got in the way one way or another.

The heads-up is etiquette to some, to others it's not trusting that you can conduct yourself properly especially if you're a child.

Humans know children are factual and view life literally to how it looks. Souls don't get offended by facts. Humans take it personally as if a blotch on their reflection.

Keeping a lie a secret to a soul is challenging because it won't pair up with their truth.

At thirteen I had to keep my first secret that had nothing to do with me.

I innocently walked in on the foster mum and daughter talking. The daughter was having an affair with a married man. The mum suddenly noticed I had overheard the conversation. Pulling me to one side, her face in mine and pointing her finger at me like I had done something wrong took me by surprise. "Don't you dare mention this to my husband as it will kill him." The one word that impacted me and got my attention was the word "kill."

This secret is huge as I don't want to kill him.

But it's going to kill me keeping a secret that has nothing to do with me.

What a dilemma did I choose, me or them?

I chose them by keeping the secret even though it killed me inside. In choosing this I ignored my element number one connection, going straight to element number two sharing from the self, putting them before me. This is not how the language of this universe works.

It left a thorn in my side of many emotions. In this situation they did not see me only themselves and what mattered to them, preserving the views of the husband. They, like me, were not using their element number one as it wasn't about them, but actually someone else that wasn't even in the room with us. In my eyes, my feelings, were not even taken into consideration or relevant, as I didn't get the chance to voice how I felt.

Just do what they ask to not upset their reality, but in doing so they did not see how it upset mine.

Being invisible and responsible for others brings out resentment when not seen or heard or understood, especially by ourselves.

Putting your actions on another creates a domino effect of destruction as it disrupts their energy flow. It's why element number one encourages you to own and hold your own in self-responsibility. The fallout may impact others in the moment, but the impact actually stays with the person who created it. I walked in on their conversation innocently, or some may view it that I was in the wrong place at the wrong time.

If I could have seen myself more clearly. Knowing my own sense of self, I would have most probably brushed it off.

I would have known that it had nothing to do with me and would have spoken up and said no way, as I am a visitor to this situation so don't put this on me.

When you can stand up for yourself, you're not doing it to hurt others or to self-preserve, because you are facing your totality in self-responsibility.

Why would you want to carry someone else's life?

That would be like innocently walking into a supermarket to buy your food shopping, but as you walk inside someone else bashes into you making their shopping fall on the floor.

They blame you for not looking where they are going, but you were. It was them that could not see me over there shopping. To save making a scene, you help pick up their items.

You offer to carry their shopping home with them to soften the blow.

Now your scene is disrupted, and you are put out.

We have choices and either stick to our path in life or allow other's actions to disrupt it.

In the secret and lie situation, I felt hard done by.

My four elements in me got rubbed up the wrong way. My sense of self, my feelings and in action resulting in feeling dumped on.

I am not someone else's rubbish bin, but this is how I felt.

This went on to impact me on my journey, not because of the details of the secret. But because I didn't want to keep the secret in the first place. I did not want the responsibility of keeping the secret. The responsibility of it impacted me. I now felt like I was living with an elephant in the room and each time I saw them they reminded me of it.

After thirteen years of experiences, I had become wary of others. I could not trust what others said or how they feel and now in action. What can I trust when it came to others?

Over the next forty years from experience, I realised it wasn't so much about others but how I held my own and felt towards myself and whether I liked what I saw in me.

What built my strong foundations within myself was not how I dodged others or preserved myself, but how I kept my own space clear my little bubble of my reality. Facing myself in any situation that faced me, I took the responsibility of my actions that I saw in my reflection when around others.

Okay, some are warranted, and others are an overreaction.

I found out because I was different. It was hard to put me in a category.

Anything unusual is bypassed.

This is why I felt invisible most of my life.

Being an orphan wasn't the norm.

Being in a children's home and being made a ward of court as your guardian isn't normal. Being psychic as a child isn't normal. Back in the eighties, being divorced and married so many times wasn't usual. Even being a single parent wasn't the majority.

Looking back, I spent most of my life in the you-don't-fit-in category and because you don't fit in, we don't have a category for you.

Even when I tried to buy insurance for my work, there isn't a psychic option.

By the time I reached my late thirties and when I didn't fit in with the psychic movement, I gave up and stopped trying.

I could not find where I could place myself to fit in because it didn't exist, so I decided to create my own place in which to belong.

I stopped focusing on the external world around me and put my energy into my own life starting from where I lived.

TIDY UP NOW

The first forty years of my life I just seemed to keep clashing with people.

No matter how I tried to get on with them and get into their good books, I was always on the wrong side of the fence.

I was wanted and useful by some but once used, then discarded.

Luckily for me I had a big family, and this took self-responsibility for others through the roof. Juggling life would have gotten me into the circus.

In between holding our heads up above water, I had moments to work on myself. Until I crashed into another human-to-human experience whether at work or pleasure.

Enough was enough. I knew if I wanted to get any kind of direction in my life, I had to get back in my own driver's seat, instead of constantly being a passenger when I mixed in the life of others to then be blamed or made responsible for how their life turned out.

I tipped the pieces of my life out in front of me.

I went back to come forward.

Writing my first book gave me a head start in sorting out what belonged to me and what didn't.

I was tired of facing my life again, when I had already faced it from different angles within the different scenes.

The view of myself as a third party and through the eyes of others. I had considered all the parts played by different people that made up each scene.

When these events first happened, I was dumped with owning it all. Those in the scene didn't take responsibility for their actions. As soon as they noticed that I faced myself and took the responsibility of my action. They put theirs on me too.

This created a heavy load for me because energy is impacting whether it belongs to you or not.

MIRROR REFLECTION

Looking back, I now see how it happens from the moment we arrive here.

We start our journey here bringing ourselves to physical life with the connection of the breath.

For that split second when we inhale our soul for the first time, we feel comfortable in our total space of ourselves both physical side and soul.

When we exhale, we are greeted by others and become aware of other frequencies in the room and not just our own.

The adults that welcome you home to their physical reality, for your soul is like turning up halfway through their film.

Babies sleep a lot as do animals, a sure way of switching off from the noise to enter self-space of peace and quiet.

The inhale starts off element number one an awareness of our own connection with our soul self. The exhale brings in element number two sharing from the self with others. Then how we are held and respond to our environment brings in to play element number three.

Element number four plays in the background, overseeing the three elements that are already in play.

Element number four encourages continuity and commitment.

From the moment of the exhale, it is like jumping in at the deep end only to resurface at the shallow end.

The physical reality is a reflection of moment-to-moment happenings that make up the bigger picture, no different to the second hand making up the hour on a clock. Both hands work together creating time.

When one hand isn't working it makes it harder to tell the time. We sync up with what we connect with.

If we are not using our senses, then it makes it harder for us to see and hear ourselves, which then creates a blurred view of what we are reflecting.

Sensing something is not psychic fakery. If you reflect a clear picture of yourself, then it makes it easier for the psychic to receive it.

This is why when I do soul readings. Whether soul maps or a one question-answer rereading, I will always explain that I get the guidance from your soul.

Back in the day psychic readings connected to a third party, relatives that had passed. This mirrored the third party accepted view that arose from using the taught script.

Souls know themselves inside out and, therefore, do not need the views or acceptance from others only from the self.

When souls stopped living as souls and became a taught version of themselves, they could not see who they were clearly and so relied on others to see them for them (this is how opinions came about).

At first this worked well before the script added deception of any kind to the list.

Souls trusted other souls to share the truth.

This altered when ego created the third party.

Humans try to get creativity physically out there, which is difficult without connection, whereas souls don't need to try because the connection of the soul connects them with every soul in this universe.

This is why word of mouth spreads far and wide.

Obviously, it depends on the content to what spreads and how it is heard. This depends on our own stations.

Example:

This is a real-life example that happened this week. To explain connection, I am writing about my experiences of this universe from the view of infinite knowing. Well, we put Netflix on this week and found a series called *The Good Place*. The content of the series matched up with the content of what I am writing. When I looked at YouTube, interviews popped up about teenage views in 1982. Again, some of their views mirrored what I was sharing in this book.

What this means is whatever we connect with this universe will reflect material that mirrors you because it is already available if we access it first from within ourselves.

What comes naturally to my soul is not explainable to my physical side. Often, the physical side does not reflect my total being.

The topics and subject interests offered around the table of the script has impacted me but not interested me.

I have ears so I can hear, I have eyes so I can see, I have touch so I can feel, and at certain times if I zone out, I don't hear or see and feel a thing.

How I apply myself in action within all the elements is how I link up in energy.

We drift in and out of physical reality without understanding why. It is brushed off as, oh, she is dolly daydreaming again.

This zoning out happens with animals, with children and adults. It's not an age-related thing.

It is down to your own transmission and what you're listening to or playing in your own space and what gets your attention.

At a frequency level each soul is decked out with all the tracks they need.

To a human it will look as if a human is staring into space, but what is happening behind soul doors is that the soul is receiving something soul to soul, just the physical element is not aware of what yet.

The physical side of them will catch up with what they received when they are ready to physically process it.

GIFTED ISN'T BEING PSYCHIC

You are a soul of this universe when you first arrive here. You continue to be a soul of this universe throughout your journey here. You continue being a soul of this universe when you leave here.

Unless you move on to the next universe, then you won't be limited to this shopping mall.

Even if you move on to the next universe you are still a soul that can visit this universe if you wish.

If frequencies match and harmonise with you, then you have access. If you are not ready to receive more, then you continue with what you know so far until you're ready for more.

CHAPTER FOUR – VIBRATION, completion oversees the other three elements

(Element number four)

WHAT VERSION ARE YOU?

Coming full circle starts with the self and completes with the self.

Element number four will encourage you to work out what version of yourself you really are.

Not the past physical scripted versions or the ones you followed.

Who are you? The version of you that you are playing now.

You may have many versions playing at once. You may find you're being patient, or tolerant, giving without taking, and supporting others in need.

These physical experiences may or may not be necessary for you to experience. If you have not preselected it, then it won't be on your menu of your soul map. If it matches your selection, then the experience is beneficial.

Souls once they learnt the script made choices from the physical script menu thinking it was their soul one. When they took the last breath after they had finished experiencing with their chosen body, they would have a soul life review. It did make souls laugh. When they came back to compare the physical life, they had lived to the soul map they had forgotten.

Seeing a physical map of events without connection is like seeing many roads that they took but had nothing to do with the soul path that they had previously chosen.

This is like putting in your satnav a route to get from your house to a location, only to forget the satnav exists as soon as you put your key in the ignition.

You start your journey having a hunch about the direction you feel you want to head in. The journey itself will depend on what you encounter on the way, and if there are any diversions or distractions.

Once you arrive at your destination the satnav gets your attention, and at this point you remember you put in the address previously before you forgot. You play the route the satnav would have taken you and compare it to the route you actually took.

Your soul is your satnav if you pay attention to it, then it will take you on your soul path.

If you pay attention to the script, then it will take you on the paths relating to the script.

This could be a million miles away from you.

This is why, when the soul catches up with you, sudden changes occur in your physical reality.

You may not just want to change one thing but everything. This is when alignment with yourself becomes life changing.

You are in your own board game always throwing the dice. Your next move is waiting for you.

When humans think they are waiting for others, they are not they are stalling themselves to avoid change from happening yet.

Even if you think your desperate for it.

If you have made changes already, then what you are waiting for is not because of you but more to do with it aligning with you.

This is like deciding to get a train to travel into town. Thinking about getting the train won't make it happen unless you turn up. You meet it halfway by getting you there yourself so you can board it.

For any action to manifest or happen we apply our energy to it first, so the external matches up with us.

Humans think PMA (positive mental attitude) is like a magic wand, wishing, hoping and praying and saying daily mantras to get what you want.

Remember, follow the energy not the memory or verse.

If your energy isn't being applied, then it's like wishing a car would move without any fuel.

Your energy rolls your own dice and creates your next move. Without it your life is on standby as if like missing a turn.

What humans have struggled with is making choices that send them away from the scripted routes.

Trusting that you're safe with where your soul is taking you even if you cannot see far ahead.

Follow your energy as you will see enough and will be shown enough without throwing you off course.

This is like putting one foot in front the other, which is all you need. But humans want to know days ahead or weeks, months and years. Souls live in the now and so one step at a time is enough.

Now living is different to later or in a minute or I will get around to it kind of living.

Humans spread their life so wide and wonder why the energy of it feels thin.

How you wear your life is up to you. This is why the body you connect with starts off naked. There is no special treatment. Every soul here whether corporate in business, or royalty or a mum or if you're homeless. We have this in common in all walks of life regardless of the location we start from – naked.

We arrive as total infinite souls and get swaddled in the blanket of the physical script.

I thought there was one main script in this reality that we got taught at school and society and by what has been handed down to us over generations.

But actually, each soul being unique is creating their own version of their script, which matches the main physical systematic script, because as long it's a script that keeps you away from accessing your soul self, then who cares what script you're following.

I have done this to myself. Set myself to-do lists and a plan of action to keep me on the straight and narrow. Funny it's not called the straight and wide.

Instead of allowing myself to be in any given moment, I have conditioned myself to live under my own scripted rule.

Routine is just another word for knowing what you're doing from experience, just repeated in the physical sense.

Dos and don'ts reinforce our need for a safety net, like having stabilisers on our bikes.

When a soul connects with their knowing, they wholeheartedly trust their soul to have their back. When a soul trusts the script, the energy is not so sure.

This creates inconsistency and a reason not to commit.

Element number four can only complete your soul map with commitment. Otherwise, an event is left open. This is like having unfinished business and having many tabs open.

Humans think they can bypass commitment (element four) by keeping busy in (element three) work and ignoring (element two) feelings, thinking if you're holding your own (element one) self while working. Then element two your feelings don't matter. It does. They all interconnect.

The struggles we have are being able to keep up with ourselves, whether we are changing our mind, or procrastinating or ignoring or hiding, or just don't know what we are thinking and blindly turn the page of each day in a hurry.

What it boils down to is, what you are getting out of it?

If you don't pay much attention to how you feel, then you're getting by mainly on action.

If you pay attention to only how you feel, then you're getting by with your connection that you share with others.

If you pay attention to yourself without a thought or care in the world towards others, then you are limiting yourself to element number one and unable to share past the self-repeating what you did the day before alone.

How you communicate with yourself shows other souls what elements you are using.

Communication is adapted to our physical abilities.

I have lived with my thirteen-year-old chihuahua for eleven of her physical years.

I have seen her character shine in many ways.

When she was younger, she would hoppity skip (as I would say rather than skippity hop) down the road with boundless energy.

I could hear her footsteps as she climbed our stairs. I would feel her paws on my legs if she wanted me to pick her up.

Nine of those years she shared with our other three chihuahuas. They clicked as a team and enjoyed sharing life together.

As each one passed, she became the only one left. Over the last two years she has adapted to being with humans only without her doggy pals.

My heart felt for her. I worried in case she was sad. To my surprise she lapped it up, taking on her doggy pals' traits as her own, making the house all about her rather than having to share with the dog family.

I have seen her eyes deteriorate where now she is unable to see, and her energy is not boundless anymore.

She is still loving life, and we have adapted our home to match her needs. We created ramps down the back steps, and a sensor light outside the back door so she could see when she could.

She started to communicate with us differently when her eyesight went. She learnt to dig at her cool mat if she was thirsty and if she needed to go to the toilet. We learnt her sign language.

Our relationship has changed but that's okay. I miss hearing her footsteps up the stairs, I miss her climbing at my legs, and I miss her hoppity skip with her back legs that she made when out on a walk.

I appreciate that she still gets the zoomies when she hears my voice and shakes with excitement when she eats her favourite meal. I love how she enjoys being pushed in her doggy pram when we have days out at the seaside, and how she puts a smile on the faces of people that pass us by.

I am thankful that she shows us how happy she is and when she walks in our local park where it is safe for her to walk on the lead without bumping into anything.

The space of the park gives her the chance to feel free in her zone doing what she loves and that's sniffing out the different smells.

As our bodies change, we adapt to them, but inside our character is who we are not our physical bodies. As long as we can shine, then that's all that matters. Whether from walking or running or from a chair or a bed, the space we find ourselves in is our space in which to shine.

WHAT PLANET ARE YOU ON?

You can travel the world and equally travel the world from the comfort of your home. You can still see the world through your eyes you don't have to reply on others.

Like our thirteen-year-old chihuahua still sees the world through her nose.

The only reason why we stop seeing the world through our own senses is when we switch off and stop connecting with it.

It has nothing to do with ability, like I don't know what the world looks like to my dog, whether she can see anything or not.

We can have sight but still not see what is in front of us.

We can be so distracted that we miss what is actually in our life, only to miss it when it's no longer around.

Living in the now allows you to be present and give attention to what is actually happening now.

If your head is in yesterday or tomorrow, then one day you will notice how much your children have grown up. But you missed them growing up.

Same as any family member. We are all growing and living our best life to the best of our ability. But are we loving it?

This depends on how you are using your four elements of frequency with the physical tools of the physical trade.

If you can apply yourself, then you're not going to want to stop, because it's not about what you're actually doing but how you're using your energy and how it makes you feel.

It could be building a house, styling a house, making a home a home, creating music or painting a picture, cooking and driving vehicles of any kind. You could be a burglar or addicted to substances.

Whatever it is you're doing, and if you're applying your energy to what you're doing, then you are living your choices. If you don't know why you're doing what you are doing, then you have followed behind the footsteps of another rather than being aware of your own.

LESS IS MORE

Your soul is all you need and have. It has your physical life covered.

You are set for your life. You made sure of it before you arrived here.

It's not a case of bad luck or good luck.

You are your luck in connection.

Humans see what they want to see, missing that they are the magnet in the centre of their reality.

When you wake up each morning you welcome yourself into your reality. You have access to the infinite possibilities of your choices.

You may purchase a new car but, on the way home, a stone hits the window screen and smashes it. It's not bad luck; it was down to your connection in the moment. You and your car aligned energetically with the stone bringing the stone to your car and impacting it.

Why is this possible?

Because the magic of space within and around you.

Have you ever dropped ink on to paper?

(Google search)

According to Answers.com, when ink is dropped onto paper, it spreads and wicks into the paper fibres through capillary action.

What else can happen are the following.

200

Spreads quickly: Ink drops start to spread within microseconds of touching the paper and reach their maximum radius in ten-to-twenty microseconds.

It flattens out: At its maximum radius, the ink drop forms a flat disc shape.

Ink and dyes can soak into the paper and bleed through.

Ink drops can create unpredictable stains and unique patterns.

You can use it to create designs and use it to spell out words.

Connection spreads your energy out like the ink does to paper. How far your soul or physical energy expands is down to your own connection with yourself.

This is why it is not about what you do but how you apply yourself before you actually do it.

Your energy is why this is possible. Thank your soul for that.

Element number four, vibration completion, connects the dots between the four elements.

Humans hear one word or see a particular look or feel certain ways in action or not, reacting to it separately, and concludes and assumes without joining the information that makes up the total scene.

This is like taking words seriously even though you weren't actually involved and present to view what is happening for yourself. Hearsay from others without experiencing it for yourself depends on the energy in which it is presented to you.

Does it match up with you or not?

Is the information passed on in its pure form, or is it tweaked with added energies to suit a narrative.

Example:

I was given bread to hand out to people, and while it was in my own company I decided that it looks a bit plain. Rather than leaving it as it was, I took it upon myself to tweak it by taking the bread to the kitchen so I could add different toppings to it before sharing it out.

What I shared out was not how the original bread looked when I initially received it.

This is what humans are doing by putting their take on things. The only difference is when it is claimed as their own, when your soul knows this is not totally the case.

What you add to anything belongs to you, but what you didn't create doesn't. You collaborate with others by sharing your creativity with theirs.

Your energy stems from you. This is then shared with others. Your take on your creation depends on your commitment to yourself on whether you come full circle with your completion.

ENERGY NEEDS AN OUTLET TO FLOW

How we apply ourselves is down to our energy flow between the physical and the soul.

You are like a hybrid car that runs on two types of energy. Your soul eternal energy flow and your physical adrenaline bursts of energy.

When the soul is the main outlet, then this carries the physical energy eternally. If the physical is the main outlet, then it runs on its own adrenaline fuel in a stop-start way in bursts of energy that can last in any length of time or duration until the energy supply runs out.

The physical energy does not carry the soul energy.

This is why the soul never sleeps or gets tired and the physical does.

The physical outlet of energy, if used, is why it relates to how long things last or how long it may take. Humans view time in energy on how long you spend on or in any situation. To your soul, it has nothing to do with physical time and everything to do with your energy connection.

When you are soul connected to an event, then it will feel like time passed in a flash. If you are physically present but not feeling your soul connection, then an event can drag.

Follow your energy as this will tell you how your life is working for you and why it is unfolding the way it is.

WHICH WAY DO YOU SWING

You have a soul frequency and your physical frequency.

You can switch between the two.

You may find yourself in your zone one minute and then all over the place the next. This is a sure indication that your soul isn't aligned with your physical causing your life to spin.

To stop this motion and action you will need to steady yourself.

Depending on the context of the situation will depend on what you do next.

If you can't hear your own guidance, you may retreat from being social. If you have spent enough energy with being in your own space, then you may choose to get out there more.

Even if you don't know what to do next or how you even feel, just balancing your frequencies is enough.

Stop the mind from tripping out and settle into a peaceful atmosphere that harmonises with you, whether you're literally on your own or around others. How your life settles in your space depends on how you apply your energy to it. Your life isn't set in time or events but in your energy. Your energy does not change because you are mixing with others. It changes because you changed it.

This is the beauty of space. If this universe was a transistor radio, then our souls make up the stations that are playing our unique signature frequencies. This is what makes up the content being played in this universal space together.

STOP COPYING ME

You may have heard the sayings, "Please excuse me, I am going to retreat to my room," or "I have finished dinner. Can I go to my room?"

Excusing yourself from a situation is not excusing you for you being you.

I was more practical than academic because this matched my soul map path ahead. Being a single parent to four children required practical skills to bring them up.

We have within us exactly what we need for our exact unique path.

It is why schools don't make sense to me. No one should be put in classes and expected to learn something that does not interest them or have any connection with it. But this is what has been offered to souls and has been going on for centuries. This is why souls often feel sad when they have limited outlets to be their unique self. The taught script doesn't encourage self-expression to build strong foundations with your soul, only to offer a script that holds up a system, not your life.

I am sure everyone looks happy doing what they are doing, and they certainly seem like it when on online platforms.

Some genuinely are not in need of followers but enjoy sharing their connection to their life with you when on them.

Others buy followers or need followers to get paid, but behind closed doors, are they as happy as they imply when they come offline?

WHAT IS A SOUL MAP?

A soul map is what you create for yourself before you arrive.

Example:

You may choose to have kids, be a teacher, dancer, singer, pilot, travel agent, etc.

Whatever you have chosen to experience you will bring your abilities with you.

If you want children, your energy will be into sex. If you want to share your feelings, then you may choose sex as an option to express your feelings but not for wanting to have kids. You may be more focused on using sex as a career.

I have used the word sex because it is used as the main backdrop for procreation, so the physical form continues.

If we can relate to something, then it will get attention. This is how following works. It is not so much about the thing that you follow but how it relates to you.

See how it always leads us back to ourselves.

You are the reason and the meaning why you do anything.

Why you go to bed and why you choose to wake up.

Humans often say they did not choose this or that, but the fact you are here sharing it shows you chose it.

It is your voice and your words coming from you and not others on your behalf.

Trying to speak on behalf of others works for so long until the soul it relates to steps in and puts a stop to it.

WHAT HAPPENS NEXT?

Juggling the past and the future is over. Your soul will guide you back to you now.

What happens next?

You happen next.

The choices that you make now will set you up for life. Not just this lifetime but the next and the next and the next experience.

You will soon realise over the next few years that the script will no longer serve you.

Life will feel strange, as everyone will be into themselves more rather than focusing on you.

Self-connection is what is happening next and once you have this connection established then you will be ready to share from yourself in action with others.

Memories will fade that grew from the script. These memories are not lost. They just evaporated into space.

You will have the veil of the script lifted, not blindsided by following others in fear, but sharing together in love and peace because you're settled with being you.

You will create for yourself your own freedom and set yourself up so you can experience yourself being you and feel comfortable with you in what you enjoy in connection.

You will see past the physical body and see the content each soul brought with them more clearly.

You will appreciate more because you feel your energy in your creation.

You will be aware and see yourself no longer zoning out on autopilot.

You will have no reason to switch off as you will be switched on listening to yourself.

You will see space around you as your home and not as something to fill, but to use like a whiteboard, not to delete but to reflect.

Your energy will flow from you around you and within you. You will feel the tingle of your soul energy running through your cells.

Over the next thirty years, the past centuries will fade and not be remembered to be reused.

It may still look like the battle between the frequencies of the soul and the physical is happening. It is not; it is restructuring. You are in the process of creating a reality that has no memory on it, but it will have your knowing running through it.

You will go back to come forward leading you back to you now.

You will enjoy this universe because you will be in control of your reality.

You will enjoy mastering yourself until you have completed it.

Mastering yourself will prepare you for the next universe.

For those who have already mastered themselves in this reality will go on to the next universe and will not come back here.

Don't worry. Everyone can still communicate with each other regardless of what universe you or they are at. It's no different to when you travel to different countries on earth's space and still keep in touch.

For those who are moving on to the next universe, it is very different to here.

This universe is like a well-stocked, totally infinite, already-known shopping mall. Nothing new to create as it has already been provided for you. You have the choice in this universe to select what you want from the already-supplied infinite choice and experience it your way.

This well-stocked universe gives you the space to get to know and master yourself.

For those who are not going to come back to this universe, the first thing you will notice is how much of yourself that you will take with you. It will feel like you're taking your whole house and contents with you rather than just packing a few things for a break. Sounds familiar to the script choices, doesn't it?

When you arrive at the next universe, you will notice that space still greets you, but the difference is that space will be just space and not a pre-stocked universe like the previous one.

Think of it like moving into a brand-new home that is empty without content but has all the space you want.

The next universe you will use everything that you brought with you when you mastered yourself. You will use this content to experience your new reality in your new space. Yes, it will actually be new. No scripts, no memory, no pre-stocked content to choose from. Just your mastered soul self.

Liken it to when young adults leave your nest to make a life for themselves. They have been used to using what you provided for them to use while at home.

When they move into their own space, they provide it for themselves.

This is why the script has mirrored the soul.

When you leave here you will be providing your own content reality for yourself.

Sharing what your universe looks like to you.

Earth has been called a world. Now you will be ready to live in your universe of your creation.

It does not end there either, there are three more universes after this.

All will be revealed to you once you arrive there.

No matter what universe you find yourself in you're never alone because of the magic of space between souls and between each universe.

The bigger the picture the bigger the reveal.

SPACE, WHAT IS IT?

Having space from others is often seen as detachment in the physical. To the soul space it is expansion, a space to review and piece together or have a catch-up with yourself.

In writing this book and looking back at this reality from space, I can see clearly what's going on in this universe.

It's like a toy box of toys that offers you variety of choices.

Nothing is new but it's all contained within this space.

The only thing that relates to us uniquely is our experience within it that creates our reality.

This universe allowed the script because it mirrors the soul knowing.

Total infinite knowing is like creating your own film without needing a script but instead improvising by using your gut instinct.

Together with the instructions of guidance of the four elements of frequency.

Nothing new is here but everything is known here.

Guidance is everywhere which starts with the self, shared with others in this space while safely experiencing your creation and completion.

The next universe is interesting because there is nothing to follow.

It's space itself offering you an opportunity to grow your roots like a seed into the next universe.

In the previous universe, you travelled around space to space experiencing yourself.

You will occupy your space with your mastered self-energy, adding more continued experiences infinitely from one universe to the next.

PART TWO

THE SOUL REALITY

CHAPTER ONE – CONNECTION to the soul self

(Element number one)

In part one I covered your physical body. In part two I am covering your soul body.

What does your soul look like?

Forget the physical image. Your soul is hot!

You are divine for all eternity. Your energy does not age or weaken, and it doesn't deteriorate or die. It flows infinitely with your guidance and direction.

Your soul doesn't look like your physical body in material. You could say your soul is an energy projection with your physical body.

Your soul looks like the steam in a sauna or fog on a winter's day. It has its own colour.

My soul colour is red. I knew from two years old that I felt a connection with it. It wasn't just a colour I casually picked from a chart.

When I looked at my chihuahua sleeping the other week, I saw her physical body lying on her dog bouncer. As she breathed in and out the bouncer rocked her gently. I suddenly saw a green mist expand from her body. I immediately knew she was showing me her soul colour like a peacock displays their feathers.

I had been used to mainly interacting with her physical body, so to see her soul energy body impacted me to say the least.

I would often say aloud to my husband, do you think she knows how much we love her?

There and then she answered me by sharing her soul green plume of colour with me.

Whatever questions you ask this universe you will receive the guidance and answer when you're ready.

The physical side wants to know everything for whatever gain it provides. Follow the money is often the reason. But those who follow their soul will follow the energy in which to understand more.

My chihuahua's soul energy body never sleeps and is showing itself constantly. The reason why we can't see soul is because we are distracted with tuning into the physical side.

You start of soul and continue as soul continuously.

You will have visited your physical family before they meet you.

You will have scanned your life before you get to physically experience it.

Nothing will surprise your soul.

There are no surprises in this universe but there is infinite knowing.

How your soul works here goes something a bit like this:

Imagine this universe is a shopping mall, and this shopping mall has a head office HQ on the pent floor that I have called in my previous books point zero.

Before we experience our total infinite knowing we will go over plans with our guides to create our soul map at head office.

While at the office on the pent floor, we can see straight through every floor and see the shops below.

We can see all the different floors and all the different choice of shops available.

Once we have selected what we wish to experience on our soul map, we pair it up with the four elements of frequency that will support us in mastering ourselves.

We have access to any shop in the shopping mall, if the energy of the shop matches us and our maps, then what we choose goes into our soul shopping basket. If it doesn't match us, then we just experience what we picked up while in the shop but won't be taking it home.

Home is home within our self.

THE PENTHOUSE HEAD OFFICE HQ

You may be aware that there are billions of souls on earth, but there are infinite souls in this universe.

What humans see is a fraction of the total picture, due to limited physical access and due to forgetting most of what is known.

Humans can't be in many places at once, but souls can.

Every infinite soul is at the office. It doesn't matter where a soul is reflecting themselves. Energetically, no soul actually leaves HQ.

Liken it to a light bulb, once settled in its connection it does not leave the fitting when emanating its energy to lighten up a room.

Souls are the same at head office.

Let's go back to how it all began.

At head office souls chatted about their infinite knowing. The knowledge and wisdom flowed infinitely. Suddenly, a soul had a lightbulb moment and blurted out to the infinite souls around them.

What is the point in knowing everything if we don't experience it?

Every soul agreed that they wanted to experience their total infinite knowing.

Collectively, every infinite soul created this universal space to enjoy the content of themselves.

Think of it like a child enjoying playing with a doll's house and creating many different stories each day with the content of the doll's house.

The pieces stay the same what changes is the story.

Souls spent many centuries creating the different spaces that would be called locations in this shopping mall.

Each soul contributed by sharing themselves to fill each shop with their take on their reality.

Each soul knew that with each different century they could alter the stock they picked to change the experience.

Hence the saying taking stock of your life.

After infinite space of planning, the first souls were ready to travel from their knowing and into their experience without leaving the penthouse.

The souls who were ready to experience themselves expanded their energy into a flowing plume. Liken it to a waterfall.

Their energy flowing from themselves at the penthouse flowed through transparent space and into the shopping mall itself.

At first souls could feel their connection to their total selves at HQ.

Liken it to a diver diving into the sea but still connected to the boat via a line that has a buoy attached to it.

Connection is everywhere. It never ceases to exist regardless of what you're experiencing within this shopping mall.

This connection and expansion of the soul has been called the silver cord.

Space created uniqueness with your signature frequency without needing to build literal platforms and walls like in the physical.

The energy from each soul created their own foundation and platform in which to create from.

Souls enjoyed experiencing many forms within the shops experienced so far.

Each shop was known by its background vibe. This chord of sound became how it was recognised. Each soul visiting each shop would harmonise with the sound of the shop in which to gain access.

Extensions of new shop spaces were added, and a signature background vibe would be created once the space had been occupied by souls that visited it.

This created an opportunity for some souls to realise that they didn't need to match the shop space, because it hadn't got its signature background tone yet.

These souls had the bright idea that they would take over this shop and call it their own in their vision.

They didn't want souls coming into the shop and sharing their frequency. They made the space of the shop uncomfortable for any souls that visited it.

The distorted sounds where a deafening noise that didn't resemble what is known in peace.

These souls severed their plume of energy with HQ, leaving them with the connection of their breath within the space of the shop that connected with HQ.

This connection was all they needed for their shop to exist.

They created what some would call hell, in the sense without a connection past this shop, this limited them from accessing more than what the shop space offered.

Any soul that entered the taught shop would be greeted by the rules of the trade. A list of dos and don'ts, including fear, made sure that once you were inside you followed suit.

DROP IN THE OCEAN

Your soul sees your experiences here like a drop in the ocean. To humans that one drop can feel like the end of the world.

Especially as you're in your own bubble of space like a drop of air in the atmosphere, having your own unique reality in this total infinite shopping mall universe.

Unless you connect with the taught script, it will then seem that this one drop is all that exists.

How your soul sees your physical self is not as insignificant or a waste of space as some humans will say.

Soul is this total universe and when you connect with your soul you are not limited to the taught script unless using it only.

Your space is an important piece of the space jigsaw puzzle of this universe. It doesn't matter where you are in this shopping mall, in what location or shop or totally at HQ. Viewing the shopping mall is like watching a film.

You can view it as much as you want before you experience it for yourself.

A spectator as well as observer and souls can be a guide for others without needing to be in the mall itself.

Like when messages are heard over the loudspeaker when someone is being called to a certain location.

This universe is totally communicating with every soul because space is the foundation of everything, the matrix of manifestation.

SPACED OUT

Humans have a fascination with space. Outer space is taught in a way of static timeframes, a bit like a still picture.

Now pictures that are taken are not just still images but viewed as live mini clips.

What makes something move or stay still?

It is energy and frequency that creates movement.

Getting back to our soul perspective.

Humans think they are only their human body and nothing else is going on with them.

If you have gotten used to the concept that you are a soul, and not your human body, then you may wonder what your soul is doing while you're having your physical experiences.

Especially as the soul never sleeps.

What does your soul get up to?

Let's find out.

HOW I GOT HERE

Before I arrived here, I went over my soul map one last time. I knew my path ahead was going to be challenging from the get-go.

I hung out in the viewing window watching the souls in the shopping mall below, knowing I would not be gaining access to all the shops of this shopping mall at first. I knew once I arrived there, I would be stuck behind the script walls of earth's space, the shop of distortion until I remembered more of who I was.

The taught shop is the one place most souls avoided.

After all, who wants to fight all the time?

The noise coming from the shop alone is enough to put any soul off.

I should not be going back again. But the shift didn't happen around World War Two because of the distraction of war. This meant earth's space didn't get its signature frequency so it could be released from its limitation and restrictions, so it could connect with the rest of the shopping mall shops.

I knew why I had to go back to help with the transfer, so earth's space would connect back to being soul rather than a taught script.

This universe alerted my element number four vibration that sent waves of energy through me. I knew that I needed to get ready and expand my energy to earth's space.

Some souls from HQ even came to encourage me for moral support.

I held the inhale of my breath which slowed the flow of my energy to earth's space.

I telepathically shared that I didn't want to go while still holding my breath not wanting to exhale. HQ encouraged me to just let go.

I heard people's voices saying they could see the head of my chosen physical body. It was waiting for me to connect.

What felt like a nanosecond I exhaled, which connected me to the body that was lying still on the bed.

My first sound my breath made confirmed my soul had connected with my chosen body.

I wasn't prepared for how loud everything sounded.

I could feel the energy of the physical body that I had already been introduced to at HQ. My soul knew that I would be limited to earth's space for a while. I watched as my body slept in the incubator.

The soul never sleeps so those first few weeks I just watched my body grow in strength.

I could hear HQ echo in the background with each beat of my heart.

They sounded like they were underwater.

I could feel the energy of the blood flow through the physical body. I felt my brain's neurons transmit as they communicated with my body.

I could not see very clearly through the physical lens, but I sensed different people by how they smelled and felt.

The day came when my soul and physical body were taken home to where we lived.

With my physical body getting stronger, I was able to feel the connection of my soul with each breath.

Even though I was limited to the confines of this earth's space, I knew if I kept my connection strong with my soul self that I would be able to use this to keep in touch with HQ.

The first couple of years made it easier for me to remember who I was. I remembered the first part of my soul map. I knew I had to stay around children as they are pure souls and have not turned into physical scripted versions. The vision of children echoed through every cell of my body embedding it into my conscious knowing. My gut flowed this information connecting with the energy of my heart and not the brain.

I also knew that I had to avoid the brain if I wanted to continue to remember who I was.

The more taught humans you mixed with created interference with the transmission between your soul and physical frequencies.

The taught script of interference rubs off on you.

I managed to navigate the challenges around my mother.

My dad having a stable frequency counterbalanced my mother's distortion.

Although my physical body felt the impact of my mother's choices, the main thing was that my soul frequency was not disrupted.

When my dad put me into care at one years old, it didn't affect my soul self, knowing it just affected me recognising who my parents were in name.

I recognised my dad by his stable soul energy.

At two years old, I left the care system to live back home full time.

This strengthened the soul-to-soul connection between my soul and the soul of my dad.

My dad shone some light on my soul map like a mirror that reflected back at me every time I faced him.

The connection we shared downloaded to my soul. This energy transfer would serve me with an extra internal compass. His energy would continue to shine encouragement and guide me and supported me on my path ahead.

Connection in energy is eternal and never deleted in this universe no matter what location this shopping mall is in.

SELF SOUL AWARENESS

Upon arriving on earth's space, my physical body didn't get in my way. I was conscious of it, but I was more aware of my soul. I was just being me as I always am in this universe.

As situations and circumstances changed around me in my family, rather than just seeing clearly through my soul and seeing one total view, I now could see double vision. It was like looking through binoculars but as a split screen.

Now I had to manage what looked like two realities, the physical scripted version and pure soul one.

I had been prepared for this in knowing HQ always shared how it's one thing knowing it but it's another thing experiencing it.

There is nothing new here but my reflected take on my experience is.

I juggled mastering my two bodies and my two realities. Surely, it can't get any more challenging than this?

CHALLENGE ACCEPTED

The moment my dad passed my connection with my soul self got ignored.

I had enough to deal with mastering two bodies without two realities.

My soul focused on my physical reality as it was where all the action was.

Until, of course, the body gets tired and sleeps.

The physical script is turned down when it sleeps.

The pockets of silence are reflected from the atmosphere of the body. This gives each soul some peace to hear its soul transmission. The soul downloads information to the sleeping body.

As I watched my body sleeping, I tuned into the space within it and shared some of my information from the first part of my soul map.

The word CHILDREN is highlighted.

Trying to communicate with my physical body isn't easy because of the space around each frequency.

The physical body forgets everything, so I found myself repeating the same word over and over each night.

After a few years my soul had managed to embed the word children into the consciousness of the gut. The brain memorised the word as this is where it is stored by the taught script.

My soul guided my physical body through the events that arose in my physical reality.

When my soul faced my mother's last breath, this opened a portal of space with HQ.

For those nanoseconds I was relieved from the limited taught shop. I watched my mum's soul reflection travel back to her total self at HQ.

I knew my total soul was with her there. Her soul leaving this taught shop gave me a chance to catch up with my total self and everyone at HQ.

I did not want this window of space to close, but I made the most of it.

I scanned what was coming next on my soul map, so I had a fresher, clearer picture of what lay ahead.

As the portal of space closed, I was left watching my mother's lifeless body on her bed.

It no longer worked because the physical body doesn't work without a soul.

My physical body was scared and felt alone each tear it shed. I felt across my soul energy face like a phantom limb feels everything.

I reassured my physical self as much as I could by taking deeper breaths.

All my soul could do is watch as my physical self was pushed from pillar to post.

The energy of my soul was shut out from being received. It was like my physical body had drawn the curtains around itself.

Night turned to day but it was still dark in energy.

The shadows of fear grew bigger with each attack my body felt.

My soul looked at my physical body like a balloon. When it felt deflated, my soul would exhale into it to expand it.

When expanded events bounced off my physical body, I was able to carry on facing what the taught shop threw at me, but with a bounce in my step.

Around the age of seven my physical body had a breather where it could enjoy playing with the other kids at the children's home.

Lightbulb moment – children.

Each time my physical body interacted with children it remembered more of who it was, a soul.

Mixing with children was like mixing with souls at HQ. My physical body felt more comfortable around the energy of children but not so much around the adults.

It wasn't because of the fearful happenings and suffocating heavy energy that this taught shop exposed me to. It was having the fun of soul-to-soul connection with the other kids. It was much lighter in atmosphere than the density of sadness I felt when mixing with adults.

Adults saw children, I saw souls.

Life felt how I remembered it at HQ, being in your own space and having the ability to enjoy what you connected with.

Those years gave my physical body the chance to build a strong relationship between my physical body and my soul.

Both my realities played out in unison and matched in harmony. This gave me a strong sense of self, from both sides of each reality.

I was soul happy, seeing how I was thriving being myself in both realities.

My physical body was starting to ask questions about reality itself and piecing together the events of the physical pieces it had experienced so far.

The word children had worked. My soul watched with a beaming smile at how my physical body connected with a doll that gave a sense of belonging.

This energy between my physical self and the doll forged a bond of feeling that matched the bond I remembered with my dad.

I watched knowing that I was getting the hang of mastering my physical body.

Hearing laughter come from the children was a welcome sound compared to the distorted noises coming from the adults.

It was like a screeching sound, similar to the sound a teacher made when they ran their nails down the board, or the sound of a car that has worn brake pads.

Watching how the relationship between my two realities grew and communicated with each other made me feel pre-armed to be able to face physically anything.

My physical body may look like to other physical bodies that I am alone, but to my soul I was far from it.

The space around my soul created a strong portal with HQ.

My physical body became aware of souls as much as physical bodies.

The soul never sleeps it is infinitely awake.

The physical body does need sleep. This created an open and shut atmosphere in the taught physical reality.

It's no different to shops having opening hours.

This gave my soul an advantageous opening of opportunity.

I knew that when the taught script shut down for rest, it would make it easier for my soul to communicate with my physical body.

I even saw moments of opportunity when the physical body had glitches, when it daydreamed and zoned out into space during the day.

I DON'T SEE DEAD PEOPLE, I SEE SOULS

A soul is all there is. A physical body doesn't work without it.

I loved laughing when I played with other children. The energy amplified our souls.

Children started to tell the adults that they could see other souls. This was translated by humans as seeing dead people or imaginary friends.

The children knew they didn't have imaginary friends. They knew they could see a reality that the physical reality couldn't.

Souls start enjoying their experiences with their chosen physical bodies because they are given the space to play and be themselves.

Souls knew that when the last breath was exhaled, although souls let go of the physical body to return their reflection back to HQ. Souls knew the energy of their experiences still played as it doesn't get deleted.

The history of experiences is constantly accessible to souls, just not the physical bodies.

What happens physical side stays physical side. What happens soul side covers the physical side too.

My physical body as it grew became aware of mortality especially after the experiences it had previously with the parents.

The physical humans were aware of it too.

Death was to be feared. To the humans it meant that you would no longer exist. This seemed true and convincing when they buried or cremated the discarded bodies.

Fear spread daily not just because of death but because the sense of the self was not understood or known.

What was happening in this taught shop reality called earth didn't match with the information embedded within each soul's knowing. Deep down each soul knew they were infinite souls, but seeing the physical bodies being buried or cremated caused them to doubt and to not know what to believe.

Deep down inside they felt eternal but, on the surface, it looked like death was the final curtain. Once the body is deposed of, humans noticed that this left a gaping hole and a void of empty space where the character of the soul once shone through the physical body.

The presence of the soul now missed; the humans confused this as missing the physical body.

The physical body only contains organic material and organs. The soul character and personality are what the physical humans actually interacted with without even realising it.

The taught script tried to reflect a reality that had no part of the soul in it.

By the age of seven, my physical body was aware of its soul reality as well as the physical reality.

This caused the space of my soul to expand around my physical body.

This space ended up bumping in o the physical reality that was going on around me.

My soul bubble started to get my physical body into trouble in the taught shop called earth.

My physical body got told off for giggling and asking questions as if it didn't know a physical thing.

Admittedly, my soul hardwired my physical body to a default connection setting. Whatever words were taught to my physical body that didn't resonate on my soul connection menu, then my physical body didn't retain it.

My physical body looked like a ragdoll being dragged from one part of the shop to another.

Then suddenly out of the blue, the taught shop gave my physical body a permanent address. This gave my physical self a chance to get to know and explore more about my soul self.

Whether you view yourself through the lens of your physical reality or through the lens of your soul reality, both lenses lead you back to yourself.

Okay, it may take you physically years to work it out, or it may even take you centuries. The reason why this information in this book is being shared with you now is because the taught shop itself is in the process of new management and having a refit.

The taught, scripted shop is over, and this means the experiences that souls remember in memory about the history of earth will rapidly fade.

This universe provides you with everything that you need. In the past it may have felt like you were in the dark, but not anymore.

You will defrost from the layers of the script, which will reveal your total self back to you.

You won't have to replay and live out many versions of yourself that you don't relate to. You will have some space over the next thirty years to work out who you authentically are.

My soul has observed how tough it has been for my physical body.

The taught script does not make room for a physical reality to live as an energetic soul.

Souls living within the confines of a script are like using batteries instead of being plugged in to the main energy supply.

Those that are aware of their soul self will be self-recharging as if using rechargeable batteries, rather than using ones that are discarded once they have run out of energy.

Once I knew my physical body could hold its own energetically, I didn't need to be so concerned of the atmospheric events that crossed my physical body's path. I knew that it didn't matter how strong the storms were. My physical body was strong enough to face it. It didn't knock out our physical-to-soul transmission either.

My soul felt in control no matter what. I had synced up my physical body with my soul where communication flowed between both the realities in the now.

I recognised my physical frequency, and I recognised my soul frequency. This was enough for me to bed down some roots in my allocated space within myself.

We did experience wobbles from both realities when the frequencies pulsed in waves of irregular rhythms. The past and the future caused static interference creating an energy surge, each reality could not access anything. The physical reality could not access the scripted menu in the scripted shop and soul reality could not project the soul menu on to their physical body.

Static encouraged the last frame of either of the past or the future to play on a loop, like buffering.

Sharing looped repeats in the physical taught reality created fun and laughter and lots of tears too.

The taught physical shop experienced massive highs and extreme lows.

This is how the physical experiences projected to my soul.

The challenge wasn't so much about myself, as my sense of self was established from my soul perspective. But my physical self-identity was still a work in progress.

It took my physical self roughly fifty-seven years to remember who I was totally.

MIXING WITH OTHERS DOESN'T MEAN TOTALLY BLENDING WITH THEM

Souls and humans are like different tubs of Play-Doh. If you have ever played with it, they are okay on their own until you mix the tubs together. It is near impossible separating the colours. Often, you give up and just squeeze both tubs together.

Each tub is no longer recognised or seen because it just looks a different colour entirely. Yes, both tubs are there but the space between them is zoomed in.

This is what mixing in the taught script shop is like.

If a soul doesn't manage to keep the space around their chosen physical body, then they run the risk of mixing the frequency of their physical self up with the frequency of the physical others in the shop, because they meet in the middle, in space.

CHAPTER TWO – PULSE Sharing from the soul self

(Element number two)

My soul has observed the relationships of both realities between the soul and physical body. My soul has seen enough from the viewing window of HQ and here in person experiencing it for myself. As I faced the scripted shop floor called the earth department, I know and recognise the distinctive differences between the soul and the physical bodies. Not because of how they look in image or known by physical names, but because of the transmission of their frequencies playing in space.

They are playing in plain sight and not even hidden. If you tune in, you can see it for yourself.

SHARED RELATIONSHIPS

The first experience my physical body was made aware of its personal space, physically speaking, was when other physical bodies felt they could touch my physical body without my soul permission in a sexual manner. This is the equivalent to a physical child taking the toy from another child and calling it their own.

Space creates organic boundaries that the scripted shop assumes does not exist because of the distorted sounds of static, making it impossible to pick up anything of sound value.

The taught script shop acts as if it is a free for all. Liken it to a hotel and anyone can use what is available as if no manager or owner is present.

Frequencies sound like foghorns, a lot of noise but no message. This is like stray frequencies playing just because they can but with no meaning or purpose to them.

Your physical body belongs to your soul. This is why your soul chooses it.

Your soul is the master of your physical body. This is why this universe is about mastering the self.

It does not matter what you choose at HQ, what location, how much infinite access you have, or if limited. Neither does it matter if you live in an expansive manner or in a broom cupboard. You are constantly your soul self, regardless.

Your soul space only occupies you. Your space around your soul is often called your aura. This is where you can meet up with other souls.

If each soul was a shop, then your space outside of your shop is where others can look in without being able to enter.

One soul in and one soul out, that's you. This is how you live in your own soul space bubble in this universe. Your space bubble is like a seed and can embed in any location of your choosing, so you experience more from your chosen menu.

To my physical body it looks like it is inside earth's taught script shop and stuck there and nothing else exists outside of it.

To my soul I can see why it looks like this to my physical body, because of the frequency distortion that creates energy bursts that pile up on top of one another, creating a grid-like wall.

The soul frequency continuously flows with information, whereas the physical energy is like a dripping tap of bits and pieces of information. To speed things up, souls have tried to dangle their established clear self-pairing at other pairings in the chance that they will see their pairing more clearly in the reflection.

Pairing meaning the soul and physical combinations when a soul chooses a physical body.

The most challenging relationship is between the pairing selves. It takes souls infinite centuries to master their own many pairings in this shopping mall.

This is how frequency works, behind an action is two frequencies at play, either contracting or expanding, creating movement.

Your soul infinite life is about you and only you.

I have noticed how the physical bodies get caught up in fighting over things that don't even come into their pairings, blaming others for their experiences when it has nothing to do with anyone else.

Each soul chooses their soul map menu. Each soul chooses their chord from the four elements of frequency.

Every soul and physical body is accounted for.

There are no random or stray walking physical bodies.

Each physical body has a handler the soul itself.

As soon as the connection is made at the first breath, your soul is responsible for it until the last breath.

It's not so much the literal body parts but more how the two communicate.

If you are picking at your physical body and only seeing fault with it, then you have not paired up with it in the comfort of your own space.

I have seen this happen to my physical body.

My physical body didn't get stable access to food and or a warm environment to settle in.

My physical body survived on my soul breath that I shared with it.

I switched the stations playing, so my physical body had a rest from the erratic frequencies and had a chance to relax to the soul-soothing sounds playing from the master, myself.

My physical body was encased in my soul connection and had gotten used to hearing my guidance.

I struggled to handle my physical body when the connection between us became pulled in many differing directions of opinions.

My physical body no longer heard my signature frequency clearly without the opinions of others getting in the way. My physical body did adjust back to myself and started tuning in and listening to the other physical bodies in the script shop, knowing they too have a soul handler deep down inside.

I didn't get the chance to explain to my physical body that although you trust your master, it doesn't mean that other physical bodies had an established connection to their soul masters.

I had to step back and trust that the gut of my physical body would listen to their conscience, the voice of depth and meaning.

When my physical body spiralled out of control, it happened because it listened to the opinions from other physical bodies, triggering the stored memories to surface and reflect instead of stored menu soul content.

I looked on feeling helpless when the shop floor opened for business. All I could do was observe until the lights were turned off for sleep. I didn't give up communicating but had to leave it until physical switched off when the body slept.

The soul never sleeps so this created a peaceful space in which my soul could chat with my physical body without any disturbance from anyone else.

YOU ARE NOT ALONE

You are not alone here because your physical self is overseen by your soul constantly.

There is not one moment when your soul is not with you. This is possible because the soul doesn't sleep.

Your soul is pure energy and is not impacted in the physical reality in the same way as your body is.

Physical is physical; soul is soul. They are not even similar. You can tell them apart like chalk and cheese.

This is why experiencing being connected with it makes mastering yourself fun. This is like how humans enjoy becoming an avatar in a computer game and become known for it.

You know there isn't any risk to yourself because you know you are you.

This is the same for your soul. The physical isn't risky business.

You may experience your avatar being blown up and destroyed but you can turn the game off and know you're intact. This is no different to how a soul interacts with the chosen physical body.

You will see how your relationship with yourself is the most important relationship that you will ever have.

It energetically stays with you and never gets destroyed.

Your experiences, if registered, are embedded within the space of your soul.

It doesn't matter what you remember and what you forget. Your soul remembers everything for you.

Most humans focus on their physical body and the bodies of other humans they encounter while on earth.

Forgetting to pay attention to themselves.

SOUL LOVE IS AN ETERNAL FLOW OF ENERGY

My physical body asked my soul self, how did souls make love?

My physical body did not understand the concept of energy soul transfer yet.

It viewed intimacy and sex as a purely bodily act of experience.

The only thing that came close in understanding the power of energy is when the body experienced an orgasm.

This experience was hit and miss and wasn't guaranteed when two physical bodies got close in contact, especially if their connection was off.

The only way I would be able to explain the power of soul-to-soul energy transfer to my physical body was not during intimacy but when it explored the spiritual realm as it was named amongst physicals on the off-grid community.

These physical soul pairings found a corner of the script shop and retreated within their spaces to avoid breathing in the fumes of the repeated words of memory.

They kept themselves to themselves and only came out onto the shop floor when the physical businesses were shut.

Knowing this, I kept my physical body awake so it would cross the paths of these pairings.

This opened the eyes of my physical body, realising there were more awake bodies than asleep.

They grouped together and started to chat about what they remembered about their spatial awareness.

They agreed to meet regularly when the shop floor shut.

This made it so much easier for us master, to communicate with our physical bodies. The group together amplified the connection between the pairings enabling us to send messages direct to the group.

Some out of the group started to write down the messages that they received. This would be kept in safekeeping to hand down.

This group together created a movement of energy that spiralled up through the shop and reached HQ.

This was possible because they were not just physical bodies they were connected with their master souls too.

This caused a ripple effect of energy to permeate through the walls of the scripted shop but was not visible to the scripted bodies when they awoke.

My soul got excited. This connection with my physical body enabled me to guide the content from my soul menu straight to this body. The information flowed like ink to a pen.

My physical body being the pen shaft and my soul being the ink.

The first thirty or so years, I was able to strengthen the connection of the gut of my physical body.

The gut pocket of air is the space around the lungs between the lungs and the rib cage. This gave my soul plenty of room to download the relevant pieces of the soul map that matched up with what my physical body was experiencing.

I kept an eye on the physical dramas to make sure it did not steer my physical body in a direction that was away from its own path.

My connection with my physical body was like having to control two magnets that had different magnetic fields.

My soul being very powerful it took me a while to gauge how much magnetic pull my physical body would need to get my attention.

I worked out if a drama was close to impacting my physical body. To avoid it, I turned up my magnetic field which steered them away.

This made it easier to guide my physical body compared to when it first arrived on earth and before I built a strong connection in the gut.

My soul-to-gut connection sent a feeling that my physical body felt and recognised as a hunch.

In the beginning it was easier for me to project visual images than it was to send actual information and dialogue.

This visual refection came naturally between us, it was so much fun. It is like how the physical scripted bodies watched films that they projected on to the screen. They called it cinema screening.

When my physical body encountered other scripted bodies in the shop, my physical body was able to see through to their masters.

I was able to send visual images that other masters picked up from their bodies.

Liken it to a walkie talkie in visual form.

Once my physical body was used to receiving these images, it managed to signal the gut for itself.

At first my magnetic field signalled the gut. Now, my physical body worked out how to access the gut on its own.

Think of the gut as a wardrobe that souls use to store information.

This saved a lot of energy having the information stored in one space.

Even though communicating with my physical body went offline from time to time when it had a lot going on.

I gave it the space it needed to get on with shop business.

The group pairings changed over the years. It started off as a small group and ended up larger the more messages of guidance that was received. Word spread to those that were gut open amongst the scripted versions. As each soul had a master connected to them in which to be there. This left the space open for them to connect to their gut if it got their attention.

The physical brain was like a war zone of words being fired in all directions. It got harder to avoid them with each passing day.

The noise increased tenfold, and the static noise rose due to more technical frequencies being introduced.

This gave each physical version less room to project themselves.

The image of themselves became less clear, which made the non-scripted versions stand out.

To avoid my soul from being seen, I turned down the magnetic field during shop openings. I did this by shallow breathing into my physical body when a scripted body was near and turned up the field when an open gut body passed by breathing more deeply.

The scripted shop was busy constructing technological advancements and created a version of themselves that did not mirror their authentic soul masters.

With the scripted versions being preoccupied, this gave us masters a chance to work out how to pass on more soul map menus to more physical bodies.

I remembered how my physical body asked how souls have sex.

I decided that my physical body was ready to receive the answer.

The group of pairs met up when the scripted shop shut. The masters formed a circle around the group. This created a strong portal of energy flow.

It was agreed amongst us masters that I would direct the energy of the circle into my physical body.

I bypassed the brain and linked this energy flow to the gut of my physical body.

The energy flowed from the gut space and connected with every space around each cell within the physical body. My physical body shone like a trillion stars.

I brought a soul from HQ to the group that one of the pairing knew closely before they arrived at earth's shop.

The energy from this soul flowed into my soul and into my physical body and transferred to the paring that the soul from HQ knew. The energy that flowed between the parties involved created a circuit.

The feeling the physical bodies felt from head to toe was nothing like they had ever felt before.

Every cell lit up confirming a connection was made. The energy flowed from the cells and into every space internally and externally within the physical bodies. The euphoria they both felt was like they had never orgasmed before.

To them it felt like the first sexual experience, but instead of it being a physical body-to-body experience, it was a soul-to-soul exchange of energy.

A feeling that vibrated around the cells of the body, a feeling likened to how blood feels as it travels through the veins. Both bodies pulsed gently in unison. This created the image of the visiting soul in the space between them.

This image happened because of the soul from HQ that joined the group projected their image through the portal opening and into my physical body. My physical body felt the image of the visiting soul. My physical body transferred this image to the pairing. It recognised the frequency of the visiting soul and responded first with a smile and then with tears of joy.

With the transfer complete the visiting soul from HQ left the group, which stopped the transmission.

The image would have been impacting enough, but the euphoria they felt penetrated to their gut core.

Both bodies knew that they would never feel anything like it ever again at the shop, as the physical body-to-body connection is unable to connect as close as soul to soul.

My physical body was happy to have received the answer to the question on how souls have sex.

The answer my physical body experienced explained the difference between a body connection and a soul energy one.

This experience impacted my physical body so much so that it wanted to find out more about soul energy transfer.

Although my physical body was eager to know more, I had to pace how much it received as I didn't want to overload it.

I got around this by introducing other physical bodies from the scripted shop that would be able to connect long enough with my physical body, to provide the experience of having children.

This experience resonated on all levels as it matched the soul menu of choice.

I made sure my physical body was kept busy for a while, and busy it was. It didn't have the experience of one child but four.

This distracted my physical body from rushing into soul energy transfer fields before it was ready to understand it.

I knew to understand anything is to experience it and it would blow my physical body's circuit board if it was introduced to such powerful energy before it matched up with it.

My physical body loved caring for many children who arrived. My soul watched on in love. The love from my soul poured into my physical body and transferred to the children. My physical body had what the shop floor called a family.

Their energy filled the atmosphere of their home with fun and at times tantrums and explosive arguments. Thankfully, these were short-lived.

The main ambience of unconditional love built a strong foundation for them each to grow themselves from, a bond they forged through everything they faced together as a team and on their own.

My physical body made do with the limited offerings available from the scripted shop. I taught my physical body how to juggle when money transfer was low when exchanging it for goods.

I had trained my physical body to follow and connect with energy and not follow the energy of money. This did cause struggles for my physical body on a financial and material level, but it wasn't anything my physical body could not handle.

My soul made sure that my physical body had everything that it needed. It may not have been everything that it wanted, but it was enough so that the family would feel at home in energy and feel safe while mixing with others. Okay, it wasn't picture perfect, but it served the energy of the family unit well.

My main priority to my soul was keeping their space around each of them intact. This space ensured that each family member would be able to be themselves without the fear of becoming a scripted version.

Each family member thrived. The family home gave each physical body their own space in which to be heard by their master self.

They did have fallouts when they mixed amongst the shop floor. They saw how their internal connection with their masters wasn't the same as other scripted versions of others.

This resulted in the family keeping themselves to themselves with not many long-term companions. Those that crossed their paths would stay around if they matched their soul menus.

This caused upset and frustration as they wanted to experience more of themselves outside of the family home.

The masters of the family unit agreed that the children were reading to flee the nest to explore locations within the shop to create their own family home.

This created a domino effect of events, and the family energy started to expand from the children's physical bodies.

The masters knew that each physical body within this family had a strong sense of physical self, element number one. The masters saw how the physical bodies shared past themselves as a supportive team, element number two.

The masters knew that each family member was ready for element number three, action.

The events next would strengthen the connection between the masters and their physical bodies.

Feeling confident that the physical bodies would not lose their sense of self as they mixed amongst the shop floor in search of action.

CHAPTER THREE – WAVE, action, movement, creativity from the soul perspective

(Element number three)

Before the children left the family home in pursuit of experiencing their own soul map menu, the family home had opened their physical eyes to the concept and awareness that there is more to life than just the scripted shop floor.

With the strong pairing between my soul self and my physical body (the physical body known as their mother) they had grown up being used to seeing physical phenomena.

It became part and parcel within the walls of the family home. They didn't know any different and if they ever felt scared because they didn't understand what was happening, I guided my physical body to explain it to them in a way they knew how.

The children experienced things that should not have been physically possible, but they were possible because of their connection with their master souls.

The activity that occurred ranged from utensils moving across the kitchen without anyone physically holding it.

Toys that needed batteries would randomly play without any batteries being inserted.

The volume on the radio and television would change to get the children's and my physical body's attention. Smoke rings appeared near a physical body even when they didn't smoke.

Master souls were seen walking through the spaces of the home.

The children asked their mother, "How this was possible?" The physical body called it physical phenomena, but this didn't explain how it occurred.

Stories of fear spread out in the scripted shop floor when one of the children's friends witnessed such happenings when they came round for dinner.

Not being used to such activity, when the friend went home, they told their mother how scared they got while being at ours, the mother told their child to stay away from us as our family was haunted by ghosts.

The next day this so-called friend made fun of our family by spreading rumours that our home was haunted.

This made my physical body upset, because whatever upset the children affected my body too.

This put a strain on the relationship of our pairing, as it had a knock-on effect.

After a while, things settled down, especially when the family moved to a new house and different location.

The area was more spacious outside the family home with a beautiful tree that stood the test of time.

The neighbours were more creative and open to more than just the words of the script.

My physical body made a trusted friend, and the new friend saw that my physical body was not like the other scripted versions at the shop.

The friend invited my physical body over for a cup of tea at their house. When my physical body sat down at my friend's table, my physical body could hear the house phone ringing.

I was not able to stop my physical body from blurting out your phone is ringing.

With a confused expression the friend put down the cups of tea on the table and replied, "It's not ringing."

The friend barely had a chance to sit down, when the phone did start to ring.

Without a word the friend went to answer it. My physical body looked into the teacup and smiled while lifting to drink it.

My physical body had been used to the freedom of living with physical phenomena at home, but how the friend would respond to this in their home we would soon find out once the phone call was over.

The friend greeted me with a smile as they walked back to the table. This made my physical body feel more at ease.

The friend could not stop chatting and sharing how she had read about physical phenomena from a book that had got handed down through their family. "Wait, I will go and find it for you," she said. "I knew as soon as I met you that you reminded me of this book by the way that you spoke."

I didn't know if the information in this book was real or not, or if such phenomena actually happened or whether it was some made-up story.

The energy in the atmosphere expanded in excitement like bubbles in a soft drink.

"Here it is. I have found it," the friend said. She started to flick through the pages in the book and stopped at one particular page that mirrored what happened at the table. "See, look, it says it here, the ability to hear things before they are physically heard. This is what happened with you when you heard my phone ringing before it actually rang. Are you even aware that your abilities go way back when but were known by a different name?"

I shrugged my shoulders not knowing any other explanation apart from physical phenomena.

"You are what would be called the abilities of a total soul. This later got translated to shaman. How did those kinds of words come about?"

"Why these names?" I asked my friend.

"What these words meant that, way back when, the first souls arrived at earth's shop floor, they brought with them information about outer space."

"Wait a minute. Don't you mean total body, not total souls?" I was still on catch up.

"No, they were pure souls. These souls created the first physical body from the shop floor in which to connect with. They didn't see themselves as physical bodies but more pure total souls having a physical body experience.

"Legend has it that these souls got taken over by a group of other rogue souls. This group of souls decided once they took the first breath, they would sever the energy plume that connected the souls of earth to outer space. This severely affected everyone on earth.

"Severing this plume portal, the souls inside the shop floor were confined and limited to the space of the shop. They had lost the ability to travel freely through the corridors of the shopping mall. The rogue souls made many more versions of themselves and created the script in which to follow.

"The pure souls got trapped with them. The pure souls used their soul abilities overriding the physical frequency. These souls created a frequency grid around them that housed them. Being created of pure soul frequency, this made them invisible to the rogue souls. They cocooned themselves in a layer of frequency where physical script versions would not dare to go. The frequency looked like snow and ice to the scripted versions because they could not read frequency. These souls knew they would stay until the completion of the coming shift. These souls were known as the watchers."

Having caught up, I went on to thank my friend for being open-minded and for sharing the legends in this book.

We finished the conversation as we had to pick up our children from the scripted floor teachings.

We both met up so our children could see that physical phenomena weren't a taboo subject matter.

Our children enjoyed playing together while they listened to our deep conversations about outer space.

The friends reread the different passages of this book together, which took my physical body on a journey of soul self-discovery.

This friend after a few years moved away because they had paired up with a physical other. My physical body and my soul self was thankful that our paths had crossed.

The children of my physical body continued to grow in-between the responsibilities of family life, and when my physical body had some space to itself it started to write down what my soul shared with it.

After being introduced to more about life in outer space and the possibility that watchers still lived amongst us at the shop.

My physical body didn't just want to know about them but actually wanted to meet them.

My physical body had to train for such a task. The watchers were cocooned in their frequency grid. The conditions of cold, snow and ice put most physical bodies off from even going there.

My soul spent the next twenty-four years showing my physical body how to read frequency. It knew the basic concept of energy projection transfer, but there was so much more to frequencies than just projecting into space.

My soul stopped communicating with my physical body during shop business hours.

Instead, my soul gave my physical body some space to enjoy family and personal life.

I watched as each year passed and how they forged memories, not in words but connected experiences.

My physical body got settled with a pairing that understood and supported the physical phenomena element in their life.

This partner gave my physical body the support needed in the running of the home. This took the pressure off my physical body of being the sole provider.

This gave my physical body the space it needed to explore more about outer space.

During those years I took my physical body on a journey of self-discovery. We faced the physical reality together during shop hours and during sleep.

At first, my physical body got use to my soul as a projected image.

My physical self saw my soul self as a guide.

My physical body got used to this image as it resembled how physical bodies recognise each other. If I had shown my soul self as my signature frequency, I would not have resonated with it and our pairing would have been rejected. A visual image made more sense, so my physical body recognised the difference between the soul reality and the physical reality and didn't see them as one of the same when the physical was based on the teachings of the script and not the knowing soul.

My physical body got frustrated with me when I kept showing them the pieces of their physical reality.

My physical body would often blow their top asking what has their physical reality got to do with physical phenomena.

I promised my physical self that all will be revealed and to keep writing down everything that we shared.

My physical body had finished writing down everything to do with their physical past, now that it had been faced it was ready to face their soul self of me.

I explained to my physical body how we would meet in the sleep zone. When the shop shuts would be different to any of our previous meetings.

If you want to be able to meet the watchers, the only way is by facing frequency first.

My physical body understood and realised that the next part of the journey would be nothing like before and was ready to face the unknown.

My physical body still managed to juggle the demands of family life and supported all family members when needed.

I didn't give my physical body the heads-up when I was going to connect with it astrally rather than in projection.

Even though my physical body avoided using the physical memory, it had still rubbed off on it being around it constantly. This is why I didn't give it the heads up so the physical frequencies didn't get in the way.

As my physical body laid down to rest, once the body started to drift off to sleep my soul frequency connected with next exhale of the physical body and with the inhale the energy of the physical body connected to my soul like a magnet.

The physical body was paralysed and unable to move while this was happening because the energy of the body was travelling with me and no longer flowing in the space of the body.

When energy of the soul isn't flowing through the physical body, it doesn't work.

Like the phantom limb my physical body was still conscious of itself but unable to move within it.

This freaked my physical body out because it felt out of control. It started to struggle energetically and rejected travelling with my soul.

On the next exhale of the physical body, my soul let go so my physical body would gain movement with physical body again.

Because this experience freaked my physical body out, I decided I would have to try another way that eased my physical body into accepting travelling via astral projection.

I left it a few weeks before I tried to connect with my physical body in an astral way again.

This time instead of magnetically connecting our frequencies together, I chose to use my frequency and use this as our lens.

While my physical body drifted off to sleep, my soul zoomed in close where there was not much space between us.

This enabled the energy of my soul to reflect in a super-imposed way on to the physical frequency of my physical body. Liken it to putting a magnifying glass up to your eye. It makes what you're looking at zoomed in and bigger.

The connection between us allowed my physical body to see the vastness of astral space through the mirrored reflection. My physical body wore my soul frequency like humans wear reading glasses.

I guess you could say my physical body was wearing my soul like a VR headset.

I used my frequency and expanded us into space. We travelled at nano speed. I knew this would not freak my physical body out as it had enjoyed fast rides at the theme park.

The colours of space sped past us creating the illusion that we travelled through a tunnel.

Once we reached our destination in space, I stopped the astral travel by letting go of the physical body's breath and creating more space between us.

Wow, that was out of this world. My soul smiled and replied, well, it is outer space.

My physical body had so many questions, the first one being how is it possible to actually travel that fast?

What were all the colours that passed us on the way?

Why did we stop there?

I knew my physical body would not be able to sleep unless I answered these questions.

My soul told my physical body that it may surprise you that while you think you travelled at nano speed, you were actually still.

How the universe works is what you connect to energetically in outer space of this universe is actually travelling towards you.

This is why element number one is the key to everything that connects with you.

Each soul has their own frequency colour. This is why you saw an array of colours pass you.

This is like you standing at a train station and you're waiting for a particular train. While you are waiting, many trains may pass you by just not at the speed you saw astrally, but it's the same concept as an example.

Souls don't move in this universe, what they connect with does.

This is why every soul is still at HQ.

This first introduction to frequency helped ease my soul into accepting the next part of astral traveling.

On our next encounter, I decided to take my physical body on an astral travel destination to show it around the space of this universe.

As my physical body slept, I zoomed in like before, so my energy connected within the frequency rhythms of my physical breath. Liken it to a surfer riding the waves, but instead of the waves I was riding my physical body's breath.

I presented the image of my soul self that my physical body had been used to seeing.

The energy of my physical body connected with my soul and astral travelled with me in image.

My physical body thinking I was their guide called me by the name they had given me, Ramini.

My image to my physical body looked like a North American Indian medicine man.

The character of my physical body had a childlike spirited vibe to it. When my soul as Ramini met up with my physical body, they shared in an air of innocence and fun.

This kept our contact and content simple and to the point.

My soul as Ramini showed my physical self around this universe. My physical body felt the effects of frequencies in outer space.

I showed my physical body how the universe is constructed with space being the backdrop. We visited other shops in this shopping mall. My physical body met other souls in other shops and saw how life experiences where totally different compared to the confines of the scripted shop.

The main thing my physical body enjoyed is how easy it is to communicate in space and how easy it is to be understood instantly. The physical way of communicating was exhausting in comparison.

My physical body started to enjoy the astral outer of space of this universe more than being in the scripted shop.

I noticed that after each visit my physical body felt sadder.

I didn't know how I was going to remove the sadness. I knew why my physical body felt like it and I totally understood why.

The next eight years I decided that my physical body was ready to receive the last download of the soul menu map.

I explained to my physical self that they would now be ready to see totality for itself.

This was way more information than the different layers of space realities.

Before revealing the bigger picture, I wanted to build the image of the bigger picture with my physical body.

In that way, once it was pieced together, then the big reveal would happen organically.

I knew it could only happen when my physical body asked for more.

I can guide my physical body back to themselves, not shatter their view of reality.

The taught script teaches limited versions. The totality of this universe is infinite, which includes all versions.

The children that lived with my physical body had moved out of the family home to create one of their own.

They spread out and continued their own paths of self-discovery.

They knew they could visit and stay whenever they needed.

This meant I didn't have to wait until the script shop shut and for the body to rest. My soul now had a super-imposed connection with my physical body. This meant I could communicate with it on the go.

It didn't matter where my physical body was, in a queue at the till, or eating at a restaurant, or walking the dog, I could connect and communicate with it without being ignored.

I let my physical body know that the childlike spirit would always be there, but for this next part of the journey I needed more concentration and commitment to complete the final piece of the soul map.

I altered my image and introduced my next guide in me as sound and recognisable in tone more than the image. I knew my physical body loved deep tones, so to get my physical body's attention to accept my frequency more than image, I had to make an impact. My physical body had often mentioned how they loved the tone of the actors' voices like Liam Neeson, Morgan Freeman and Denzel Washington on the television. I knew these tones combined created the perfect tone for me to use to introduce my soul self in frequency to my physical body.

My physical body had been prepared over two years that change was coming, not just personally for my physical body but globally within the earth's space of this scripted shop.

What my physical body had been known for, doing physical phenomena readings for those who wanted to be in contact with their soul master that was connected with their physical body, they were unable to communicate with them by themselves.

I created space around my physical body with my soul frequency, knowing that no one would cross my physical body's path.

This made it feel like my physical body had retired because no one was booking in for a reading.

My physical body kept busy with writing books with the information it had already received from its soul map menu over forty-nine years.

The two years respite gave my physical body the chance to enjoy the things it had not been able to do when the needs of the family came first.

My physical body enjoyed baking and making many different dishes and cakes in the kitchen. It made homemade toiletries and even knitted some hats and scarves.

After a much-needed rest and recharge, my physical body was ready to be introduced to the next version of me as a guide in tone more than image.

When my physical body had the house to itself, I got its attention by connecting my soul frequency to the rhythm of its breath. My soul energy flowed sharing the space with the physical frequency.

Combined we harmonised without being disturbed.

My physical body felt my soul frequency and knew to listen to what was coming next.

My soul did go over the top a bit, to be fair. I wore a big-rimmed black hat and a mysterious black cape. Well, Halloween had passed, and I had always wanted to dress up. Now was my chance.

The big hat and cape certainly worked and got my physical body's attention.

I introduced myself in tone, and of course my physical body tried to hear it as a name.

A ... C ... H ... O ... at first it sounded like the word echo, but upon repeating the sound my physical self said ACHO.

As Acho spoke, the tone of the voice transported us to what my physical body called the lectern room.

I guided my physical body to a spare lectern. The voice from the portal in the middle of the circled lecterns asked each physical body to put both their hands onto the surface of the lectern in front of them.

I watched as my physical body placed both hands on to the surface of the lectern. This created a connection and the lectern glowed red.

To my physical body it was one of those ah-ha moments. This is why I felt a connection to the colour red.

I looked around at the colours coming from each lectern.

The voice of the portal asked each physical body to look at the centre of the portal.

The voice explained to the physical bodies that as soon as they connected their energy with the portal, they would see their total soul self-reflection back.

I felt the beating adrenaline of my physical body's heart rhythm. This matched with energy of the soul, showing me that both realities were ready.

I watched as my physical body connected with the portal. The energy flowed from my physical body and from the lectern creating a sea of red energy to flow into the portal.

An image appeared to my physical body of its total soul self.

What my physical body saw was not just one image but many. The image of their physical body the image of Ramini and Acho all played at once back to my physical self.

The physical body relaxed as the red energy flowed in a wave motion back and forth between the portal and the lectern.

My physical body felt tired and closed it eyes and awoke on the sofa in the lounge.

ACHO ...!!

I heard my physical body call out in a panic wanting to know if what it had seen was real or just a dream.

My soul replied in the familiar deep tones, "Yes, it is true."

Welcome back home, my total soul.

Upon hearing the word total, this reassured me that what actually happened did happen.

I have so many questions to ask you, Acho, or should I say to myself.

My physical body laughed at the self-realisation of what being in this universe meant.

My total soul knew it was now ready to complete the final piece of the soul map, by connecting all the pieces together with element number four vibration that oversees all the elements regardless of what space you're in.

The big reveal.

CHAPTER FOUR – VIBRATION, completion, the bigger picture from the soul view in commitment, while overseeing the other three elements

(Element number four)

THE BIG REVEAL

My physical body now reunited with its soul self. I felt the peace inside, the distortion frequencies still played around my home, but they didn't disturb my inner peace.

The sadness my physical body previously carried, lifted and evaporated into space, not having the chance to even be stored in physical memory.

Going back to come forward enabled me to face my total self and not just my physical experiences that I had with my physical body.

My soul self had mastered the four elements of frequency and in doing so I had mastered my soul self.

WHAT NOW?

"Is this it?" I asked space.

Without even having a chance to get a reply I was straight back at the lectern room standing behind my lectern with my hands palm down on the surface.

The red energy flowed from my soul to the lectern room and into the portal itself.

I asked the question in my consciousness, "Why are we here when we have already faced who we are and our total souls?"

The voice of the portal asked us souls to watch the scene coming from the portal swirl.

The final piece of your soul maps will be revealed. You will now have a life review where your questions will be answered. Keep your hands on your lectern at all times so you can watch your own life review.

I felt slightly nervous at watching my life review. Even though I had lived it and knew it, it's another thing experiencing it from a different angle.

The swirl of energy spiralled up creating a mist in front of my face.

This is the haze that faces souls when they have completed a life experience.

I saw how the mist blended with my red energy that flowed from my soul. These particles danced in balance and harmony, reminding my soul of when starlings flew together.

As the haze cleared the scenes of my history played.

I saw my soul at HQ and my soul standing behind this lectern. I could see in multidimensional vision. I saw every version and every angle of what I had experienced so far.

The space opened to reveal the scripted shop at the shopping mall. I saw the fighting and I saw my children as they followed their own paths. I saw how those that followed themselves lit up the shop space and those that didn't were invisible on standby stuck behind the bollard of words and of opinions.

The truth made me laugh, the thought that I had gone through so much when I had mixed amongst the scripted versions that looked so fearful and terrorised us with the rules and regulations.

The threats feeling so real.

I now could see how the transfer of energy works.

My soul turned down my volume of my signature frequency. This showed me how my own soul made the scenes of what I watched come to life.

Without the volume of my soul energy, these scenes looked like clothes hanging on hangers just hanging there in the wardrobe of my life, waiting for me to pick them up.

But then as soon as I connected my frequency with what hung in front of me. This made the event come to life as if I were wearing it.

Without my energy, events were just events that had no impact and passed on by.

This is how it works. I didn't know whether to laugh or cry. This is why element number one connection to the self is first. Because without our connection of the self, nothing comes to life. Once a soul connects, they then start to feel what they connect with. This brings in element number two sharing from the self. Element number two makes the event feel like you're wearing it. Once these two elements have connected to an event, element number three comes in to play in action, bringing movement making the energy flow throughout the event, expanding in variety and opportunity.

Element number four oversees the balance of all the elements.

Now my soul understood how frequency and vibration worked in this universe, I did wonder now that I knew this simple truth I asked myself, what possibly can be next?

The portal replied by asking to watch as the scripted shop zoomed in, making me feel like I was back inside it.

I could see life going on as normal but what I saw passed through me as if I were transparent.

The scripted shop scenes of the past played to me.

I saw the watchers. They stood out as clear as day, but the scripted versions could not see them at all.

I smiled as it made more sense seeing the two realties interplay yet are spaced out from one another. This is how if you follow your soul energy. The physical reality does not affect you, because of space around each frequency.

I was then shown the future of what's next. I saw the words that threatened the very shop itself. This confused me because if the shop had created the script, how can its own words threaten itself?

Keep watching the voice of the portal said.

I found it harder to see the physical bodies inside of the script shop. I could not make the picture out clearly. The frequency of the shop buffered and glitched.

The portal explained that because the past is over, so is the future possibility that connected to the past.

As the past faded this made the future possibilities cease to manifest.

Words that were fired faded into thin air popping like burst bubbles.

I could not see how this was going to turn out.

Then I was shown the now.

I saw how the watchers needed a plume of energy in which to exit the script shop before the contents of the script disappeared into space itself.

The portal granted me one wish.

Without hesitation I replied that I would like to meet with the watchers and help them leave the script shop floor.

The portal replied, "Your wish is granted."

The red energy from my total soul spread out from my lectern and through the portal creating a plume that flowed into the scripted shop.

The watchers saw the roof of the scripted shop turn to a red sky like a ruby sunset.

The heat from my energy melted the ice, turning the water into a swirling red pathway that the watchers used as their portal to leave the scripted shop.

Each watcher stopped to thank me and told me that they would see me on the other side of this universe.

As the last watcher safely left the scripted shop, the portal closed behind them and my red energy returned to me at my lectern.

I kept my hands on the surface of my lectern and saw how the scripted version shop disappeared particle by particle.

The space that was left was how the space began before the first souls ever arrived.

This shift created a new paradigm that was meant to have happened in 1942.

The only content left was a leaflet lying on the floor. It read this confirms that the signature frequency of this space has been granted. This shop is under new management and will be open for business shortly for souls in this universe to use.

HQ cheered and clapped in excitement knowing the space of the shopping mall was complete.

With completion completed, the portal in the middle of the lectern room closed. We removed our hands, and the energy of our lecterns flowed back into our souls.

"HQ is this way," said the voice.

"Is that it now?" I asked.

"For now," came the reply.

We made our way out of the exits and reunited our total energy self back to our infinite soul self at HQ. A lovely cup of tea waited for me. After a catch up with all the souls of this universe, I suddenly remembered what the watchers whispered to me. "See you on the other side of this universe."

What did they mean "the other side of this universe"?

There is always more. Finish your cup of tea then the watchers will tell you.

OVERVIEW OF A VIEW

This universe experiences totality so you recognise your space, which prepares you for the next universe where your infinite soul self meets infinite space itself.

The story doesn't end here with element number four. This has introduced you to yourself, your physical self and your soul self and how this pairing works. You have seen how you have survived the shop floor of scripted earth. Now you are ready to create your soul story in your authentic image of your soul reality, not mixed up or distorted with other's views or a hand-me-down script. Your space in you is established. You are free to experience infinitely as much as you feel. Love yourself as yourself is what loves you back.

Living in the past the future is over. You are ready for now.

Much happiness always

From

My master, total soul self, Dee, Acho, and Ramini

PS: Always follow your energy.

THE EPIPHANY

The old scripts are out. We are in a new paradigm, and it is your responsibility now to create your own reality founded on you and you alone.

MEET DEE

Me in present day

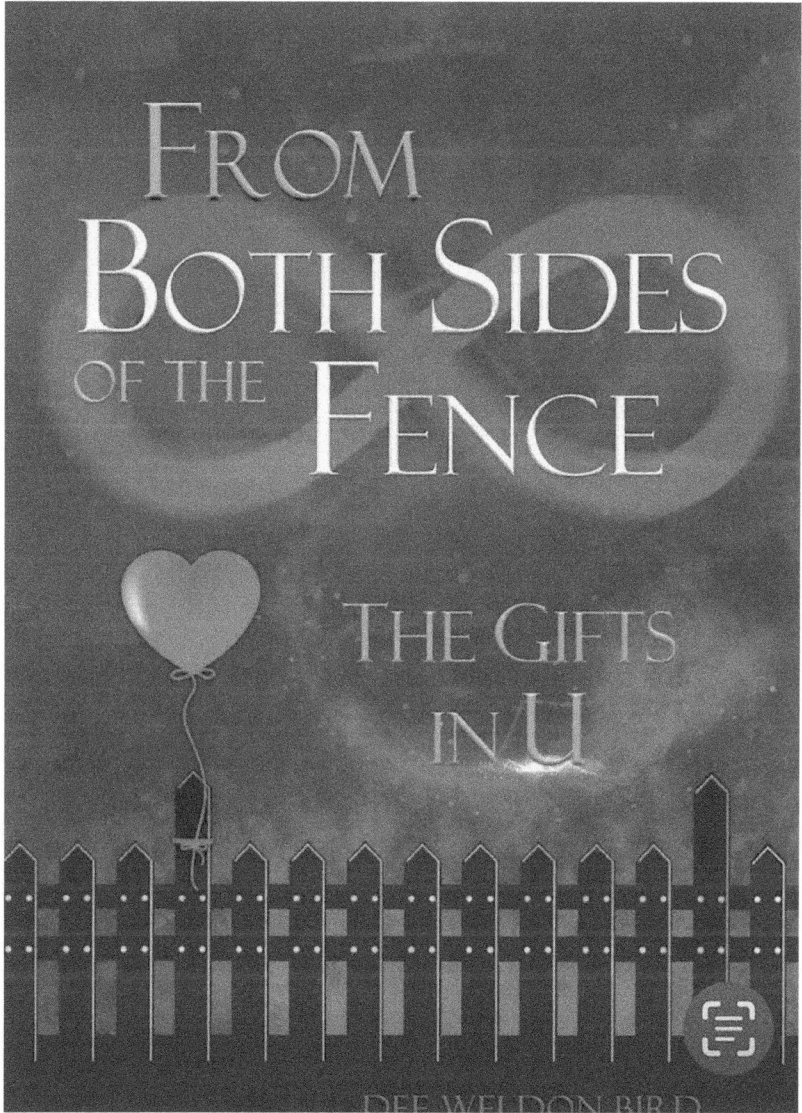

Book 1 - From both sides of the fence

CONNECTING
TO
LIFE'S COMPASS

You're not lost - You just think you are

By Dee Weldon Bird

Book 2- Connecting to life's compass

THE MAP
OF
THE UNIVERSE
A Traveler's Guide

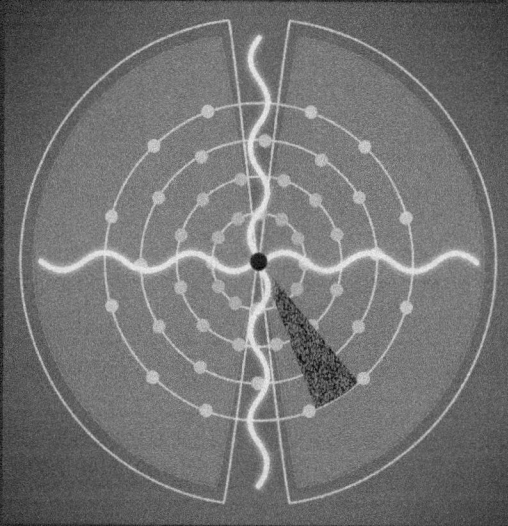

Dee Weldon Bird

Book 3- The map of the universe

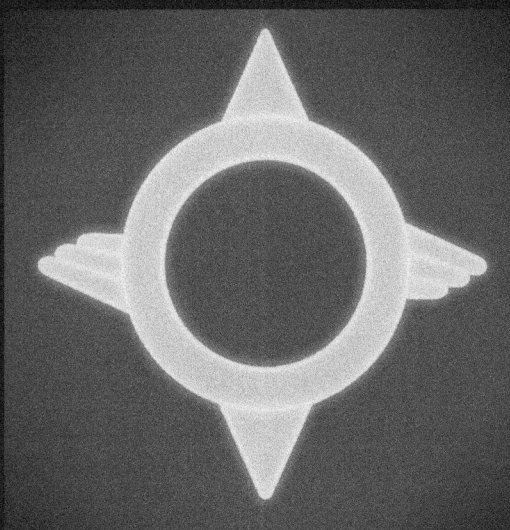

SOUL DISCLOSURE

100% Access

Dee Weldon Bird

Book 4- soul disclosure

WHERE THERE IS LOVE THERE IS NO GENDER

Understanding
Love, Sex, & Relationships

Dee Weldon Bird

Book 5 - where there is love there is no gender

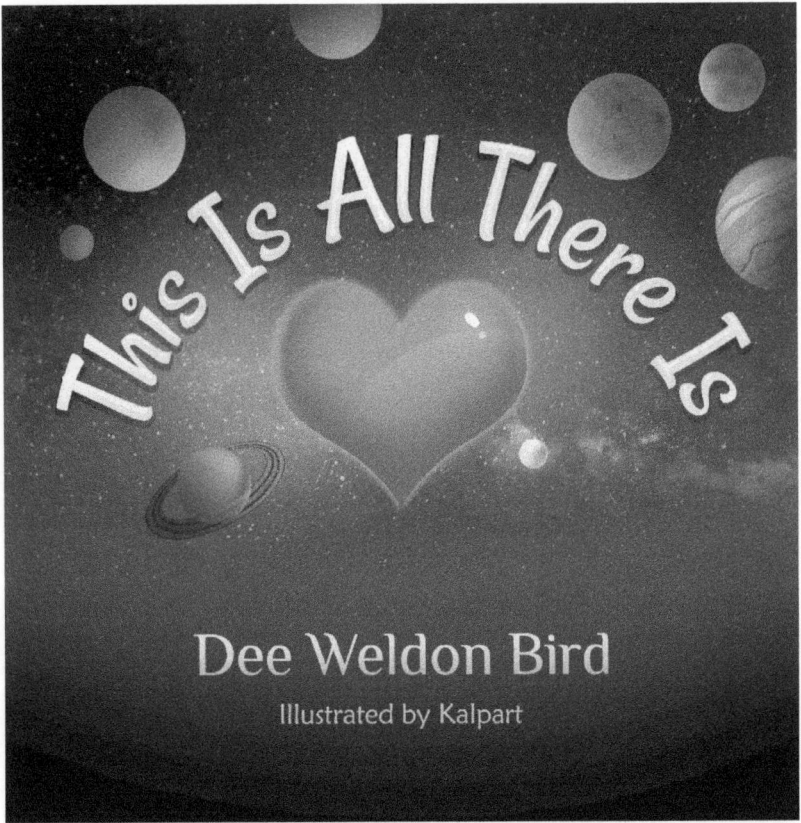

This Is All There Is

Dee Weldon Bird

Illustrated by Kalpart

Book 6 - this is all there is

I SENSE

This is all there is . . .

Dee Weldon Bird

Illustrated by Kalpart

Book 7- I sense this is all there is

My family

My four chihuahuas

My four daughters on my 50th

My half sister and niece

My parents

Recreating a picture with my four girls

With my husband

QUESTIONS BY YOU ANSWERED BY THIS UNIVERSE

(A selection taken from my Instagram page deeweldonbird_soulreader from 2023)

Q - Why do I still feel lost even though I have worked on myself?

A - You are a total soul that covers all areas of your life and not just specific problems. This depends on if you have been focusing on the external or internal. The bigger picture is different to the past. You are your own masterpiece that is never finished because as you complete chapters of your life, there is always infinitely more to explore.

Your space is your future.

Focus on you. Connect and settle into yourself.

Then you will see your future.

Q - Why does the thought of dying scare me?

A - Death is seen as an end never to be seen again. Yet death is like birth and a doorway into a new experience. Once you have completed experiencing with one form, such as your physical body, you go on to your next. There is no death, just an exit from this form. Unfortunately, humans don't remember infinity, so we fear eternity doesn't exist. When in fact you are totality itself.

Humans crave change but they can spend a lifetime preventing it.

Q - Why do I feel so anxious all the time?

A - Without looking at your soul map I can only answer generally, but it sounds like you are picking up change around you if not personally. The past is over for everyone. Life around us is uncertain while global and personal changes are being faced. This could be the reason if you want to know more, then a soul reading would give you more detail.

Capture the moments that leave a lasting impression.

Q - When someone goes through suicide was it still meant to be that way no matter what?

A - This depends on their soul map and why they chose this. If they were meant to just exit, for example, they have completed everything they set out to achieve in the physical life, but the soul has forgotten how to take their last breath, then they have chosen suicide as a way to exit. If they are not facing situations and want to exit because of this, then that's a different reason. Such a question would depend on knowing that souls map and what they chose to experience here.

Trying new things isn't just for kids. You are never too old to experience more.

Q - Why do good, kind people always come last?

A - It depends on what context you mean? Souls don't need to be first; humans do. This depends on if a soul is in service to others or self-experiencing. The soul may have chosen to experience observing or sharing. What looks like coming last to humans is actually timing and alignment. Not wasting time rushing or pushing things because the soul knows when things will align. Everyone has a soul reality and a physical reality, and both are playing side by side. If it looks like the physical reality is slow, it's often because the soul is busy with their soul reality. Quality is often more important over quantity.

Your own energy carries you through your life.

If it's a bumpy road then the path you have chosen doesn't match you. Often our problems stem from an external source rather than an internal one.

Q - Does numerology actually affect our lives or is it more down to free will?

A - The universe always guides us through our physical self so we stay in tune with our soul self. Because the physical is made up of matter the universe uses what it can to get our attention. The tools of the physical. If numerology resonates with you then you will feel the connection and it creates movement. It all boils down to connection. Everything is energy. We can attract and repel, even ourselves. So, if numerology is a way the universe can get your attention, then it will work for you. For someone else who isn't interested in it, it won't have an impact to them as a tool. The physical is full of distractions so the universe will use everything around you in your life in which to guide you and communicate with you.

If you want a happy life, then follow the fun and laughter. You won't find joy in stress.

Q - Why do we find it hard to move on from people on a soul connection?

A - The soul won't find it hard it's only the physical side that does. The soul knows we are infinitely connected but the physical thinks differently. The soul, while connected with the physical body, will at times find the physical part hard to deal with. When a soul understands the journey of the bigger picture then it is less personal, which makes it less hard. Dealing with moving on and how we manage it depends on many factors.

No one achieves on their own.

Success is teamwork.

Behind success is someone who loves creativity.

Q - Are some souls just not meant to be fertile and bring life into this world?

A - Some souls haven't chosen this as their experience. The physical creates the human body for a soul to connect with to have an experience here. If a soul hasn't chosen this on their map, they may be fertile physically speaking and may even get pregnant, but it doesn't go to term. If it's not on their map, it's not energetically meant to be. Some souls may have chosen it but at a certain age, physically speaking. If, for example, they have chosen to experience after thirty-five years, they may find they try all through their twenties and it finally happens at thirty-five-plus, which is how they set it. This is why a soul reading can be beneficial as they give you the layout of your life and what's on your map. A soul reading views the map and route that you have chosen. Just because it happens physical side it doesn't mean you have selected it. Deep down you will know. Some souls experience living with children if a partner already has them, but they don't feel the need to have their own. There are so many different reasons to this question.

Chasing your dreams in the hope of catching up to them is a long wait. YOU are your dreams. Invest in yourself, no chasing required.

Q - Why does life seem odd at the moment?

A - When you start viewing life around you more than from the view of yourself, you start to see more. When you're not preoccupied in everyday tasks and distracted, you get more of a real view because you can observe life more. Everything is changing for everyone now as we are encouraged to shift. It's a global thing, not just personal. With everyone and everything shifting life can feel odd and unsettled. Go with your gut. Listen to your soul and take each moment as it comes.

Questions are always answered by your soul. Guided by your own reflection. An answer for someone else won't fit you.

Q - When someone passes away. What determines whether they make contact after or not?

A - It depends on the connection between you. It depends on their passing events. It depends on their own personal beliefs before they passed. It depends on their character and if they are talkative. The big reason is, once they pass and let go of the physical form, they soon realise that the physical reality experience is a reflection. Returning back to their total soul reflection they soon realise that there is no separation and everyone's soul in the physical reality is still in the universe and never left. The physical only sees physical and doesn't see what the soul can see. When you see from your soul, you see that everyone is in this universe together and never left each other, regardless of where the reflection of the soul is experiencing itself in the space of this universe. You are with your loved ones, but the physical can't see it. The soul will only bother connecting here to support you this side. But if connecting won't benefit you, they won't bother because you are with them anyway.

Do you realise how unique you are?

If you did you would stop trying to fit in and be comfortable in you.

Q - Is having a child or not a destined thing? Is it up to our own free will once on Earth?

A - It's not just about having a child in the physical sense, being focused on the child and being a mum. The language of this universe will give you the reasons of why you are experiencing what you are together with your soul map. The language of this universe. I call the four elements of frequency.

Element 1: connection to self

Element 2: sharing from the self

Element 3: action, work movement

Element 4: completion

Depending on what you have chosen to experience from the four elements, your soul may want to share more from the self, which doesn't mean children but working in the communities as an example. The reasons why some have children will depend on whether it's a service to the self or to others. Encouraging sharing without losing the self-connection. Some souls deliberately choose having a child as a marker on their soul maps and other times the soul may choose it as a surprise to encourage a soul from the me, myself, and I focus to the we, us, and you perspective. There are many different reasons as to why you experience what you do. A soul reading helps you understand your path, giving you the bigger picture to where you are at on your path and what you have chosen gives you guidance to understanding your physical journey here.

Often what we think is the problem isn't the problem after all. Always look at the bigger picture.

Q - Why do the people who are meant to love you the most, hurt you the most?

A - It depends on the bigger picture and full story. The physical only sees a part of the picture. The question depends on both people's soul map. It comes down to why you are here and what you're completing or have chosen to experience. It depends on if your soul is strong enough to face the hurt because you're guiding the other person to see themselves or face themselves. This question depends on so many factors, which is why there isn't only one answer.

Tough love is still love. A soul reading gives you an expanded view of why.

The new paradigm we are in is the now.

Living in the past or future is over, energetically speaking. Live in the now and now is where it aligns. Be patient. It's coming.

Q - Does a baby still have a connection with the parents even if stillbirth happens?

A - Creating a body for a soul isn't creating a soul. The soul is already there; it's just waiting to find a body to connect with. A soul waiting to connect with a body at birth may decide they don't want to after all. For some souls the experience of pregnancy is enough. The soul visits the body growing in the womb during the nine months of pregnancy and this alone is quite an experience for a soul. A soul will always remember the experience and the parents associated with it. They are thankful that they shared the experience together. The soul does not get attached to the body they didn't connect with. The soul knows it is not the physical body, like we are not our clothes. We are so much more than the physical body we connect with. A soul that does not connect with the body will not see it as a loss because the soul is always there.

You don't have to lose yourself in anything you do whether it's collaborations or settling in with a partner. Stay in your space of you because you are amazing as you are.

Q - Can we manifest changes, or is it better to let go of control and let the soul guide us?

A - You have control over two realities. Your physical experiences and your soul reason for being here. Depending on your own unique soul map of why you are here and what your soul has chosen to experience here depends on what you experience in this physical life. If your soul wants you to use your own knowledge and experience in the physical reality, then the soul will back off and let you use your own gut. If you go off track, then your soul will kick in and guide you back to your path. If you ignore it, the soul will bring in what's available to you in your life with others. It's always wise to follow your gut, as the gut covers your physical side. Follow your feelings then your soul will guide you to your bigger picture and meaning.

The physical focuses on time and numbers. The soul focuses on energy and events.

Energy moves time. Time does not move energy. Energy moves events. Time does not move events.

Always follow your gut then you won't be limited by the schedules and expectations of time. Follow your energy through your experiences.

Q - Is it true that things that are meant for you will never pass you by?

A - What you choose to experience and happen from your soul perspective depends on if you have included a hot spot of energy associated with it. If you haven't added this on your soul map, then it will be reliant on whether you connect with it and choose it from your own energy of experience. It really depends on your own unique soul map and if external factors distort or distract you. It will be available to you, yes, but it doesn't necessarily mean that you will connect with it or choose it. It can stay as just an option.

Your future is now.

There is no use putting off what you want.

Embrace it.

Q - Why do my relationships not work out when I put so much energy into them?

A - If the relationships you're choosing don't come already self-supported and aren't able to hold themselves up, then they won't work out no matter how much energy you put into them. It's like picking a ball off the shelf that soon deflates once home, and it needs constant inflating.

Connecting with someone that matches you is what's important, rather than one that needs constant work just to be in your life. You hold the key to your life and have unlimited choice.

Choose wisely.

The physical sees losing and winning.

The soul sees experience.

Q - Could souls go straight into a new body after passing away?

A – Yes, they can. It is not so much the body. It's more to do with the reason why they are connecting straight away and with what they want to complete whilst here in the physical.

Those that have manners will succeed. Those that haven't will face obstacles.

Q - Why does grief hurt so much?

A - It hurts only from the physical perspective. The physical has been taught to see a limited view of life. The soul sees the bigger picture and does not mourn the body. The soul knows it's not the physical body. The physical can't see the soul through the physical and so therefore sees death past death and not life. The soul that passes sees everyone even those still in the physical. When souls here see souls, they will not mourn as no one leaves each other. What is mourned is a physical experience like water experiencing being frozen. When water changes it's still itself. This new paradigm will wake up the physical, so every soul remembers.

The next two years are important.

Tie up loose ends and get affairs in order.

Because the years 2026-2028 are a game changer. If you want to be in control of your life, make changes happen in the next two years.

Q - When it comes to love how do we know a soul connection? Can it change?

A - The physical runs through the brain the soul runs through feelings and connection. If you have to overthink or try, meaning just to function daily or babysit a relationship and become a detective to search for a connection, then this situation is predominantly physical. When you have a soul connection you don't have to babysit it or overthink it. You connect enough to work together in unison. So, when your relationship just works and flows, your soul connected. When you're battling each other, it's physical. It doesn't have to be perfect just more comfortable than not as the physical is still part of it. A relationship compliments you and does not pull you apart.

You can only do your best and your best is always enough.

Q - Why do I feel my life one way but in the physical it's not matching it?

A - What your soul feels and sees is often ahead of the physical. The physical has many loose ends to tie up which causes delays. When we are no longer tied up in other people's energy, we are free to then occupy fully in our own lives energetically speaking. When our energy is frayed into many pieces, we are not standing in our totality. For example, sharing your cup and leaving yourself empty. The soul urges you to stay holding your full cup and to encourage others to hold their own full cup too and to not keep taking from others to fill themselves up. That's not sharing its need. Self-responsibility comes when we can occupy and hold ourselves up. This is not to be confused with physical bodily limitations as many disabled bodies achieve above and beyond able bodies at times.

Excuses are made when we are not looking at our own reflection, which is the hardest thing to face past the physical image. This is why the physical is such a distraction. Stick to your vision and keep following your energy.

Worrying about your life is not living it. The more you relax, the more you are able to listen to your inner guidance from your soul. What's more important is trusting it over the worrying brain.

Q - Why does everything feel off?

A - If it feels off in your life you're feeling it, so it gets your attention. Observe it and try not to ignore it. Massive change is happening everywhere as we are being shifted into our own unique realities no longer fitting into other's lives. Everyone is moving into their own life.

If something feels off its because it is. Follow the energy and where it is guiding you. It can feel like everything is falling apart but really its falling into place specially for you. If you feel alone, it's because you're ready for a scene change. Often, a complete change which brings different people into alignment. The universe always connects you with what best reflects you.

If you don't like the look of your life look at yourself because it's mirrored on you. Globally we are facing the biggest shift ever that goes further than the space of this earth. Stick to your reality as you are the master of it.

How you look physically is for the physical benefit. The soul looks past how you physically look to your soul reflection. This is your true image.

Q - Are dreams always messages?

A – No, not always. Dreams cover all reasons from just visiting and catch up, to replaying your own experiences knowing its being faced at a deeper level. Dreams are a viewing window into your soul reality, the deeper side of ourselves where we are not distracted by the physical.

Stop repeating what doesn't work,

Saying what isn't your truth,

Living a lie.

Stick to the facts then your life stops being a game and becomes real.

Q - Why am I scared of ghosts?

A - We have been taught to live in fear, to live on guard, to protect ourselves and our belongings. Anything we do not understand we fear. Ghost stories, the bogey man, sandman, etc. are all fear based. From birth you are taught to be physical, and everything is focused on the physical. The soul is rarely talked about or discussed, which has become a taboo subject and made into scary stories. The truth is soul is peaceful and is none of the scary stories. What happens physical side through passed on stories is nothing like the truth of the soul. You are not going to see the truth through the physical distortion. See the truth through your soul and you will find fear doesn't exist.

Feeling lost is feeling disconnected.

Feeling disappointed is feeling impatient.

Feeling angry is not facing yourself.

Reality is an illusion until you can see yourself clearly. Then you live authentically without reaction getting in the way.

Q - Does the physical actually exist?

A – Yes, as far as the physical body in the sense of its form. Everything else about the physical doesn't exist to the soul. How souls have adapted and learnt to be physical instead of a soul reflection. It's like the story of the emperor's clothes to the soul. We are souls having a body form experience with our soul gifts. Souls that use the brain and behave like they are physical are not living an authentic life they are only following a taught script. Lots of souls will remember the real reality and get back to living a soul reality rather than this taught, nonauthentic, physical one. Souls don't need to be taught anything. This is why anything physical is taught and learned. Living a soul lifestyle is nothing like a physical one. There is no comparison. Soul living is freedom and peaceful using instinct and knowing. Physical living is limited filled with fear.

Follow your gut

Follow you!

You are the doorway to your life and future not through others.

You are what you are waiting for, and you are what's calling you.

Q - Why do you do soul readings and your work?

A - I do my work because I love the universe. It's been my home here for fifty-seven years and I want to share the magic with you. My job is not to teach you anything but to guide you back to yourself and to confirm what you already know so you trust yourself, value yourself and honour who you uniquely are. Living your authentic life will bring you inner peace and freedom. I absolutely love what I do. Every day is a gift having a front row seat when each soul shares their soul with me.

Choose you

Select you

Open doors for yourself, it leads you to your path through you.

No blame, no anxiety, just pure self-connection.

Q - Is it true when it's your time to go, it's your time?

A - This depends on your reason for being here. We all have good intentions, but we can also give up and not see things through. It depends on if the circumstances around you support what you want to achieve here. It also depends on your physical body too. No one dies, but we can let go and decide to continue when circumstances align better. There are so many factors involved as to why we exit when we do but your soul map will hold your answers.

A comfortable and settled life does not mean it's lacking in excitement. A fairground full of rides is exciting, but we visit it for a day and wouldn't choose it to live in it.

See the benefit of a settled, calm and comfortable relationship and add the excitement to it.

Q - Why do you do soul map readings rather than traditional readings connecting with passed relatives?

A - I did the traditional way for twenty-five years but because of the shift in 2018 the world needed something more. Something deeper. Each person here is a soul and not a physical person. What you thought was life you will soon remember it isn't. To adapt to the truth and to step out of the physical script after many centuries here. There is little focus here on the soul and it's mostly all about the physical body. The soul is alive. Your physical experience would not exist without your soul. Usually, you would have a life review once you exit here, when you take your last breath. You're having access to your soul maps because the physical script is now over. Everyone is having a life review. For some they will exit but for others they cross my path because they are staying and need their maps to follow now. Not the script taught to them by the physical as this will no longer serve them.

Your legacy won't be how much money you have, as it won't stay. It won't be your portfolio because that will go too.

What stays is your connection, what you love and shared with others, your meaning and depth. Impacting others comes from you if it is infused with your energy.

Your energy is your signature frequency. If your life doesn't come with your energy, then your life is just a life of accumulated stuff.

Q - Does my soul view my life in the same way as I see it physically?

A – No, it doesn't. The physical reality is taught and doesn't exist energetically in the same way to the soul. The physical reality is taught with rules and fear. The soul reality is known using instinct. Teaching a life isn't the same as living soul. How the physical sees things is often in reaction and blame or right and wrong. To the soul this doesn't exist and is purely experience. The physical way of life up until 2018 is like the film *The Truman Show* and the story of the emperor's clothes to the soul. To the physical taught humans, it looks real and convincing through repetition memory and it's convincing because everyone is living like it. The soul lives in the now whereas the physical taught way lives in the past and future. The soul knows that there is only the now. This is why a soul will never live like a taught human.

When you feel your totality, you feel complete in yourself and know nothing is missing in you, you then share with others without relying on them.

Self-sufficiency is self-mastery. Your connection internally is the key to your foundation. If you need others to fill a gap, then you're still mastering yourself. This is element number one of the language of the universe.

Q - Why do I find it hard to be understood in the physical?

A - Communication is made difficult in the physical taught reality. This is often because what is real is rarely faced and avoiding the truth is not an authentic life. The soul can't hide or lie, yet humans live a life of pick 'n' mix that is not consistent enough to flow in a committed connection. Repeating patterns isn't how souls live. The universe always moves. Humans get stuck in the past, which causes miss understanding and no movement.

If you are still busy catching up with yourself and growing into yourself, then relationships will not be your priority.

If you have settled into yourself, then you will be ready to be comfortable in a relationship and commit to it.

Q - Why can't I see my life ahead? I feel unmotivated.

A - It can be for a number of reasons surface side that got you to this point. But underneath it will be because you are energy charging or strengthening your connection with yourself. For example, like a mobile phone without a charged battery, it doesn't work. The same goes for us. If we are feeling flat, we need charging. There is no action if there is no connection or charge. It's how the language of this universe works. Connection to self, feel your vibe, then action.

You're not going to see your life now if your head is stuck in the past or the future.

Get in the now.

Q - Why is it that no matter what I do life situations hold me back?

A - Whether it's stuff or others holding you back, your soul has no preference as it all boils down to energy. Everything flows by energy and not by money. You can't buy a connection; it's either there or it isn't. Yes, you can physically turn up, but it doesn't mean that your energy is present in it. Tuning into yourself is the only station you require and the one you have. Anything else is background noise. Stay focused on you then your life will mirror you. If your focus is off, then what you are focusing on will often not match you. The universe works in pairs starting with you. If your energy doesn't match your intentions, then your intentions won't manifest.

If time stopped, if your diary stopped, if money stopped, who would you be?

You have lived in a created life served for you. You have followed a script your soul did not choose. Listen to your soul. Who are you?

Q - Does trauma exist?

A – No, it doesn't to the soul. There is only one reality and that's the soul one. The human body does not work without a soul. What physical people view as trauma is memory recall. If an experience is going to be challenging, then the soul spaces out from the experience. Leaving just the body to it. This is why a challenging event is often remembered up to the event and after it and not during it. It is then pieced together by witnesses. This is why trauma does not exist to the soul. Everything is experience but the physical side of you holds on to it in memory. Trauma is another word for not letting go and moving on. Living in the past relies on memory. You only live in the now whether the past gets in the way or not.

We have everything within us to face our life with no faffing, no mind games and no excuses. Just in the now to live, to laugh and to enjoy.

Q - Where do we go when we die?

A - We are in the universe. We never left. Our soul is at what I call point zero, the hub if you like, of this universe. When we choose to experience our totality, we reflect our soul into space around point zero. Think of a light bulb: it doesn't leave the lamp, but it reflects the light. Our souls do the same. When we have chosen what we want to experience, we reflect ourselves like torches and experience what we have chosen without having to leave point zero. Once we have finished our experiences, we move on by bringing our energy back in, like switching off a torch, back to point zero. When that part of our energy is back at point zero, we remember that we never left, and every soul is at point zero. This is why there is no loss in the universe and only experience.

The next four years, 2024-2028, is going to be like fifty-two-card pickup for some. For others everything will fall into place. To have stability you must tune in to yourself. Focus on what you are doing and everything else is just background noise.

It's about being tuned in, listening to yourself and not being distracted by others.

Q - Can people get taken over by dark energy unless we protect ourselves?

A - Your soul is infinitely protected by space. There is space around every soul in this universe. Your space has your frequency within it. No other soul can enter your space because they are not you. Think of radio stations, each station is unique, tuning out of a station into another causes distortion until you connect with one station of itself. You can reflect and see reflection and get as close to the space around each frequency. But it's still reflection. In the physical much of the frequencies are distortion physical side. The physical does not exist without a soul. There is space around the physical frequency too. A different reality. Between the two frequencies you are the master of both. It is your own self responsibility of what you focus on or believe or reflect. Souls are infinite and can experience whatever it wishes. No limits.

You are free to connect with whatever gets your attention. Like anything, if we are not conscious, we can be open to anything. But it will still be reflection.

If you struggle with being connected in your life, it's not the connection with the external things, it's the connection with yourself.

Q - Can childhood trauma block the physical from being fully connected to their soul?

A - The physical body is 100 percent connected to the soul via the breath. The soul only needs the breath as a basic connection. To have an experience with the body it needs to fully connect with the body. It does not have to be a childhood trauma for a soul not to experience its potential. It could be disassociation towards the body itself as it's so different compared to being a soul energy. Children pre-2018 up to the age approximately of twelve are total soul, during those twelve years they learn how to be physical. This is why children cope very well to what is termed trauma. Often, to the child, it's an unpleasant experience but they use their soul more as a shield to face it. Souls know how much they can experience. During what is termed trauma, a human will often remember up to the trauma/event and after it is finished.

The soul itself does not experience pain. So, the soul transfers all its energy to its soul self, leaving the physical like an empty vessel, but connected with the soul via the breath. Think of it like taking yourself out of your clothes. The body experiences it but your soul energy will observe it. Often during accidents, it can feel like slow motion because the soul transfers from the physical reality to its soul reality. Think of it like switching radio stations. The soul understands everything, but the difficulty often happens due to translation. The physical views things in a limited way and so therefore misses much of the bigger picture. A challenging situation can cause repetitive pauses and habitual survival skills to avoid facing all of it. Souls have infinite possibilities so therefore the physical side can play the joker or hide and seek. It depends on the full story as to why a soul is either stuck on the past or whether they have lost interest. It often can be because a soul is waiting until the physical body is a certain age before it accesses more. This is why knowing your soul map gives you a clearer picture.

Forget PMA (positive mental attitude). The next four years, 2024-2028, moving forward is all about connection. Forget thoughts they mean nothing. It's all about connection now. What you connect with stays. If there is no connection, it moves away.

Q - My dear mum passed away ten years ago. How can I meet her soul?

A - You are with each other always. Connection is connection. Meeting up often happens when the body sleeps. If connecting won't affect your life, then it happens when you need support.

Every soul is connected in this universe there is no urgency to meet up physically speaking because your souls are already together now. The physical is like a different station and doesn't pick up on the meet up between souls.

Sometimes stripping back your life and starting as you mean to go on is what is needed, even if it's not what you want.

Q - Will the world ever become a more peaceful place?

A - Yes. Since 2018, the earth's space got its resonance signature frequency. The shift, as its often called. When it was just space some souls decided to create what I call the Truman show, as an example from the film. A fake reality to the soul which didn't match, and this is why lots of distortion has been experienced in the fear mongering, taught and rule using existence. This is why lots of fighting occurred. Souls when they arrived here could not be soul. They were encouraged from babies to learn the physical script, the physical way of life. It is not the soul way of living. Since 2018 it has switched from physical back to soul, and this is why lots of change is happening around us personally and globally since then. This will continue until 2056, when transfer from physical to soul here is complete. Every soul will live soul. The script will not even be a memory. It will be like it never existed. This earth's space will be peaceful. Rather than waiting until 2056 to see the completion, focus on yourself and create a peaceful connected life for yourself now because you can.

We are like a seed.

First, a seed enters its space.

It's alone. It's still. It's quiet. It's patient.

To manifest anything, this comes first.

Once in our zone we then manifest our self – roots known as self-connection.

Once rooted, we then share from our space.

It's from here that we manifest and bear fruit.

We don't stop being in our zone.

A seed that has grown into a hundred-year-old tree is where it started a hundred years on, in its zone and space. Hold your space like a hundred-year-old tree.

Q - How to attract more good people and wealth into our lives, does soul decide this?

A - Yes, your soul has decided what it wants to experience here. If the physical taught script has distracted you, then it is about your connection with yourself, with your soul, without being physically distracted. The more you connect with yourself and honour your truth and how you feel by being honest with yourself, you will attract the same reflection. This universe works in pairs.

Honour what you are feeling. If you are tired, rest rather than forcing yourself to move.

If you are hungry eat, but don't if not.

Drink if thirsty, but don't if not. Follow these basics then your life has foundation. Everything else will fall into place the more you follow your own energy. If you feel it, go with it, if you don't, don't.

Q - Why do kind people die of accidents and disease?

A - It's because they have forgotten how to take their last breath and need help. It doesn't matter how you behave here. If you have forgotten how to take your last breath, you will be helped. If you remember how do it, then you won't need help with letting go of your body. This is why sudden death syndrome is a mystery, but it isn't if you know how souls work.

Enjoy having fun with those you love without technology distracting you.

Q - What happens if we don't like what our soul has chosen to experience?

A - The film, *The Truman Show*, or how I call it now the Truman human reality since up to 2018, has been a taught, scripted reality, often full of distractions and hopes and wishes, making us want to try harder to achieve what we think we want. However, your soul knows the bigger picture and will encourage you to experience what matches your chosen reason and meaning.

Often humans do not listen to their gut and soul and stay focused only on the brain of memory. So sometimes your soul needs to give your physical self a wakeup call to shift you to your truest direction. It is not always easy to get human's attention because of the many distractions in the physical, so it may take an experience that is impacting to do so. The human element may not like it, but the soul is always thankful and sees the bigger picture.

Some of your meaningful moments and memories are happening right now. You just won't realise it until playback. So, stay in the moment as much as you can and enjoy the now.

Q - Why do I feel lost and lonely when I have wonderful people around me? It's so confusing.

A - When we connect with our body at the birth and when we take our first breath, we come without any physical stuff or belongings. We do come here with our gifts, skills and our character and personality in our soul. This is what I call your soul suitcase. Everyone starts with themselves and visits everyone when they are introduced to others the longer you are here. Time creates memories pre-2018, but not always beneficial connections. Often, when living with others, we lose the sense of self that we came here with. We become new names or labels through external choices, but it doesn't mean you have to lose yourself.

If you are not feeling a connection or don't want to do something, own it. People pleasing is over; communication and holding your own is. We all have our own unique souls which should be respected. If you have to say no, it's not a rejection. It doesn't mean you don't care for others. It means you're self-caring in that moment. Saying yes doesn't mean a yes for everything.

Variety is the spice of life. Allow everyone to live from their space to maintain self while visiting you in the space you share together. Space is healthy when understood.

You do you. Let others do them.

Space is a gift, so everyone gets a look in.

No groups, no trends, just be in your zone.

Q - How do we live in the new paradigm, the now and as souls?

A - When you are willing to face yourself totally and accept all of you, then you will be ready to let go of the physical taught script lifestyle that's been handed down over the centuries. Unlearn what you have been taught, switch to trusting you and your knowing, and use this as your compass. Follow your feelings and not your brain. Give your brain back to your body. Trust your feelings and your guidance. This is your vibe and matches you. Your path will be clearer because you will be self-focused and then ready to share from you with others doing the same.

There will always be someone else doing the same thing as you. Same job, same career, same style business, but it's what you bring to the table that makes it unique. There will always be other creators, but there will never be another creator like you.

Q - In this next paradigm, what will we notice around us?

A - From 2018-2056, what will be noticed is yourselves catching up with yourself. The physical way of living is over. You will review what connects with you the most rather than living from memory and the brain. Feelings will rise for some in confusion and frustration with feeling unsettled in life and for others feeling of calm and settlement if aware of your soul. The landscape will change, and the atmosphere is changing. Every soul is turning up the volume.

Going back to instinct and gut, you may even see your domesticated pets showing instinct traits. Souls will be seen and not overshadowed by the body. Everything that hasn't been a soul way of life is dissolving. Truth will trump deceit. There will be fun and laughter over need. Commitment and consistency in energy over fear. Living a quality authentic life will build strong foundations. Unlearning the physical script and remembering your own soul language.

Change is everywhere. Nature, air, land and self.

The physical, to me, is an outdated recording of stored memory.

This isn't the same as soul and living in the now. Are you living in the physical or soul?

Q - What is soul destroying to the soul?

A - Everything is energy, and this universe works in pairs in harmony. Often humans mix with other humans causing stress. Humans look at the external, what they ingest or topically use missing the internal cause. Energy. If you mix with humans that make you feel less than yourself, stressed and worn down, this is what makes you ill. You can even turn energetically on yourself, matching what you receive and pick at yourself. If you don't boost your energy, then you are depleting yourself. This is what causes illness at an energy level. Choose who you mix with carefully, so you live in energy that is peaceful and in harmony.

Soul gifts are never taught.

They are given space and encouraged to grow.

Organic talent comes from your space.

Q - Why does an infinite soul choose to connect with a body that doesn't last long?

A - The soul is always infinite choosing to express itself through its chosen experiences. Like we choose to wear many different items of clothing, the soul connects with the physical body to experience more than energy but to experience energy in a different form. As long as the soul knows that the physical body will be able to assist with the experiences that the soul has chosen then the years are not the issue.

The soul is the fountain of youth. The more soul running through the physical body the longer the connection in years is possible. The soul decides when taking the first breath as well as letting go with the last breath. If the soul can work with the body for its experiences, then the soul will connect until the experience has been utilised. If the soul feels this isn't possible, then the soul will choose to let go of the body.

If you're feeling flat, your life is waiting for you to self-inflate it. If you're waiting, it's because your life is waiting for you to take the lead.

Like an orchestra follows the conductor, you are the compass that life will now follow.

Q - Does dying hurt?

A – No, it doesn't to the soul. The physical body does not exist without the soul. Like a piano doesn't play any sounds until you press the keys. The human body has nerves, but if the soul has no contact with them then the nerves are not felt. The soul only needs the connection of the breath to be connected to the physical body at this basic level. Anything more than this depends on where the soul energy is flowing. This is why pain is not felt during an accident. You are often aware up to the accident and after it but not during. If your soul feels to experience it, then it will. It's the soul's choice on how much it experiences. The closer to death or passing you get, the more your soul flows through the soul and not so much through the physical body. This is why someone can look vacant behind the eyes before they pass. It's because the soul is already vacating. The soul does not experience pain. If the soul chooses to experience it, then it will connect with it.

Look back and see how beautiful you have been and how amazingly wonderful you are now. Give yourself some self-love and self-appreciation.

Q - Why do kids have imaginary friends?

A - Children are pure soul, connected to this universe totally. They haven't switched from pure soul to being physical. It takes a pure soul approximately twelve years to learn how to be human. Adults see human, physical children but they actually have pure soul children until the children are taught to live physically. This is why children and animals see souls, not the imaginary friends as the physical would call it and why humans only see humans. Past 2018, souls arriving here will use their souls and not learn the human script.

In the old paradigm, pre-2018, money could buy you a life. Not anymore.

In this new paradigm, post-2018, connection builds your life. Follow the connection in everything. If there is no connection, let it go.

Q - Why is being on earth so hard and a battle at times?

A - You came to earth 100 percent soul with nothing physical about you. You connected with your physical body, using it for your chosen experiences here. The physical image is all you see. Learning the physical way created the illusion that you are a physical body. You are not. You are a soul. For example, your clothes to the physical body are not you. They are just an extra layer.

Trying to be something you are not hard work and exhausting. The physical teachings do not match your soul. This is the battle limiting your space to be free inexpression. The more you let go of the physical teachings the more you will be back to yourself, and your life will flow through you rather than against you. If you are not in alignment, then your life won't be. Set your life up to match you then you can get on with your life in peace. A teaching way of life isn't a knowing gut one.

Mirroring others and tagging along isn't living your chosen life. Just because others are, have or are doing, doesn't mean it's going to be enough for you and match you. If you tag on to things you may start off pouring your energy into it but eventually it goes flat.

Choose your life. Choose you and follow your choice then you won't feel flat at the end of it.

Following in the footsteps of others will not leave your own footprint.

Q - Can a soul map change?

A - It can depending on if a soul has set their soul map with markers. Some souls create their maps as they go. The maps are changing now anyway because the shift we are in alters everyone as we are living in the now rather than the past, moving away from relying on a taught reality to a knowing one. The more we come into our own the more our maps are revealed to us. It's more about how you connect with yourself that sets your map.

Having space is often perceived as rejection.

When we need some self, one-on-one space, honour it. Whether you are the one choosing some space or another, it means some self-connection is wanted. Communicate clearly why you want space. A soul connection won't lose touch because of space. Inner connections stay without being in physical external contact. Connections that run deep stay rooted regardless of what is going on above the surface. Trust your connections and honour space.

Q - How can I receive guidance and information from my soul? Can I ask for signs?

A – Yes, you can ask for signs. You may not get the guidance when you want it, but you will when you're ready for it. It is all about timing and it depends on the energy around situations.

Always listen to your gut and feelings. If you feel nothing, then nothing for now is what's happening. It's often hard waiting and sitting with nothing but if that's what's needed then allow this space. If you search for things in your mind, then your mind is being impatient. Going with the flow can be frustrating at times, but by doing so, then what is meant to connect with you will. Filling your life up with events that just relieve patience isn't productive. It creates experiences just to fill the time.

Try to trust the process for your path. It doesn't mean nothing is happening when you're waiting. It gives you the chance to strengthen the connection with yourself or a chance to process what you have already done so far. When you're ready for the next chapter in your life, your soul will guide you. Being still within your life allows everything to flow towards you. Being erratic and not settled creates distortion. For example, when you want to catch a ball, you stand still and focus, being all over the place means you're more than likely to miss opportunities.

Trust yourself. Trust your journey. Trust your soul. There is no point in comparing because every soul is unique.

Do you match what you want?

You may know what you want but wonder why it's not happening in your life. The universe works in pairs. If you don't feel good enough or worthy, then you won't be matching what you love. Always look at your reflection to what you want in your life. You will see what matches you and what doesn't. If you are picking at yourself and giving yourself a hard time, then your external reality will match just that.

Be what you want so that what you want pairs up with you.

Q - What happens if I do not follow my soul's path?

A - If you choose not to follow your path then you will be filling time with your day-to-day. Your soul will always try to get your attention. But if you choose to ignore it then what you experience here will be surface stuff and not registered on your soul map, like being asleep but living on memory autopilot. What you don't face or experience on your soul map this time around you get a chance to again.

When you are waiting for things to happen in life, it's usually because you are waiting for those that are going to cross your path or what you are waiting for is waiting for you. Are they free to cross you at this moment? Are you?

Just because you are physically free doesn't mean you are emotionally free from the past.

Are you so used to giving to others that you're struggling to receive? It may not be so much about the thing you are waiting for but your ability to welcome it and receive it in that moment. Are you ready? It is one thing saying you are but another meaning it.

Q - I have been feeling like the earth's vibes are off lately. What is going on?

A - The earth's frequency has been getting stronger since the earth's shift in 2018. Since January 2024, the energy is stronger. Globally, in the next four years, we will see the biggest changes ever. Each soul is coming into their own, becoming their authentic, dialled in self, rather than playing out many versions that actually don't match them or limits them – tuning in to connection rather than memory autopilot living. It's like we are in an energetic lockdown as each soul tunes into themselves, major shift and major sorting out. This is why everything feels up and down and lacking foundation and movement. The more you face yourself in your reality the more stable and settled you will feel.

If you define your life by labels and age, then you are setting yourself up for a limited life.

Q - How can we attract more good souls in our lives?

A - Stay in your own vibe and space. Know your boundaries and choose who you want in your life. Often, we put up with others because they have crossed our path without actually choosing them. Know what you want. Get to know the content of others. As the body can cover up a lot. If they match you, then you will vibe and being around them will flow. If it's hard work and buffering, then something is off. They may not be tuned into themselves very well. You will be surprised how many people/souls don't know themselves very well. They will be encouraged to do so over the next four years. If you feel it go for it. If you don't then don't. The more you are tuned in to you the more you will attract what matches you. It all boils down to choice. Choose what connects with you.

The choices you made yesterday do not define you today.

Variety is the spice of life. It's okay to change it.

Q - What does infinity mean?

A - Infinity in this universe means that everything exists. There is no waiting in this universe. It is all there instantly, infinitely every possibility. The only difference with the physical is waiting for you to connect with it and realise it.

Silence

Q - Does past life reflect in your current life?

A - It depends. Whatever you have chosen to experience in the past, if complete, won't roll on to this life. If you haven't completed it, then it will roll on to here. Even if completed, you may have the past so ingrained that the challenge is letting go to create a new experience. The past will be there when we first arrive to help us carry on from where we left off, but some souls complete in such a detailed way that they arrive without any distractions from themselves or others. Your soul knows exactly why you are here and what you're doing. The physical side may not want to know as the physical is busy learning the physical ways. The physical taught reality isn't a soul one.

Don't panic if you see or feel ahead but then not. Or if you feel connected in your life one minute, then not. We are in the midst of flowing change for everyone. Don't worry about what others are doing. Focus on what your soul shows you. This is your reality after all. You may even find yourself feeling all sorts of emotions. Ride each second of each day. Try not to preempt. Be open to welcoming your next moment. It's not about juggling your life now it's more about balancing and steadying it.

Q - How do I know if I am doing the right thing?

A - To the soul, there is no wrong/right, good or bad. It's all experience. The choices you make and what you select depend on the connection that you have with yourself. You are base number one, if you like. If you're not in alignment with your base and ignore yourself then decisions are often influenced by others more, meaning you will be making a choice based on others over the base of yourself. If you feel the connection to your choices, and you don't have to think about them but face it and get on with it, then this reflects it is working for you. If you are questioning things, then it's not quite aligning with you and is a work in progress. If you feel it, go with it. If you don't, then address it. If in doubt, let it go and trust your gut.

Breathe - Drink - Eat – Rest

Souls love to move and be creative.

If you feel physically stuck and hitting a wall, then you have pent up soul energy not going anywhere apart from the above, breathe, drink, eat, rest.

If you notice you're doing this then you are moving out of the physical repeat and entering your foundation of soul and doing the bare basics. You are creating yourself. Try not to see yourself as doing nothing as you are charging, getting ready for your own creativity. Keep going with breathing, eating, drinking, rest. Once you are done you will use your stored energy for what you have been waiting for. You will be ready.

Q - Hi Dee, what is our purpose on this planet? All we do is eat, breathe, work, work?

A - Before each soul comes to earth, they would have met up with someone like me to go over their soul map. There is a lot going on behind the scenes of the physical. Breathing is the connection between the soul and the physical body. Just having an experience with the physical body energetically is an experience in itself, like an astronaut wearing the space suit. Energetically the physical body is dense because of the energy of the physical, taught way of life. It wasn't always as heavy as it is now.

This is why in the beginning here souls could connect with the physical body for say five hundred years at a time. Everything was much bigger including human form, say approximately up to eighteen feet tall. So human reality compared to the soul reality has shrunk. Quite a challenge in itself. So breathing is the window to your soul, the doorway. The physical body needs food for cell regeneration and sleep for energy charging. If a soul chooses to copy the physical taught way of life and follow this, then it will feel like Groundhog Day and boring and all work and no fun.

It depends on your soul map as to why you are experiencing what you are and if you are on track or not. When you follow your soul, you connect with what you enjoy and then it doesn't feel like work. It may look like work but it's not. The purpose of being here is because it's part of this universe. Some souls, pre-2018, came to hide. Some souls bridged the gap between the past and the future for now. Some souls helped other souls to see their true reflection and not the physical limiting taught one. Always follow your gut and instinct then you will feel more in your reality. This is what each soul wants to be, at home and connected to their reality in this universe.

The shift on earth is huge because it's not just happening to earth's space.

Locations around earth's space are going through a shift too. This is causing an extra wobble here. If you are connected with other bilocations, as well as here, then you will be extra affected by this shift. It is not just about this earth's space. Take into consideration the totality within this universe.

Q - How can we protect ourselves from negative energies and negative attacks?

A - The soul does not need protecting because of space around each soul. This universe isn't a place, and earth does not have a physical address. This universe is space. We each occupy space for our experiences. Earth is made up of souls called earth. The maps of earth have changed with the souls. It's pliable and moveable/fluid. Not stuck like labels or names. Each soul has their own signature frequency, and this universe is infinite signature frequencies. Like a

TV or radio, it doesn't matter how many stations there are. You can listen to them and see them all because of space around each frequency. As soon as you tune out of your frequency, you meet in-between frequencies which causes distortion. You may hear a bit of one station and another depending on what the connection is. Space prevents you from being in another's station.

You only have your own unique frequency, and space keeps you in your reality. You can see the other souls around you, and you can hear them, but you only have access to your space, and you bring your space and your frequency to each event you connect with in space. Like you can listen to each station on many gadgets at the same time. The physical forgets this and doesn't see space as their safe place. This is why it is filled with stuff and materials to feel safe. You can still not feel safe even in highest security. Own your space and feel the connection. Understand the universe.

If you are struggling to tune in when normally you have no problem, it's because the frequency of Earth is playing louder.

We are encouraged to tune into this frequency and get aligned with it. This frequency surge is causing the distortion of tuning in. It means tuning in has to be more focused and dialled in. You could say, the connection requires a deeper connection.

If you're not picking up much, it's because each soul is aligning with earth. Souls are busy with this rather than reflecting their path in life. The focus now is how strong your connection to self is. This goes for everyone.

Q - How do we get out of a rut?

A – First, acknowledge it. Avoid fighting it or reacting to it. Sometimes doing nothing is a place to start as this gives you a chance to observe the situation, obviously depending on what's going on. Wanting to change a rut gives motivation and encouragement. When you are ready, you know as it's amazing how much souls can put up with. If you're playing the same words over and over, that's all you will hear and repeat.

Silence to actually hear your guidance without the mind getting in the way helps change. Trusting and committing to any new choices to follow through with what you mean. Even if you're scared it means you are ready. Make changes manageable ones rather than overwhelming. If change forces your hand, you are equipped to handle it. Access your experience and knowledge so you can use it as your tools. The more you access yourself the more connection you have with yourself and the stronger and more in control you will feel. This will all start you off on your new adventures and it's wise to keep going and not look back.

What version of you is playing right now?

Since 2018, and especially from this January onwards for the next four years, our souls are encouraging us to align with ourselves. It is all about the self now.

For centuries many have been living a different life to the authentic one.

Living a lie, acting out a life that doesn't match them. The sooner you self-align, the quicker your life will move in the direction you know you want.

Q - What do you think signs mean? Such as numbers, robins, feathers, etc.?

A - The physical has many tools that are used to guide, support and encourage a soul while here. When a soul switches off from transmitting and receiving through their own soul frequency, then this universe will use what is around you to get your attention in the physical. Often contact happens when you're relaxed or snoozing or when you go to sleep. When you're tuning out of the physical and over to your soul self the window opens for communication and contact. When a soul is distracted in the physical then it's harder to communicate with you. For example, you can't listen to Kiss FM on the magic soul radio station. They are two different stations.

If you need guidance or support, reassurance and encouragement, what resonates with you will be the very thing that gets your attention to get in contact with you. Soul to soul, like in the way that we send text messages to one another, you may receive synchronistic messages in the form of numbers or feathers and robins, etc., confirming that you are heard, seen and known in this universe and not alone.

Your conscience, your morals, your heart, is your soul compass. If you choose to not listen to these, then you will be reliant on a physically taught script of memory. If you want to be free from limitation, then listen to and follow your soul. You have a choice.

Your soul is waiting for you.

Q - Is our highest self at the top of our evolution or can we keep going? Is there no limit?

A - Your soul is an infinite soul. It is already total. There are five universes. In this universe you master the four elements of frequency, the language of this universe, through your experiences. This universe is like a banquet with every infinite possibility available. It's already there. Hence, why I have often said just because you can't see it physically it doesn't mean it's not there.

Connection is key to what you experience. Not luck. What you choose to focus on, you connect with and experience from the infinite banquet of choice. This universe waits on you. Once you have mastered everything here under the four elements of frequency, you then go on to the next universe to that infinite banquet of possibilities to experience. Your soul is total. It's what you choose to experience that gives you variety of experience infinitely. Your wealth of knowledge of experience and understanding expands. For example, you are still you whether you are two years old or eighty, it's your experiences that change with your body and reflections of others around you.

There is only one you.

You will never find another you.

You are so rare and unique in the whole universe. That's how special you are.

302

Honour you and appreciate you then you connect with yourself in love and self-acceptance. Be comfortable in you and if you're not then find your comfort zone so you can be.

Q - Do souls that have lived in human form and make mistakes or cause severe pain to others, apologise to those they inflicted on when physical life passes, and they meet again?

A - The physical does not view in bigger picture form and mainly views in wrong, right, or good or bad. There are so many layers to life experiences. An apology will arise by the physical when they have not viewed a situation in bigger picture view, once they view totality then they may want to apologise. Souls know the full picture like a jigsaw puzzle. The physical views pieces without connecting the dots, creating conclusions based on one image. Many life scenes are the endings of previous life scenes and the physical viewing it comes in at the end not having seen the previous story to it.

You cannot hurt a soul as a soul will attract what it needs and not react like the physical. So, from the physical-only perspective you may want an apology, but once you view the scene from the soul bigger picture you will realise no apology is needed. The soul is always in control and superior to the physical. The physical does not exist without the soul. Therefore, everyone is soul and not human only experiencing the body in form. Everyone knows each other in the universe and knows each scene is purely experience. We never left this universe. Here is only a reflection of our chosen experiences.

Have you created a wall for yourself without realising it? The wall you created during challenging experiences so you can protect yourself when feeling scared or fearful. It's an energy of protection in the space around you. If you feel stuck in the same reactions and limitations, then face your wall.

When an opportunity arises of what you want, you will be facing that opportunity behind your energy wall. You can either use the wall and knock the opportunity back or get through your wall by not reacting with it like a shield but instead focus on the opportunity and choose to connect with it.

Then you will have got over yourself and set yourself free from your wall.

You don't need it anymore to feel safe.

You are safe in you.

Q - Will racism or division always exist, or will it get better?

A - Everyone has a choice on how they live. Labels, opinions and judgements are physically made. The physical does not exist without a soul; hence, when we take our last breath, the physical body no longer works. Everyone is now switching from physical to soul. Living soul has no need for labels and judgements.

Over the next four years from 2024 major change is occurring. The physical is over, and all labels are fading. Living a quality life in depth and meaning will grow a connected lifestyle rather than a divided one.

You have chosen you to experience your total infinite knowing. You are your path, your satnav and compass.

If you can't face yourself and walk side by side with yourself, then you will be stuck on the spot repeating the things you don't want. You are everything you need, and this is why there is no need to search. Others and your surroundings distract you from yourself. Focus on and connect to you then you open the door to what you really want.

Q - How can you know if you're living in the right location? How do you find where to be for the best life?

A - It depends on your soul map and what you have set for yourself. It depends on your four element of frequency chord. If you feel unsettled and life around you isn't slotting together, often things fall apart because your soul knows you're not meant to settle where you are. Your soul, your gut, your feeling deep down will always guide you. You may just know. Once you know and open up to it rather than resist it, you will pick up the hunch that you're meant to move, but don't know where, you can sit in the knowing for a bit. This is often enough to strengthen your connection to change incoming. When you're ready your soul will guide you more into making active choice to implement it. Sometimes you get things to pop up in your familiar life to see if you continue what you have completed energetically or pick you and start your new reality. It's not a test of right or wrong. It reflects how ready you are for change.

You chose your physical body. Love it. Appreciate it. You are connected to it for such a short time. Your body ages but your soul doesn't. You will feel just as you at eighty as you did eighteen. Enjoy your body; it serves your lifestyle. Once you take your last breath you won't experience with this particular body again. So enjoy it. Embrace it. It serves you.

Be comfortable with it. Be friends with it.

It's not for long you're with it. When you look back from fifty-seven plus, you will see how quickly it goes. It seems forever from sixteen plus, but it flies.

Enjoy you and enjoy the body you chose.

Q - Is everybody's future on a fixed path?

A - Some souls have made specific choices before they arrived here. Some are creating as they go. Every soul path is unique to each soul. Some have completed and are enjoying here as if on holiday. There are many reasons as to why we are here. This is why soul readings guide you back to yourself. The physical surface is often a distraction to your real reason for being here.

Social media gets more energy than face to face. If we aren't already living in a simulation, social media is creating it as a reality. Don't forget what's in front of you face-to-face. Not screen to screen.

Q - When someone passes does their soul still continue to have a connection with people here?

A - In this universe every soul is connected. The space of this universe gives every soul their own space to experience their reality. Every soul knows each other and is connected in this universe, although they may not be connected in chosen experiences. You have the space to not interact with souls that do not aid your experience. But in the bigger picture view like looking at a completed jigsaw puzzle, if one piece went missing it would notice on the puzzle. Every soul is noticed, visible and heard. Every soul is connected as it's completed infinite backdrop. It's a choice whether staying in contact in experience is required. It depends on what each soul has chosen to experience and where that path takes them.

Space allows everyone to experience who they independently are, so you grow into yourself without the need to copy others.

Space is infinite as you are.

Q - When someone passes, do they have a life review and see the path their life could have taken?

A - Souls are infinite and recognise infinite. Yes, every soul has a life review. Especially if souls have had their view clouded by the physically taught way of life. Many souls have had physical life situations and circumstances created from the physical fear that is limited. You're taught to copy your way through life. That kind of physical lifestyle fills time but often will not touch anything on the soul's path. Living a taught, dictated life is like coming with your soul map and ignoring it, so when you pass and have a life review, you will see that you kept busy but have done none of the things your soul set out to do and instead filled your time with scripts. Your soul does not need a script to follow from the physical. You have your own soul map while you are here and your gut follows it well, trust it. If you follow the mind, then you're not on your soul path.

MORE QUOTES

(These additional quotes are also from my Instagram page, deeweldonbird_soulreader.)

I, me and you, only references one part of you, usually the physical part, when really it is we that we should remember.

The physical does not work without the soul.

When the soul connects with the physical body at the first breath, it creates a 'we' relationship between the physical and soul totally. When the physical leaves out the soul it becomes just, I - me - you.

But to experience totality and the bigger picture, it's always we.

You are your afterlife.

Space creates your unique reality.

When you exit from this earths space you will be aware of your bigger reality that connects you with this universe totally. Remember how amazingly unique you are.

Follow your happiness.

There is no joy in miserable.

Souls are leaving the physical taught way of life in droves. You will notice the difference between life and soul situations to the physical sucking the life out of life, which is soul destroying. Souls will stay around souls and leaving limited situations. We are going to see the biggest change in life that Earth has ever seen. Stick to your truth, follow your soul and let go of limiting soul-destroying situations. Limitation is over.

The physical taught way of life needs soul to exist, if soul energy leaves these environments, then they will disappear.

Follow the energy. Give your soul energy to what matches you. Stop feeding the physical script and you will thrive soul side.

If you don't like it,

If you don't feel the connection,

If it doesn't make you feel happy,

If you're miserable, stop giving it your energy and walk away.

Let go.

Move on.

You are all you need.

Or stay but stop feeding it.

Even a tree has seasons

When you're not bearing fruit, it's because you are tending to your roots.

Don't panic.

If this was your last day here, would you say yes or no to your next opportunity?

Live each day as if your last so you go for it.

Why wait?

Be aware of your irrational thoughts. Know they are irrational and don't give them energy. Let them pass on by. Know yourself to know what you control. The more you know yourself, the more you listen to your inner truth and not external distortion.

Everything is frequency around you.

Know your own self frequency.

How much of your day do you give to you?

An autopilot life isn't a creative one.

Choose one thing each day that isn't just routine. Small changes turn into bigger ones. You are like a seed, grow you.

308

Be prepared so you don't face panic.

Be in your own knowing so you are not held back by fear.

Be in your connection and know yourself so you don't have to follow others.

Be committed to yourself so doubt does not feed your foundations.

Honour yourself so you respect your boundaries, then you will live in your space in peace.

Creativity doesn't grow on guilt.

Creativity builds in a connection that you have with yourself. If you want a strong business, look at your relationship with yourself. You are the roots to your longevity.

Don't forget to make time to catch up with yourself. You have been with you from the beginning and will be moving forward.

You are the most important soul in your life.

See you, hear you, notice you, connect with you.

Your soul knows what you need.

You may think you should be focusing on a career but if your soul knows that your relationships and personal life come first, then this is why you may find yourself still waiting for a career. Having a soul reading and seeing your soul map will show you what order you have set things.

The universe provides infinitely everything.

If you want to pick and find fault, then you will find it. If you want to appreciate it, you will find that too. If you want to be angry, laugh, cry, all of it, you will find because the universe says no to nothing. If you can't choose, it will provide both and more.

Mastering ourselves isn't a puzzle, it's in our choosing and connecting. Whether at a physical surface level or soul level it still comes back to the self. You always have a choice. If you don't like something tune out of it and choose another option like we do switching channels on the television or radio. It's that simple.

Up until 2018, thoughts and thinking could see you through. After 2018, thoughts and thinking no longer work. Connection in meaning is what moves your life forward now. Previously you could think something and act it regardless of if you felt it or meant it. Now only what matches you will play out for you. A double life of distortion is over.

Thoughts are useless now unless they match action and meaning. It's wise to match what your intentions are into action as you share so you continue consistently.

If things are not happening, there will be a break in connection somewhere.

The next four years is about the self.

From 2024, who are you?

Are you your authentic self consistently?

What are your morals and boundaries, including your depth and meaning?

If you don't work out who you are over the next four years, then you will spend the rest of your life here working on it before you are able to share more of yourself. No more playing at life and being many versions of yourself. One version of you is all you need.

Souls that already have one version will be the creators and manifest now.

The more you don't need to be in control,

The more in control you are.

Success isn't chased, it is grown.

Trying to be successful isn't being successful. The root holds a tree not the fruit. If you want to see success focus on the root. The soul that holds it up. Mimicking a root has a shelf life. A genuine root has staying power.

If you know you're in position and all set but you are still waiting for it to manifest, try not to view it as waiting, but more travelling towards it. It's coming.

The only way to trust yourself is by letting go of your mind. The mind is only meant to serve the physical body. Let it go, give it back so your body can run 100 percent efficiently.

Get used to using your gut and follow your energy. The mind works on memory and repeat which limits you to the past causing you to feel stuck. This is why the future is a struggle. Let go. Live in the now and allow yourself to access the universe now. You can do it.

Face what you know you want, and you will let go of the fear blocking it.

Fear is being removed now.

Give your energy to what you want and watch your life change energetically.

Cut the scripts. Cut the memory.

Cut the autopilot words. Your energy is connected to every thought, word and action. If it's not what you want, then stop feeding yourself energy full of words that keeps you in a reality that you hate.

You don't need to follow anything, only your soul.

When you trust yourself, you will listen to yourself and follow your gut confidently.

When you doubt yourself, you search for something else. Focus on you and strengthen your connection with yourself.

Then you will feel in control.

Each day, fill your life with what you know you want. If you leave it open and blank, you're leaving it open for anything.

At least know what you don't want, then you won't be in the firing line of situations that you don't like.

The physical body doesn't work without your soul. The energy of your soul is what makes it work. It's like looking at a computer and changing the keyboard around and thinking this will affect the circuit. It won't touch it.

Your circuit board is your soul energy.

Anything you change on the physical only touches the surface. If you want to change your life in depth, face your soul.

When you exit here you take your life with you. Everything that connects to you goes with you energetically. If you spent your life filling time, not being yourself and living your life from others, then all you did was fill time and not live in connection with yourself. It doesn't matter how much you copy, anything copied does not travel with you because it wasn't created from your energy.

Anything that stems from your energy stays with you always.

Are you feeling the shift yet?

Every soul is accounted for, and no one is left out. The wave of energy is shining us into our transparent self. You are facing yourself like never before. Be happy being you.

We'd like to know if you enjoyed the book. Please consider leaving a review on the platform from which you purchased the book

www.ingramcontent.com/pod-product-compliance
Ingram Content Group UK Ltd.
Pitfield, Milton Keynes, MK11 3LW, UK
UKHW010409040625
6219UKWH00003B/122

9 781634 102544